NEW ORLEANS AS IT WAS

SOUTHERN LIBRARY SERIES

New Orleans As It Was

Episodes of Louisiana Life

By
HENRY C. CASTELLANOS,
A.M., LL. B.

Foreword by
Charles L. Dufour

PELICAN PUBLISHING COMPANY
GRETNA 1990

Pelican paperback edition
First printing, 1990

Library of Congress Cataloging-in-Publication Data

Castellanos, Henry C.
     New Orleans as it was : episodes of Louisiana life / by Henry
  C. Castellanos; foreword by Charles L. Dufour--Pelican pbk. ed.
          p.   cm.
     Reprint. Originally published: New Orleans : L. Graham, 1895.
     ISBN 0-88289-787-X
     1. New Orleans (La.)--History. 2. New Orleans (La.)--Social
  life and customs. I. Title.
  F379.N557C28   1990   89-26568
  976.3'35--dc20   CIP

Manufactured in the United States of America
Published by Pelican Publishing Company, Inc.
1101 Monroe Street, Gretna, Louisiana 70053

IN GRATEFUL REMEMBRANCE
OF MY FATHER AND MOTHER
THIS BOOK IS AFFECTIONATELY INSCRIBED.

FOREWORD

In 1895, Henry C. Castellanos, a distinguished attorney and judge whose avocation was writing about the New Orleans he knew for a period of seventy years, produced *New Orleans As It Was*.

Quite naturally, Judge Castellanos wrote in the flamboyant style of the nineteenth century, but what he had to say was revealing of the era that his life spanned. As a source of material for the history of New Orleans, its value is attested by the fact that the present printing of *New Orleans As It Was* is its fifth. The printing firm of L. Graham & Son, Ltd., published *New Orleans As It Was* in 1895, and reprinted it in 1905. In 1961 Pelican Publishing Company produced a facsimile of the 1905 printing. The book's fourth appearance was in 1978, under the auspices of the Louisiana American Revolution Bicentennial Commission. This particular Pelican printing in 1990 is a paperback edition from the 1961 volume.

There is no "story line" in *New Orleans As It Was*. There is no relationship among its seventeen chapters; it is rather a miscellany, a collection of personal experiences or inherited traditions. Castellanos denounced "the infamous woman, Lalaurie," whose cruelty to her slaves created the "Haunted House" legend in New Orleans. He describes some famous duels and duelists; Marie Laveau and Voodoo rites; Parish Prison hangings; the famed Père Antoine and Abbé Adrien Rouquette; the strange case of Jean Gravier, "possessor of untold thousands," who died "in a condition of abject indigence." Castellanos took a dim view of the police and blamed them for "the spirit of lawlessness then rampant in our poorly guarded city."

The development of American New Orleans, under the dynamic leadership of James H. Caldwell and Samuel J. Peters, evoked this meaningful comment from Castellanos: "While leading and wealthy Creoles . . . were listlessly dreaming of the possibilities in store for their native city, the Anglo-Saxons . . . were at work with tireless energy."

Several generations of New Orleanians have known the French Quarter as the "Vieux Carré" and the assumption has been that this designation dates from the early years of the American domination. Judging from Castellanos's nonuse of the term, it could date from a decade or two into the twentieth century. Castellanos several times refers to the French Quarter as the *carré de la ville*.

Charles L. Dufour

PREFACE.

A preface is generally expected by the reader; without it, a book may be likened to a sermon with the text omitted.

The following pages were mostly written during a long spell of sickness, not only with the view of whiling away the tedium of convalescence, but of contributing my mite to a neglected branch of the literature of Louisiana. Conscious of their many defects and imperfections, I still hope that the students of our old-time institutions will find in them matter for instruction as well as entertainment.

Under the form of narratives I have, among other matters, attempted to illustrate the various phases of slavery that obtained in our State before the war of secession. The subject is an interesting one, not only to our Northern brothers, but to the friends of humanity at large, and is presented in unprejudiced and truthful language. I have stated facts and left the reader to his own conclusions.

A peculiar feature of the work is the descriptive history of the city's buildings, monuments and customs since its foundation to within a short time before the year 1860. Under proper headings in the index column the reader will readily discover the information he seeks upon that branch of the subject. As far as the compass of the work has permitted, I have omitted none of the salient episodes which constitute the charm of this unique metropolis of the South. Some of these incidents are so startling, romantic and improbable that, were they not authenticated by undeniable proof, they might be taken as the vaporings of an exuberant imagination.

I have drawn many of my facts not only from old records and disused archives, but from oral recitals and traditions.

Having reached a period of life which has made me, in some measure, a connecting link between the present and a generation long extinct, I have enjoyed the rare opportunity of knowing and hearing some of the men who once conspicuously figured upon the shifting scenes of life's drama. To my mother and grandmother, also, have I been greatly indebted for many particulars related to me in my boyhood's days, of which they were eye-witnesses. To revive and to perpetuate these recollections, which may be termed the "Unwritten History" of New Orleans, has been my aim and sole ambition.

Should I succeed, even partially, in this endeavor, I shall issue, I hope, at no remote time the "Unwritten History" of Louisiana, than which no subject can be more grand and soul-stirring.

THE AUTHOR.

New Orleans, September 1, 1895.

CONTENTS.

CHAPTER I.

THE LABRANCHE-HUESTON DUEL.

RECALLING A DRAMATIC AND FATAL ENCOUNTER UNDER THE OAKS.

The overwhelming cyclone which had burst forth with such fury upon the heads of the Louisiana Whigs, in the congressional elections that occurred in the summer of the year 1843, was destined to produce a bitterness of feeling seldom displayed in previous times; and, as a natural result, a series of personal difficulties followed throughout the State. The Locofocos, as the Democrats were then styled in derision by their opponents, had literally swept the State in that memorable campaign, and had elected John Slidell, Alcée LaBranche, Gen. Dawson and Gen. Bossier over George K. Rogers, ex-Governor E. D. White, Judge Elam and Judge Moore, the opposing candidates. As was to be expected, the victors were exultant, hilarious and boisterous. With the exception of the occasional appearance of a roughly drawn caricature representing a rooster discomfiting a coon, and of other harmless pleasantries, their joy and boasting do not seem to have exceeded the bounds of decency and

good nature. Different, however, was the temper of the
opposite side and of its chafing and impetuous Hotspurs.

They refused to accept the result with anything like
good grace, paticularly the one which involved the defeat of White in the Second Congressional District, acknowledged to be their stronghold in the State, and
which, but a short time before, had been carried by the
Whigs by a maority exceeding two thousand! The pill
was too bitter for digestion, and they refused to be com-
forted.

Alcée LaBranche, the victor in that contest, the man
who had so unexpectedly dashed their hopes and humbled their party, as they conceived, in the eyes of the
whole nation, became, of course, the centre of attack.

Brave, intelligent and impulsive; well versed in the
knowledge of public affairs, acquired in positions to which
he had frequently been elevated by the popular will, he
was undoubtedly the type of his people and of the creole
race. Against him, therefore, were hurled the shafts of
calumny and detraction, not only in the streets and other
public places, where politics were usually discussed, but
eventually in the columns of the public prints. As
long as his enemies had merely confined their abuse to his
political life and actions, he, like a sensible man, laughed
them to scorn; but, when articles began to appear reflect-
ing upon his honor, his manhood and his character, he
did not stop to hesitate. With him, to determine and to
act were synonymous terms.

It happened that in the month of August, 1843, in the
town of Baton Rouge, there appeared in the *Gazette* an
article so personal and vindictive that no man with any
sense of self-respect could possibly overlook its trend and
object. By many it was deemed entirely uncalled for,
even if justified by the facts, inasmuch as several months
had already elapsed since the election, and the occasion

for any such ebullition of temper and passion had long
passed away.

The writer of the objectionable publication was Mr.
Hueston, a gentleman of Northern birth, who, after having edited various papers at divers times at Franklin,
Mobile and New Orleans, had finally settled down in
Baton Rouge and taken charge of its leading Whig journal. He was an enthusiast in the cause of "Harry of
the West"—a veritable monomaniac in his hero-worship.

Withal, a man of agreeable manners, engaging presence and great popularity. His record was, after his
death, graphically written by Mr. Wilson, his quondam
associate in the conduct of the *Planters' Banner*, in a
feeling and well tempered article. It represents him as
a man of a generous but somewhat erratic nature.

To say that the article was abusive is to use a mild expression. It was directed against the whole congressional
delegation elect, particularly against General Bossier
and LaBranche. There is no doubt that if the latter had
not hastened to chastise Hueston, Bossier would not
have been slow in resenting the insult hurled at him and
his people. He was represented in that publication as
destitute of talent, acquirements or industry. It said
that the people of the fourth district ought to blush at the
contrast between him and Judge John Moore; that Gen.
Bossier could neither read nor write; that he was so ignorant, that he would find it no easy task even to vote,
without the aid of a prompter ; and that, with some one
to pull the wires, any French automaton could do the
same thing. Indulging in a similar strain, the editor
went on to say: "We will wager our white hat, which we
would not lose for one thousand such generals as he, that
when called on to vote, he will oftener say 'oui' than aye!
How an intelligent people could have been induced
even by party considerations to elect a man so perfectly

destitute of qualifications for any office as Gen. Bossier in preference to Judge Moore is strange, passing strange! But he is a creole" he concludes; "he once killed a man, and for that he is now qualified as chivalrous, and a good man for Congress."

The diatribe against Mr. LaBranche was still more personal and indecent, and the reference to a difficulty in which he was once engaged with Col. John R. Grymes was well understood by the general public as a reminder of a scandal in which the honor of a lady had been seriously concerned. That part of the publication was, therefore, unwarranted, and, as such, cowardly. "By a parity of reasoning, Mr. LaBranche will make a very ordinary congressman, for, although a creole, he has never killed any one. He is not qualified or 'chivalrous,' and it is said that once, when the wrath of John R. Grymes was being hotly discharged against him, he valiantly took to his heels, and implored shelter behind the skirts of several passing ladies."

A French contemporary, commenting on the above effusion, gave vent to his indignation in the following terms:

"We confess that never have insults been heaped in a more outrageous manner than by this editor upon Mr. LaBranche and the entire creole population. The representative of the second district is not only attacked in his public character, but even his private life is intruded upon without decency or scruple, and thrown open to the contemptuous gaze of the whole population."

In the meantime, Hueston had taken a steamer and come down to New Orleans. He was received with open arms by his enthusiastic admirers and became the lion of the hour. He had taken his quarters at the St. Charles Hotel, and, mingling in the gaieties of the town, seemed to court notoriety. As chance would have it, La-

Branche happened to be in the city at the time, and was about to engage his passage for his plantation home, when a friend hurriedly approached him, and placed into his hands the scurrilous attack. It was more than human nature could endure, and, deferring his departure to another moment, he at once, accompanied by friends, hurried in quest of his traducer.

This was on the 16th of August, 1843.

On the evening of the 17th, the following "card" appeared, explanatory of the rencontre between the parties:

"TO THE PUBLIC.

"The undersigned have perused with surprise the statement given by the *Herald* this morning by Mr. Hueston, editor of the *Baton Rouge Gazette,* relative to the chastisement inflicted upon him by Mr. Alcée La-Branche, yesterday, for a false and shameful publication respecting that gentleman. In the statement of Mr. Hueston there is not a single word of truth. He asserts that Mr. LaBranche struck him, while he was being held by one of the friends who had accompanied him, and that when he disengaged himself Mr. LaBranche was hurrying away. Such is not the case. The following is a true and correct version of the affair, from the beginning to the end.

"Mr. LaBranche had intended to leave town at 3 o'clock on Wednesday last, when one of his friends placed into his hands the paper containing the article from the *Baton Rouge Gazette,* in which he was so infamously abused. Hearing that Mr. Hueston, the editor of that paper, was in town, he immediately went in pursuit of him, but was unable to come up with him until the evening of that day, when he found him in the billiard saloon of the St. Charles Hotel.

"The undersigned, perceiving the excited state of Mr.

LaBranche's mind, and aware of his great bodily strength, accompanied him for no other purpose than to prevent him from using too much violence.   Mr. LaBranche entered the billiard room, some five or six paces in advance of one of the undersigned (Mr. Bouligny), while the other was still further in the rear.   Mr. LaBranche went up to Mr. Hueston and said: 'Are you Mr. Hueston, editor of the *Baton Rouge Gazette?*'   Mr. Hueston, holding a cue in his hand, answered 'yes,' offering his hand to Mr. LaBranche.   The latter said: 'I am Mr. LaBranche,' and instantly struck him a severe blow with a hickory stick across the face.   Mr. Hueston was stunned by the blow, and Mr. LaBranche repeated the blow several times, when the undersigned interfered, in order, as they supposed, to preserve the life of Mr. Hueston, who was saved from falling by one of the undersigned (Mr. Bouligny), who, in doing so, received a blow on the arm.   Mr. Hueston was quite insensible for some time, during which Mr. LaBranche remained in the room, and was with some difficulty induced to retire by one of his friends, who, apprehending that Mr. Hueston was dead, wanted Mr. LaBranche to avoid the police.

"According to this plain, unvarnished statement of facts, it is plain that Mr. Hueston's account of the matter in this morning's *Herald* is entirely false—infamously false.   So far from being held while Mr. LaBranche was striking him, the truth is no one came near him until he was senseless under the blows of Mr. LaBranche; and so far was the latter inclined to run away that he was with difficulty persuaded by a friend to retire while Mr. Hueston was insensible.   On the next day, he sent two of his friends to Mr. Hueston to inform him of the number of his house and the street in which he lived, and to express his willingness to furnish any satisfaction that Mr. Hueston might think proper to demand.   The undersigned conceive themselves bound by a just regard to truth and by a sense of their own integrity to contradict in this formal manner the base falsehoods contained in Mr. Hueston's statements, which are as revolting to a man of honor as a blow from a cane.

"GUSTAVE BOULIGNY.
"ARTHUR GUILLOTTE.
"EDMOND GANUCHEAU."

Appended to the foregoing statement, appeared an "addendum" from the pen of a gentleman, who for a number of years occupied the position of Recorder of the First Municipality, and died lamented and regretted by the whole community. It was couched in the following terms :

"The undersigned was not present at the commencement of the beating given to Mr. Hueston by Mr. Alcée LaBranche, but came into the room while the former was stunned, and Mr. Bouligny supporting his head. Fearing that he was killed, the undersigned expressed his apprehensions to Mr. LaBranche, and begged him to retire to avoid arrest. After much argument, Mr. LaBranche complied with the wishes of the undersigned, on condition that the latter would represent him in his absence, in case any one should wish to see him. When Mr. Hueston was restored to his senses, he called out : 'Where is the damned rascal?' Then the undersigned told him Mr. LaBranche was ready to give him whatever satisfaction he might demand, and could be found whenever he chose to look for him.

"JOSEPH GÉNOIS."

On the following day, an editorial appeared in a paper friendly to Mr. LaBranche, which was evidently inspired by him and left no room for any adjustment or compromise. Public excitement had naturally reached the

acme of fever heat, and gloomy forebodings were expressed on every side.   Both of the parties numbered their
friends by the thousands.   They were known to be brave,
cool and sincere in their convictions.   Hence, nothing
but a bloody, terrible conflict could ensue under
such conditions.   The Whigs were proud of the grit and
pluck of the doughty champion who had unexpectedly
brought himself into prominence by his zeal and impetuous ardor in their behalf ; while the Democrats, confiding in the icy coolness, indomitable will and just cause
of their idol, calmly awaited the result.   The following
is an exact reproduction of the article, which appeared in
the French side of the *Louisiana Courier:*

" The *Tropic*, at the request of Mr. Hueston, states
that he has no disposition to enter into a controversy
with Mr. LaBranche.   From our knowledge of the latter
gentleman, we feel very confident that he would consider
himself humbled were he to thus honor Mr. Hueston,
and of this he has given proof by resorting to the summary way of expressing his indignation at the slanderous publications that called forth such a public castigation.   Mr. LaBranche has done nothing since to make
that affair public.   He has ever manifested a wish to
settle it privately with Mr. Hueston.   With regard to
Mr. LaBranche's friends, to whom allusion is made by
Mr. Hueston, through the columns of the *Tropic*, they
are equally reluctant, we know, to enter into any discussion.   Their statement of yesterday was called for by a
regard for truth, so that the public might be disabused
of misapprehensions that might possibly be entertained in
reference to Mr. Hueston's personal account of the affray.

" Whether Mr. Hueston will or can settle this ' private
affair ' is a matter for him alone to decide; but it is
manifest that if it has at any time been obtruded upon
public attention, the fault lies with that individual him-

self. In exhibiting so much delicacy and repugnance to
any public allusion to the occurrence, he is rather incon-
sistent, inasmuch as he has himself given to it great and
unnecessary publicity, and has, according to the declar-
ations of eye witnesses, falsified the truth for that purpose. Besides this, he made an indecorous, wanton and
slanderous allusion to ' a private affair ' between two gentlemen, with which it had nothing to do, and which was
not a legitimate subject for newspaper remarks, and, in
fact, raked up a disagreeable past for no other purpose
apparently than to gratify a malign and unworthy propensity.''

After such a terrible arraignment, no other alternative
was left but a resort to the code. Notes were immediately exchanged, and the seconds selected. The grounds
agreed upon were the '' Oaks,'' near the intersection of
the Gentilly Road and Elysian Fields. The weapons
were double-barreled shotguns, loaded with ball, and
the distance forty yards. The word of command was to
be : '' Fire – One – Two – Three – Four – Five,'' each com-
batant to discharge his barrels after the word ''Fire,''
and before the word '' Five.'' Gen. John L. Lewis and
Joseph Génois attended LaBranche and Messrs. Richard
Hagan and Col. W. S. McArdle, one of the editors of the
Tropic, represented Hueston.

The appearance of the antagonists was such as might
be expected, and, until the weapons were put into their
hands, they were cool, collected and passive. Upon the
rigid and marble-like features of LaBranche not a passing cloud of emotion could be traced, while on the countenance of his opponent a spasmodic, muscular twitching
occasionally betrayed the fires of concentrated rage
that burned within his bosom. There they stood awhile,
silently confronting one another, while awaiting the
signal to proceed to their deadly work.

At the word of command, which was given by Col. Mc-Ardle in a slow, impressive manner, both raised their guns and discharged their barrels. A second of cruel anxiety to the spectators ensued, when an examination by the seconds resulted in the announcement that neither was hurt. The balls of Hueston had gone astray, while of those of LaBranche one had perforated his adversary's hat, and the other had grazed the lapel of his coat.

Hueston demanded a second fire, and the guns were again loaded. The same formalities were gone through again, without any definite result. Hueston had missed once more, but the bullets whizzing in close and dangerous proximity to his head attested the not to be despised accuracy of his enemy's aim.

Four shots had been exchanged by each of the contending parties, and the crowd who were witnessing the unusual scene thought that enough had been done to vindicate honor and attest their courage. But Hueston was obdurate and determined. His Anglo-Saxon nature was fully aroused. He had come, not to observe a vain punctilio, but to seek redress, revenge and satisfaction, and nothing but blood could secure his desire. Under the laws governing the duello, LaBranche could not refuse under any circumstances his opponent's request to continue the combat, subject, as he was, being the challenged party, to his orders and demands, and hence all parties proceeded to reload for a third time.

At this stage of the proceedings, the seconds began to betray symptoms of irritation, and Col. Hagan excitedly exclaimed that, if this stage of things continued, he would urge the shortening of the distance, a right, by the way, exclusively belonging to the challenger. The preliminaries, however, were gone through once more, and again were the combatants put face to face. This third ordeal came very near proving fatal to the gritty American, for, while his bullets flew wide of the mark, his cold-eyed antagonist had inflicted a scalp wound from which streams of blood were freely flowing. It was now evident that LaBranche was aiming not to maim or cripple, but to kill outright.

Stanching with his handkerchief the crimson tide, and maddened by the stinging pain, Hueston demanded and insisted upon a fourth round. To this the now excited spectators and some of his own friends strenuously demurred, but nothing could shake his dauntless spirit, and, with gleaming eyes, turning to a medical attendant, "Feel my pulse!" he cried out, "and see if it does not beat with normal regularity." It was nearly 6 o'clock in the evening, and the duel proceeded. Nothing can reproduce or photograph on paper the wild, gruesome and painful scene. The shots again rang out against that bright summer sky, and the falling form of the unfortunate Hueston proclaimed that death had closed the final act of a drama, full of sickening horror and blood-curdling interest.

Tender and loving hands lifted his inanimate body from the ground, and gently placed it in a carriage. Conveyed to the "Maison de Santé" of Dr. Warren Stone, on Canal street, he breathed his last, far from his home and idolized wife and children, among sorrowing friends and political admirers. The fatal bullet had entered his lĕft side, in the direction of the lower rib, and passed out at the right side, in a direction nearer to the back.

His remains were conveyed by boat to his desolate home at Baton Rouge, where they were interred with pomp and civic honors. His paper was taken charge of and conducted in the interest of his widow by J. R. Dufrocq, who for many years became so well known at home and abroad as the popular Mayor of our present Capital.

Thus died a noble, gifted but erratic man! In looking over the files of old papers published in Louisiana at that period, I stumbled, some time ago, upon a copy of the *St. Mary Banner,* which furnishes an interesting account of Hueston's life and previous career, and as it may prove of interest to the Louisiana reader I close this sketch with its republication. As to LaBranche's public record and services, they are too deeply interwoven with the political history of our State to require at this time any special mention.

"We knew poor Hueston well. He lived with us, and labored with us in conducting this paper nearly a year. He was generous-hearted to a fault, remarkably industrious and energetic, but rather eccentric in his character, acting frequently on the hasty impulse of the moment. He was born in the State of New Jersey, where his father, we believe, is now engaged in farming. He was a self-made man. He has often mentioned to us that he had spent many a day in plowing, and would devote his evenings to study. Well advanced in manhood, he became acquainted with Prof. Palfrey, late editor of the *North American Review,* to whom he acknowledged himself indebted for acquiring some knowledge of the classics. He spent some time in different printing offices at the North, as compositor, and left for South Carolina. He then went to Georgia, and was for some time connected with the press in Augusta. About the year 1836 he went to Mobile, Ala., and that year, or 1837, commenced the publication of a small daily paper called the *Examiner.* We well remember the ability with which it was conducted. About the latter end of 1837 he sold out the *Examiner* to Mr. Ballantyne, and sailed for France. He spent nearly two years in Paris, in literary pursuits, and visited England, and, in the beginning of 1840, returned to New Orleans. In

March, 1840, we employed him as French compositor
and assistant editor of the English side of the *Banner,*
and our friends are well aware of the ability which distinguished his writings. He remained with us until he
took charge of the *Baton Rouge Gazette.* During the
last six months he was with us he was engaged in the
study of the law, and would, we have no doubt, have become a distinguished member of the bar. The industry
with which he pursued his studies was surprising. Poor
fellow! Through his great failing, the want of pru-
dence and forthought, he has been cut down in the
prime of manhood and the vigor of intellect, leaving a
wife and young family and a wide circle of friends to
deplore his untimely end."

CHAPTER II.

LOUIS PHILIPPE ROFFIGNAC.

REMINISCENCES OF AN OLDEN TIME MAYOR.

In the latter part of the year 1846, the subject of this sketch died in France under circumstances of a peculiar character. He had been suffering for some time from some chronic disease, and, while resting in his invalid's arm-chair and in the act of loading a pistol, he was suddenly stricken down by an apoplectic attack. Just as he was about to fall the pistol was discharged and several small buck shots lodged behind his ear. This circumstance gave rise at first to the supposition that he had committed suicide, but a medical examination at once dispelled the suspicion.

Count Louis Philippe Joseph de Roffignac's life was strewn with eventful and romantic incidents. Born at Angoulême, his godfather and godmother were the Duke and Duchess of Orleans, whose son, Louis Philippe, subsequently ascended the throne of France as "King of the French." At the age of fourteen, he was appointed a page in the semi-regal household of the Duchess, and, at seventeen, obtaining from Louis XVI a commission of lieutenant of artillery, immediately proceeded to Spain for service under his father, who was then holding an important command in the French army operating against that nation.

At the age of twenty-four, he was promoted for meritorious service and gallantry to a captaincy in the Queen's Regiment of Dragoons, upon the field of battle. From these active scenes he was transferred to America, and found himself in Louisiana in the year 1800, the period at which Spain ceded this country to France, and still later when the latter sold the territory to the United States. Availing himself of an article of the treaty of Paris, which allowed French subjects equal privileges, those of naturalization included, as those conferred upon actual residents, he became thereby invested with the rights of American citizenship. In the course of his long sojourn in New Orleans he was employed in various positions of honor and trust. His attachment to the country of his adoption was sincere and profound. He became a member of the legislature, during ten consecutive years; a colonel in the Louisiana Legion; then a brigadier general (an honor conferred upon him for his intelligent and effective co-operation in the defence of New Orleans); next, a director of the State Bank of Louisiana, and, finally, was several times elected Mayor of New Orleans from 1820 to 1828. In the latter year he resigned his office to return to his native France, where he died at Périgueux, under the circumstances above narrated. Such is a brief epitome of his long and useful career in the " Crescent City."

The administration of Roffignac as Mayor, notwithstanding the almost insuperable drawbacks which he was frequently compelled to encounter, was highly successful, and emerging, as New Orleans then was, from a chrysalis condition of stagnancy to a new era of advancement and progress, he gave to its affairs an impetus which to the timid savored of extravagance. Contemporary journals are filled with accounts of the hard work done by that honest man. He restored order to the finances of the city, always an ungrateful task, particularly when the pruning knife of retrenchment is to be applied.

He attended strictly to the policing and cleanliness of our streets. He remodeled the organization of a semi-military police, called "gendarmes," whose main duty was to put out fires, to repress disorder and tumults and to suppress all attempts at insurrection among the slaves. He improved our public parks or squares, and encouraged the establishment and endowment of institutions of general utility, education and charity. Of course, there were growlers in those days, as numerous a class now as then, prone to oppose all innovations, but their gloomy forebodings never caused him to falter for a moment, or to deviate from the line he had mapped out for his guidance.

There was in the city, at that period, a constant influx of strangers, particularly from the western country, who repaired here every year to sell or barter their produce and commodities, for which they usually found a profitable market. They were in the habit of descending the river in barges and flatboats, laden with flour, corn and other cereals, besides immense quantities of cured meats. But in the wake of these honest farmers and traders could always be seen a horde of bandits and gamblers, which it was difficult to extirpate.

Licensed gambling was then in vogue, and the dens of its votaries were kept open at all hours of the day and night. From them issued a stream of criminals and ill disposed persons, whom it was necessary to constantly watch. Incendiary fires were matters of frequent occurrence. More than once was the city in great danger of total destruction. The night police were very inefficient. They were few in numbers, and the territory which they were required to cover was large. The papers of that period teem with accounts of assaults, robberies and felonies of all kinds committed in the very heart of the city, under the very eaves of the old Cabildo or Town-House. But to these constant menaces to the peace and good order of the community, Roffignac opposed an energy and courage characteristic of the man.

As we have already said, the coterie of croakers and grumblers was not wholly extinct during the period of his administration. It was said by those who disliked him, that he was very vain, conceited and shallow, addicted to giving to himself all the credit due to others. As illustrative of this foible, the following anecdote was told of him:

At a time when the Cathedral bell was summoning almost every night our drowsy citizens from their slumbers to assist in subduing the fiery element, Mr. Roffignac received from the Mayor of Mobile information that a woman, who had just reached that place, had made a declaration implicating certain individuals of New Orleans, who designed to fire the town from one end to the other. The woman, in her affidavit, had minutely specified the names, residences and occupations of the suspected parties. Armed with this documentary evidence, he summoned before him the Captain of his Guard as well as the *Commissaire de Police*, secured the services of a number of hacks, stages and coaches, and sent them forth to search the city and suburbs. As prisoner after prisoner was brought in and locked up, Roffignac would ascend and descend the stair case of the Town-Hall, with the air of a Cicero who had just detected a lot of Catalines. Then grasping the arm of some gazing admirer, he would shout forth: "I hold them, I shall have every one of them this blessed day!" and when complimented on his Vidocq-like abilities, he would reply: "Ah! *mon ami,* you can't imagine the trouble these scoundrels have given me. I have not closed my eyes for nearly a fortnight. My unceasing vigilance in ferreting out this vile conspiracy, etc."

Whether the story be true or not, I do not pretend to say, but one fact is certain—that the arrest of the suspects and their subsequent banishment from the city relieved our denizens of many apprehensions, and put a check for a time to further incendiary attempts.

The usual punishment for minor offenses and mis-demeanors was exposure at the pillory, a custom inherit-ed from our ancient colonial laws. The *modus operandi* was as follows: The culprit was taken to the Place d'Armes (Jackson Square now), and made to sit on a low platform, directly facing the Cabildo or City Hall, from early morning to the setting of the sun. Suspended from his neck, and overhanging his breast, a large placard was placed, on which, in great big letters, were written his name and crime—thus: "My name is———; I am a thief" (as the case might be) : "I stole from———; sen-tenced——— days, to exposure at this pillory." As this was about the most frequented thoroughfare, being in a direct line to and from the public markets, multitudes habitually gathered around this place of punishment. As a general rule, this system of discipline became very ef-fective, and it is said that, with very few exceptions, the culprit seldom remained in New Orleans, to avoid being hooted at, jeered and, perhaps, re-arrested. This prac-tice, as far as whites were concerned, was subsequently abolished, but as to the blacks, it remained in operation as late as 1847, or thereabouts.

It was in the first year of Roffignac's administration

that trees—sycamores and elms, I believe—were first
planted on the Place d'Armes, the levee front and Circus,
better known as Congo Square. This was in 1820. In
the following year, Mr. Montgomery, a member of the
City Council, successfully introduced a resolution, ordering the planting of sycamores all around the city, that is
to say, along Esplanade, Rampart and Canal streets,
which was done, thus girding the town proper with a
beautiful avenue of umbrageous trees. The same coun-
cilman also urged the necessity of substituting rock
pavement for mud streets. A correspondence to that effect with some Northern contractors was thereupon
opened. Backed by the Mayor's influence and authority, a Mr. Scott consented to come to New Orleans, and
was the first contractor engaged to do the city paving.
The materials used were cobble stones, covered with sand
and fine gravel. Square block pavements replaced them
at a much later period, some thirty years thereafter.

At about the same time, a fine substantial levee front
was begun. This work the City Council opposed for
want of a sufficient appropriation, but Mr. Nicholas
Girod, Mayor at the time when the battle of New
Orleans was fought, and whose name fills a wide and
long page in our city's history, being bent on the construction of this much needed revetment, swore that he
would pay the expenses himself, if nobody else would,
and such was the persistence of the plucky Frenchman
that the levee was built.

In 1821, the system of lighting the city was first introduced, and this was done by means of twelve large lamps,
with reflectors attached. They were hung up within
the limits of the *carré de la ville*, from a rope fastened to high posts placed obliquely across the streets.
This innovoation was hailed with pride by our predecessors, particularly by belated pedestrians, whose

sole guides at night over flatboat gunwales and slip-
pery walks were trusty bull's eye lamps! As late
as 1837, this practice of carrying lanterns about the town
was not uncommon in New Orleans, especially above
Canal and below Esplanade streets.

Towards the close of Roffignac's administration, an
event occured which finds an appropriate place in these
pages. I refer to the destruction by fire of our erstwhile
neat but modest State House. It was situated on the
down town side of Toulouse and Old Levee or Front streets.
Erected in 1761 under the French colonial régime, two
years before the cession of Louisiana to Spain, it was used
at the time of the disaster, which I am about to outline,
as Governor Pierre Derbigny's official residence, and
within its precincts were held the legislative sessions of
our early Solons. It was then in a rather dilapidated condition, sadly needing repairs, and it was a wonder to
many how the people, in throngs, would venture to go
up the ricketty old staircase, when anything like an interesting debate was going on in the two chambers of the
Legislature, sitting in the upper rooms.

The offices of the various State authorities were situated
in the basement. The business of the Executive, through
his private secretary, was transacted on the lower floor
and consisted mainly, in addition to the duties of ordinary
routine, in issuing pass-ports. Adjoining the damp and
gloomy apartments reserved for the use of subordinate
employees, was the public library, if a very scanty collection of books could be so called, rich, however, in rare
and valuable manuscripts and old historical records.

It was a quaint, old, historic building, with its broad
galleries in front, overlooking the river. Nor was its
little garden wanting, with its *parterres* of flowers and
small groves of tropical shrubbery. Truly, indeed, did
it stand forth as a revered monument of a dramatic past!

Here it was that every act of cession had been acknowledged, and every "Ordonnance" or "Bando de Gobierno" promulgated, and there it was also that was signed
the warrant, that, within a few squares of it, consigned to
an untimely death, upon the banks· of the Mississippi
River, and in front of the Spanish Barracks, the patriot
LaFrenière and his brother martyrs.

Since the acquisition of Louisiana, this edifice had always been used as a State House by the American authorities. It was looked upon with reverence by the latter settlers for the important incidents which it never
failed to record. Within those walls it was, that in 1806
Gen. Wilkinson and Governor Claiborne had frequently
conferred to checkmate the designs of Aaron Burr to establish a vast empire from the Alleghanies to the Sierras
of Mexico, with New Orleans as its glorious and brilliant
capital. Here it was also that Gen. Jackson concerted
and executed those high-handed measures—the dispersion
of the Legislature at the point of the bayonet, among
others—which he claimed to be necessary to defeat the
machinations of alleged traitors. These and many other
circumstances of a like interesting character had enshrin-
ed the venerable pile in the hearts of the people.

The origin of the fire, whether accidental or designed,
baffled investigation. The flames blazed forth from the
lower portion, and rapidly consumed the entire building.
The conflagration then spread along Old Levee street,
devouring everything in its path, including the mansion
of Baron Pontalba, from which point it ranged towards
the corner of Chartres, when it was finally checked.
The residence of the Baron stood at the corner of St.
Peter and the Levee, and was anciently occupied as a
hostelry by a Mr. Trémoulet. It was a handsome, ornamented structure, in the old colonial style of architecture,
with a wide gallery in front, which commanded a view

of the whole river expanse.   It was the resort of our refined society.   Within its antique and arched parlors,
the daughter of the Spaniard, Almonester, was wont to
dispense her hospitality with queenly grace, ere those
troubles arose in her private life, which eventuated in after
years in so much Parisian gossip and scandalous litigation.

The progress of the flames was only arrested by the entire destruction of this and a few adjoining properties.
Had it proceeded further the entire row of low-roofed
buildings, belonging also to the Baron, would have met
with the same fate, thereby endangering the Moorish
building, (still existing at the corner of Chartres and St.
Peter,) the City Hall, the Parish Prison or Calaboose,
(now occupied by the Recorder's Court and Arsenal),
and most probably all the houses on that square would
have been razed to the ground.

The loss of property was estimated at about $150.000,
and although only five houses were burned down, more
than twenty families lost their all.   The loss of the State
in the Government House amounted to about $10,000, ex-
clusive of a like sum for the Code of Practice, the edition
of which was almost entirely consumed.   Of the new
Civil Code not more than one hundred volumes in good
condition were saved.   The furniture of the Legislative
Halls and of the different offices was of but little value.
The City Library, with its historic treasures, was reduced to ashes.   The loss of Baron Pontalba was fully
$30.000.00.

Numerous accidents occurred.   A negro child was entirely incinerated; a negro died from the effect of falling
timbers; a white man was asphixiated by drinking *aqua
fortis* in mistake for wine; another, dreadfully mangled
by a tumbling wall, was borne off in a dying condition,
in addition to other lesser casualties.   Among these

may be mentioned the scores of men who, volunteering
as assistant firemen, were found lying dead—drunk.

A cotemporary, commenting on this disastrous fire,
thus reproved the city authorities. I reproduce his observations textually :

"The corporation of New Orleans possesses but few
fire engines, and two of them could not be worked, being
out of repair. This is an act of most culpable negligence
on the part of our authorities. We are daily spending
enormous sums for the embellishment of our city, yet, so
improvident are we, that no care is taken to preserve it
from the most terrible and destroying element. We have
not one regular fire company in this city, and but three
or four bad engines; it is not, therefore, surprising, that
fires are here subdued with so much difficulty. The city
should immediately purchase two or three first class
engines, and procure a new supply of buckets, ladders,
hooks, etc.

"We understand that an engineer and mechanician of
this city has offered to build engines on a superior plan,
for the city, at the reduced price of $700.00; he will war-
rant them to throw more water and further than those
from Philadelphia and New York. Why does not the
City Council make a contract with him, in preference to
sending to the North and paying $4200? It is time that
the Council should take this subject into serious consideration, for this city lately is oftener visited by this
dreadful scourge than New York itself."

So well acquainted have we become with new and improved devices for the strangling of the fiery fiend that
these recommendations appear comical and strange to us
now; but, over sixty years ago, hand machines of a most
primitive construction, with buckets to supply the tanks
from the walled up gutters, were the only appliances
known. It was many years thereafter that long leads of

hose were adopted, and as these necessitated greater suction power, the engines had to be modelled with longer and more powerful brakes. The houses in New Orleans were generally one story high, those with balconies being the exceptions. Hence, hand engines, when properly constructed, served every purpose.

On the day following the fire, the Legislature, which had been in session, assembled, on the invitation of Mayor Roffignac, in his public parlor, to consult as to the selection of a suitable building in which to continue their deliberations. It was decided that both branches of the Assembly should occupy temporarily Mr. John Davis' spacious rooms. This *locale*, the former site of the old Opera House and Orleans Ball-room, is now consecrated to pious and religious purposes—an Asylum and a Convent.

A joint committee, a few days after, reported that Mr. Pierre Derbigny, as President of the board of Regents of the Central and Primary schools, had tendered the use of that portion of the building in the upper story occupied by the Central Department, which offer was gratefully accepted.

This structure, the oldest building now in New Orleans, once the Convent of the Ursulines Nuns, and now the residence of Archbishop Janssens, was situated on Condé street, between Ursulines and Hospital streets. Our old inhabitants will remember that that portion of Chartres, which extended from Esplanade to St. Peter, was then known as Condé street. I remember the building distinctly and, recalling my school-boy days, am unable to note any difference in its physiognomy, except in such changes as have occurred in its immediate surroundings.

The church, or rather the narrow and elongated Chapel, erected in the last century as an annex to the Nunnery, still exists, though greatly altered, and is now

used by an Italian congregation. The entrance opened
on Ursulines street, and over its solitary portal hung a
marble tablet, commemorative of a Spanish King's liberality. It extended along that street to within a short
distance of Levee street. Tall Gothic windows, with
panels of stained glass, admitted air from above and
light from without. Though originally constructed for
the use of the Convent, the sisters, with the exception of
the cloistered space, reserved for their devotions, had
thrown it open to Catholic worshippers. In this holy
shrine, the Bishop frequently officiated.

St. Mary's Church, on Chartres street, is of modern
construction, and its site occupies a portion of the large
playground, once attached to the schools. Below it, and
on the same side of that thoroughfare, were the buildings
used as Barracks by the United States troops stationed
at this post. (Hence the name given to Barracks street.)
Here were also the headquarters of their commanding
officers, Col. Zachary Taylor and Major Twiggs, who,
by the way, signalized themselves at the fire, and received officially the grateful thanks of the City Council.

The upper part of the building, dedicated to the Central School, was under the direction of a Mr. Santi Petri,
a Spaniard by birth. He was reputed a man of great
learning. A corps of assistants, supported him. The
lower portion was divided into junior classes, in the lowest of which the writer was not a very apt or ductile
scholar, if one may judge from the frequency and vim
with which his ears were pulled. This was a common
practice among the teachers of those times—the French
especially—resorted to in order to jog the memory of dul-
lards. It was here that Mr. Bigot presided, whom some
may yet remember, with his silver snuffbox in one
hand, and a dreaded ferule in the other. His wife occasionally aided him. She was a daughter of the cele-

brated Gen. James Wilkinson, and, as Principal of our young ladies' High School in after years, achieved great distinction. He was withal, a good, kind-hearted man, an excellent scholar and an artist of merit. His department, besides rudimentary studies, embraced landscape, portrait and linear or architectural drawing. Among several of our noted living artists, I remember George Coulon, Hortaire Guénard and various others, as young and promising scholars.

It was in the upper story of this massive structure that the General Assembly concluded their labors.

The reader will excuse this digression, but, as illustrative of the times, it could not well be omitted.

But, besides the military and administrative talents, which Mayor Roffignac's life discloses, how many are aware that as a man of letters he particularly excelled. He was in frequent communication with some of the leading statesmen of Europe, and maintained an unbroken correspondence with Lafayette. His attentions to the exiled princes, the future King of France included, both in this city and Havana, are matters of record. The papers, which were found after his tragic death, contained curious and precious autographs of the great men of that historic period, and it is a matter of note that de Lameth, the Duke de Broglie and Count de Roffignac were at one time class-mates at the Chateau of Belleville, under the tuition of the Abbé Duruisseau—three men who wielded in Europe and America, an influence, more or less important on questions affecting individual and national freedom.

Taken all in all, his retirement from office was deemed a matter of regret, and on the eve of his departure for his beloved old home, he was complimented with a grand public banquet. His parting with the members of the

City Council, as described by the public prints of the day, was affectionate and tender.

And yet in this year of grace and progress and universal enlightenment, who mentions the name of Roffignac except at a soda water stand? He is only known as the inventor of a fashionable beverage. Such is fame!

CHAPTER III.

GENERAL HUMBERT.

A DASHING HERO OF TWO CONTINENTS.
HIS SPLENDID SERVICES IN FRANCE, MEXICO, IRELAND
AND NEW ORLEANS.

The trite adage that truth is stranger than fiction is strongly exemplified in the simple narrative of the life and vicissitudes of the singular man, whose achievements in both hemispheres form the ground work of the present sketch. Without the adventitious circumstances of birth, fortune or education, this hero rose from the humblest spheres of citizenship to a dazzling position of honor and dignity; and, but for his inflexible love of liberty and of republican institutions, would have soared in military preferment to the lofty plane occupied by the Murats, Neys and the Soults of the Empire.

An exile, for opinion's sake, he sought an asylum in New Orleans, in whose defence he fought like one of those plumed and helmeted knights we read of in ancient Romance. Wherever Freedom called upon his doughty arm to strike, whether under the frowning turrets of Castlebar, or in the mountain recesses of Mexico, or along the shores of the blue Rhine, or on the banks of the turbid Mississippi; there we hear of his prowess, his loyalty and his cheerful obedience to cherished principles. And yet, notwithstanding his just claims to our eternal gratitude, he died in our midst, poor, neglected and unhonored, and even his place of sepulchre is to this day forgotten and unknown! Such, alas, is too often the fate of the patriot and the lover of the human race.

Jean Robert Marie Humbert was born in Rouvray, Lorraine, on the 25th of November, 1755. At the time of the breaking out of the French Revolution in 1789, his condition in life was an humble one, being that of a dealer or peddler in rabbit skins; but, endowed with great intelligence and undoubted bravery, and favored by nature with a stature of colossal mould and a prepossessing appearance, he plunged headlong into that career which was opening at that time to the patriotic spirits of his country the avenues that led to glory and wealth. His success was phenomenal. From a simple soldier in the army of the Rhine and of the West, he rose by gradations to the position of Major General in 1794, having participated in every battle fought during the memorable campaigns of Wurmser and the Duke of Brunswick. His attack on Landau forms one of the boldest feats of arms ever recorded in history.

It seems that, after suffering several defeats, the army of Hoche, the left wing of which Humbert commanded, had reached Keiserlauten. The Prussians, anticipating the movement, had stolen a march on him three days before, and had fortified the position by planting cannon at the head of the ravines leading to the plateau. The Prussians numbered forty thousand, the French thirty thousand combatants.

The assault began on the left, led by Humbert in person. Scaling the heights under the protection of a ravine, he marched the now maddened *"sans culottes"* in serried columns, without a perceptible waver or break in their advancing lines, under the spiriting and soul-stirring strains of the "Marseillaise" hymn, despite the din and rattle of the enemy's musketry and the roar of his belching guns. Higher and higher, amidst the deafening uproar, rose and soared aloft the inspiriting words of the national anthem, until, reaching the edge of the coveted plateau, Humbert, waving his sword above his head, gave the command to charge, crying out in stentorian tones: *"Chargez, mes enfants,* Landau or Death." The cry was taken up and repeated by his men, whom now nothing could resist. On they came, like an Alpine avalanche. The enemy, aghast and dismayed by the coolness, audacity and impetuosity of the onslaught, made but a feeble resistance. Landau was captured!

His strategic movements on the enemy's flanks at Froschwiller and Worth decided the victory in favor of France and put an end to the campaign by disconcerting the manœuvers of Wurmser, the Austrian, on the lines of Wiessenbourg, and, completely routing him at Gersberg, forced the Prussians to retreat to Mayence and the Austrians on Gemersheim.

His success in the pacification of the Vendée, devoted to the Royalist faction, is mentioned by historians in laudatory terms, though most of the credit is bestowed on Hoche, his ranking officer. These two men were deeply attached to one another, and always acted in perfect concert. What Stonewall Jackson was to Lee, or Sheridan to Grant, Humbert was to Hoche—the man of action, of surprises and of celerity.

Thus it was that when, in 1798, the French Directory determined, as a retaliatory measure, to attack England in her own stronghold, by sending to Ireland an ex-

peditionary force to assist the insurgents in their attempts
at independence, Hoche, to whom had been assigned the
chief command of the enterprise, asked, as a special
favor, for the appointment of Humbert, as his lieutenant.
The request, coming from such a source, was readily
granted, and with it his promotion to the rank of Lieutenant General. The plan of operation was soon mapped
out in council. Humbert was to effect a landing with a
small vanguard, to which, it was expected, large acces-
sions from the Irish peasantry and their leaders would
lend strength. Once a lodgment secured, it was further
agreed that Hoche, with the bulk of the liberating army,
would, co-operating with a formidable fleet, make a descent upon the coast, and, uniting with the small force in
the field, take personal command. From this, will be
seen the confidence reposed in Humbert's audacity and
judgment. But the combination, though feasible and
well matured, signally failed. The period selected was
an unfortunate one, for, the English government had
just quelled with fire, sword and confiscation a formidable insurrection, and the inhabitants, stripped of their
arms and other means of resistance, were ill prepared to
renew the perils and incur the risks of another revolt.

In this condition of things, while the Viceroy was actively engaged in plans for putting the militia into such
a train that it might be speedily dispatched to any part
of the Kingdom which expediency might require, the
intelligence of the disembarkation reached Dublin.

"Happily" says an English writer, "for the integrity and safety of the island, perhaps of the British Empire, the French government at this time was guided by
men of feeble character, incapable of taking a decided
part at the momentous crisis. They suffered the period
when Ireland was in a state of active rebellion to pass
by without affording any aid to the insurgents; and now,

when it was quelled by the firmness of the government, they dispatched an inconsiderable force thither, from whose co-operation no important result could possibly flow."

Humbert effected a landing at Killala, on the 22d of August. He entered the bay under English colors, and the stratagem succeeded so well that two sons of the Protestant Bishop of that diocese, who had thrown themselves into a fishing smack, were surprised to find themselves prisoners of war.

"Humbert," says the same writer, "was one of those revolutionary Generals, who had risen from ignorance and poverty to affluence and command; yet, though he could scarcely write his name, he was an excellent officer, prompt in his movements and decisive in his operations."

At Killala, he was joined—I will not say re-inforced —by a mob of peasants without leaders or organization, ready, however, to avenge their country's wrongs at the peril of life. The forces of the enemy did not exceed fifty men, and they were all Protestants. They fled after a vain attempt to oppose the entrance of the French advance, leaving two of their party dead and twenty-one prisoners, among whom were all their officers. On the following day, Humbert forwarded a detachment toward Ballina, seven miles distant to the south, defeated the enemy's picket guards and took possession of the town on the night of the 24th, the garrison of which retired to Foxford, ten miles further to the south.

Though the military arrangements of the Viceroy were far from being completed, a force more than sufficient was quickly dispatched to the point of danger. On the 25th, Gen. Hutchinson arrived at Castlebar from Galway, where he was joined on the following night by

Gen. Lake, the chief commander of the West. Upon being advised of this movement, Humbert notwithstanding the fearful odds against him, did not hesitate to advance. His whole force consisted of only 800 men, wearied by long marches and want of sleep, and about 1,000 undisciplined and unequipped yeomanry. He had no other artillery than two small curricle guns. Opposed to him was an army, fresh and vigorous, advantageously posted, with a well served train of fourteen cannons. The number of this army has been variously estimated from 6,000 to 11,000 men, The lowest computation, consistent with probability, places the figure to 2,300, though it is thought by a writer likely to know the truth (Rev. Mr. Gordon), that it exceeded at least 3,000. Before this numerical superiority defeat seemed more than probable, but Humbert was inclined to test the mettle of his troops. He, therefore, directed an attack on the enemy's flank with such impetuosity, that a disgraceful panic seized the royal troops, who hastily fled in all directions, leaving their artillery and ammunition behind them. It is said that they ran eighty miles in twenty-seven hours, nor did they stop until they reached Athlone. Perhaps, indeed, they would not have halted there, had they not been met by the Viceroy in person, who was so deeply impressed with the danger attending this invasion, that he had left the capital to conduct himself the military operations of the campaign. He was informed by the fugitives that the French had pursued the army of Gen. Lake to Tuam, driven it thence and seized that post. Such was the demoralization caused by this daring feat of arms, that even at this day throughout Ireland this affair is jocularly spoken of as the "Castlebar Races."

From the capital of County Mayo, Humbert moved on to Sligo. Shortly afterwards, however, he found himself, after crossing the Shannon, confronted with an overwhelming force under Lord Cornwallis, who had recently succeeded Lord Camden, and held the double office of Lord Lieutenant and Commander-in-Chief. After several skirmishes, for none deserved the names of battles, Humbert found himself hemmed in by fifteen thousand veterans, and, notwithstanding a desperate resistance, was compelled to surrender, with the honors of war. The event occurred at Ballymuck. After the capitulation, his troops were found to consist of 748 privates and ninety-six officers, thus showing a loss of 256 men, nearly one-fourth of his original force.

The English refused to include the revolted peasantry within the terms of the surrender. To these quarter was denied, and a scene of butchery ensued that appalled the civilized world. Fleeing in dismay, fully five hundred were slaughtered in cold blood by their relentless pursuers. Dark and troublous times followed; and it was during that sad and gory period that a boy of thirteen—one of the future illustrations of Louisiana—resolved to leave home and country, after casting a long, sad and wistful look at the form of his father, a Gospel minister, dangling from a gibbet in front of his own church! That boy was Alexander Porter, erstwhile Senator of Louisiana and Associate Justice of the Supreme Court.

Thus ended an enterprise, which failed through no lack of energy on the part of the man to whom its achievement had been confided. As was before said, the small force of Humbert was only designed as the advance guard of a more extensive expedition, which sailed too late to be effective. Reinforcements failed him at the proper moment, through adverse and unexpected circumstances. Had these reached him in season, the power and prestige of England would have received a shock, from which she could not have easily recovered, and mayhap might have transferred the theatre of a sanguinary warfare from the continent of Europe to her own sea-girt borders. Humbert and army were kindly treated by their victors, with whom they at once became very popular, and, being admitted to parole, were prisoners but in name.

As soon as an exchange had been effected, he returned to France and was given a command in the army of the Danube, where, at the close of 1799, he was seriously wounded. Two years thereafter, he was recalled to Paris to advise with Gen. Leclerc, Napoleon's brother-in-law, in regard to the projected expedition against the insurgent colony of St. Domingo. This was in 1802. Accordingly, an army of 33,000 veterans was assembled at Rochefort, and a fleet of eighty sail under Villaret-Joyeuse transported the troops to their destination and co-operated in the campaign. Three divisions were formed, of which one was intrusted to Humbert. On their arrival, the country was found to be in full revolt. The blacks, under their famous negro leader, Toussaint L'Ouverture, had set up a mongrel government of their own, pillaging and firing the plantations of the whites. Murder and rapine were the order of the day. Under these circumstances, the iron-gauntleted hand of repression became inevitable, and the war on both sides was carried on with great barbarity. The story of that African revolt is a blot upon civilization. Appointed Governor of Port au Prince, which he had reduced to subjection, he ruled his province with a rod of iron. The words of Tacitus are here applicable:

Solitudinem faciunt, pacem vocant.

Thence, he hastened to the relief of Leclerc, who was being closely besieged at Le Cap, and aided him to repel his assailants and to compel the swarthy chief to acknowl-

edge the sovereignty of France. Amid the horrors of
this internecine strife, an additional misfortune threw
sombre clouds upon the scene. This was the sudden
breaking out of the yellow fever scourge, which more
than decimated the unacclimated Europeans. The hos-
pitals and camps were soon filled with thousands of the
plague-stricken victims, many of whom died for want of
necessary medical treatment. Even the Commander-in-
Chief was prostrated by the fell disease, and died a victim
to it in the island of Tortugas. Then chaos reigned
supreme. The objects of the expedition had signally
failed. Though L'Ouverture was a prisoner himself in
France, the work of pacification was far from being complete, and Napoleon found himself compelled to abandon further operations in that direction. An order to
that effect was, therefore, issued by the home government, and Humbert, availing himself of this permission,
set sail in advance of his companions in arms, and returned to Paris, having taken charge of his late General's
widow, Pauline Bonaparte, now his acknowledged mistress.

Napoleon received him coldly. Rumors of his
"liaison" with Pauline had already reached his ear,
and caused him great irritation. Besides, Humbert's
ultra republican principles clashed with the Consul's
ambitious views, who apprehended in the fearless Jacobin the possible embodiment of an avenging Nemesis or
a threatening Brutus. "A decided Republican," says Le
Bas, "he was ill received at court, and public rumor accused him of being on the best terms with Napoleon's
sister." This short and pithy sentence summarizes the
situation. Be this as it may, his disgrace became public
and he began to be shunned by the throng of sycophants
—the Reds of yesterday—who fawned and cringed be-

neath the trappings of the Consular throne. But Humbert had friends, strong and faithful, and their representation induced the relaxation of a severity that seemed unduly harsh. Napoleon sent for him on several occasions, and at each interview strove to convert him to his ambitious schemes. He represented to him the unstable condition of the country; the plots and reactionary intrigues of the foremost men of the nation; the aspirations of France after the blessings of peace and commercial amity with her continental neighbors; and finally, the immediate necessity of an iron-mailed hand to crush out every trace of anarchy or disloyalty. But these arguments failed in their intended effect. The United States, he would unhesitatingly reply, had offered a model government to the world, and a republic, based upon a similar constitution, would be a crowning reward for the noble and generous blood that had been shed by the martyred patriots of France. The interviews, supplemented by alternate threats and promises, resulted, as was to be exepected, in an open rupture, and, as a consequence, he was exiled to Brittany. There, smarting under the injustice of his sentence, he gave free vent to his feelings, but being apprised in time that he was to be arrested and tried for seditious language and practices, he hurriedly made his escape and proceeded direct to New Orleans, about the time of its purchase by the United States.

There can be no doubt that had Humbert, at this period of his life, consented to forego his cherished convictions, and listened to the syren song of worldly grandeur, the star of fortune would have led him to dazzling heights. When we recall the career of such "parvenus" as Murat and Bernadotte, one wearing the proud crown of Naples and the Two Sicilies, the other conquering

with his own trusty sword the heritage of the Vasas—
the kingdom of Sweden—what is there to make one
deny the possibility that by marrying Pauline, as he
could have done, he might not have reached a position
as glorious and as exalted? This result, it must be admitted, was within the range of probabilities at the time
when he was obstinately persisting in following the dictates of his conscience, and had resolved to cast his lot
with America and her infant Republic.

And this fact he well knew. In his frequent and convivial intercourse with our citizens in after years, he
loved, in language more expressive than polite, to refer
to the seductive offers, the corrupt habits, and the scandalous practices and morals of the Consular Court. From
those with whom in his post-prandial hours he would
unbosom himself—"déboutonné," was his favorite expression—I learned that his conversation was piquant,
anecdotic and charming, combining the rough bluntness
of the soldier with the charming grace of the courtier.
With the peculiar idiosyncracies of the men of his period
he was thoroughly "au fait." Of Sieyès' visionary ideas
and Utopian system of government he spoke in terms of
dissent, though of deference and respect. Fouché he
despised, characterizing him as a trimmer and a "chen-
apan." Carnot, the organizer of Napoleonic victories,
was in his eyes the personification of loyalty and political progression. Cambacerès he looked upon as a mass
of putty, molded and triturated at will, provided he was
allowed to enjoy his ease. Napoleon he denounced as the
prince of egotists. The intrigues of the erstwhile celebrated coterie of the rue Clichy were the frequent theme
of his gibes and sarcasm. He never forgave this notorious clique the lampoons with which they had once assailed him on his humble origin and calling, in the times
of the Directory. It is to be regretted that the reminis-

cences of the late Bernard de Marigny, to whom I delighted to listen in my early manhood, jotted down on
fugitive and detached leaves by this quaint and amusing "raconteur" have not been preserved or are now inaccessible, as they would at the present time, when the
lapse of years is throwing dark shadows upon the receding views of the past, have thrown floods of light over
the early days of Louisiana.

The actual date of Humbert's arrival in New Orleans,
notwithstanding diligent research, is now forgotten, but
it must have been a few years before the period when
our mothers and grandmothers were quaking in their
shoes from the apprehended invasion of Aaron Burr's
men in buckram. His advent here was acclaimed by
the colony of French birth or descent with delight and
pride, and his tall form soon became a central and imposing figure. Contemporaries describe him as a man of
herculean build, of free and easy manners, with decided
proclivities to dissipation and, later in life, to habitual
intemperance. He was not quite fifty years of age, with
hair, originally black, profusely sprinkled with streaks
of gray. His cheeks were ruddy, and his nose as rubicund as the color of his favorite Burgundy. His habits
were decidedly democratic, as he always preferred the
companionship of the "plebs" to that of the mushroom
adventurers who were wont to flock hither in quest of
affluence and notoriety. He, therefore, went little into
society. He was fond of places of amusement and public
resort. Among his usual haunts was a "café" kept by
a cripple, named Thiot, a St. Domingo refugee, who had
introduced a new beverage, known as "le petit Gouave,"
of which the General was particularly fond, and to
which he had become addicted during his sojourn at
Port au Prince. This establishment was situated on St·

Philip street, nearly midway between Condé (now Chartres) and Old Levee, on the right hand side as you go towards the woods. There he would usually spend his evenings, sipping his moka and "pousse café" at a friendly game of "piquet" or dominoes.

Another favorite resort was Turpin's *cabaret,* at the corner of Marigny and the levee, on the site of what has since been known as the "Fire Proof" house. It was a long, wooden tenement of rough exterior. Opposite to it was the Marigny mansion, and from one of its actual occupants, a garrulous old gentleman of the "ancient regime," the little that I know of this primitive period has been partly gathered. This cabaret—I might call it a groggery—was a house which combined all the features of a grocery, a liquor shop and a general caravansary, and, among the gay and boisterous blades that patronized "mine host," Humbert was no laggard. In later years, Turpin's corner became the chief rendezvous of the Baratarians, as the jolly freebooters who sailed and fought under Lafitte were then styled—a motley, fighting, roystering crew. Here, in revelry, song and drinking bouts, the Spanish doubloons, that had rewarded their audacity and crimes upon the high seas, were scattered to the winds, or rather, I may say, were raked with avidity within the money drawer!

In connection with this hostelry and its patrons, a characteristic anecdote is told of Humbert. "Si non é vero é ben trovato." It is said that on an occasion, when the anniversary of some event connected with the glories of the fatherland was about to be commemorated, a grand dinner was tendered him by his friends and compatriots. Turpin, as a matter of course, was selected as the Amphitrion of the feast. The board was spread in the spacious dining hall, and to it were invited the French convivial spirits of the town. The Baratarians, as you may infer, were on hand, and took a prominent part in the affair. Among the celebrities, were the two brothers Lafitte, Jean and Pierre; the celebrated Beluche, destined to become a Commodore in the Bolivian navy; Dominique You, whose pompous epitaph adorns a mausoleum to-day in the old St. Louis cemetery; Jean Baptiste Sauvinet, their banker, whose counting room was in the faubourg below; Huet, the planter at Bayou St. John, and "homme d'affaires;" Thiac, the blacksmith, the Damon of the Lafittes; Paturzo, the Genoese, whose after-life proved a model of industry and parental affection; Vincent Gambie, surnamed "nez coupé," from the partial loss of that facial appendage, a type of ferocity and brutal force; Jean Ducoing, who so skillfully handled the solitary mortar we possessed at the battle of New Orleans; Constantini, the last survivor of the band, whom I saw but one year ago, sitting on his door steps and basking in the sun, in a vain endeavor to revive his desiccated frame; Laporte, Sauvinet's book-keeper; Marc, their notary; St. Gême, one of Jackson's most trusted officers in the repulse of the British at Chalmette, and a host of others, who were all, more or less, connected with the then mysterious establishment on Grand Isle.

At the appointed hour, Humbert made his appearance in full uniform, with the tri-colored scarf of the defunct Republic girded around his waist. Applause greeted his presence, and, by unanimous request, he was escorted to the seat of honor. The work of reoicing began. The luscious viands and succulent hors d'œuvres vanished, and wines of the rarest and raciest vintage—plundered from some unfortunate Spanish gallion—followed in copious draughts. Then followed the bacchanalian song, the ribald jest, the pungent anecdote, adding zest to the general revelry, when finally patriotic toasts were announced as the close of the programme. It was at this moment, while the entertainment, fast verging into a debauch, was reaching the acme of gaiety and folly, that an unlucky wight, more enthusiastic than his fellows, proposed a sentiment in honor of the General, and preceded the same by a fulsome eulogy of his life and services. Humbert listened to him without interruption to the end, when, rising to his feet, his cheeks flushed with wine, anger and shame, slowly responded. Every eye turned toward him, and every sound was hushed. "Your words," he said, with quivering voice, "remind me of what I was, and what I am. I must not remain here as an associate of outlaws and 'forbans.' My place is not here." Then turning to Beluche, whom he particularly disliked, he poured forth such a scathing denunciation as that worthy had seldom, if ever, heard.

It is impossible to describe the confusion that ensued. Words of menace were outspoken and many a dagger leaped from its heath, but a single glance from Lafitte sufficed to quell the storm, as Humbert deliberately strode away. "Il est saoul," (he is drunk) said one. "No," responded a solemn voice: "His conscience spoke!"

It is needless to say that, yielding on the next morning to the force of habit, he had again lapsed into his usual course of dissipation, and had resumed his relations with the same class of people whom he had the day before so bitterly denounced.

Teaching was his sole occupation; at least, he was not known to have any other. One of his boy pupils, the late Pierre Seuzeneau, who for a number of years graced the Recorder's chair of the Third Municipality, and who died before the war while performing Consular duties at Matamoros, frequently entertained me with interesting accounts of the man's peculiarities and system of instruction. His passion was for the science of applied mathematics. Self-taught, the soldier-pedagogue, though strict, was not severe, and his school was well attended by urchins of whom he was extremely fond. He also gave private lessons in the scantily furnished room which he occupied in the attic of a low frame building on Frenchmen street, opposite Washington Square.

In addition to the paltry emoluments derived from his profession, a pension from the home government enabled him to eke out a modest existence. The collection of this stipend, doled out to him every quarter by the French Consul, the Chevalier de Touzac, afforded him the occasion for a great official ceremony. Attired in his old costume of a General of the Republic, the same, perhaps, which he had worn on the heights of Landau or at Castlebar, with his faithful sabre resting across his arm, he would repair, erect and proud, to the Consular office on Royal street to receive the pittance allowed by Bonaparte, as the price of his blood on the fields of Europe. Thence, he would gravely walk down the pavement towards his friend, Thiot, and, after partaking of a glass or two of his unique "petit gouave," he would return to his humble lodgings and doff his military trappings. On those occasions, every one knew his errand, for it was then only that he indulged in military display. "Humbert has got his money to day," people would say; "look out for a protracted bamboche," (spree). And such was invariably the case. Hardly had he laid aside the insignia of his former rank than he gave himself up to every form of enjoyment, until his last cent was spent.

Thus, between his professional labors by day and his usual nocturnal debauches, varied at times by games of cards or dominoes at the Petite Bourse or l'Hôtel de la

Marine, he spent his uneventful days in New Orleans, resigned to the fate which Providence had decreed. With Napoleon's accession to the Empire and the apparent consolidation of his vast projects, all his hopes of an early return to France were completely abandoned; and, even after the restoration of the Bourbons in 1814-15, whenever urged by his friends to avail himself of the amnesty offered by Louis XVIII, he would indignantly spurn the suggestion, preferring, he would say, the proud title of an American freeman to that of a subject of a King!

He was now getting old. Three score years had silvered his erstwhile jet black locks, but his spirit was as undaunted and his intellect as unclouded as in his palmy days, His form, still erect and imposing, towered like an aged oak which the storms had failed to bend or break. But the measure of his life of usefulness was not yet filled, and destiny was preparing for him noble work.

It was about this period that a dark speck—a distant war cloud—began to hover athwart the horizon, portending danger and ruin. Every indication seemed to point to New Orleans as the objective point at which the thunderbolt was to be hurled. The English fleet were at our doors. It was the same that had devastated the shores of the Chesapeake, and reduced our Capitol to ashes. Consternation, the mother of discord, pervaded our councils. Claiborne, usually timid and halting in his policy, though imbued with the noblest intentions, was at a loss to act with that precision and intelligence which the momentous occasion required, hampered in a great measure by the race prejudices which the clash between the newly emigrated Americans and the old citizens of Latin origin frequently engendered. Of the latter there was a gallant and formidable array in our midst. But the spirit of patriotism prevailed. Then, the men of action came to the front. To the enlarged ideas of such civilians as the Livingstons, the Grymes, and the Davezacs were added the practical plans of the Roffignacs, the St. Gêmes and the Humberts, all of whom had seen military service on the tented fields of Europe. Among these, Humbert, in the organization of the committee of public defense, took a commanding part. His services in placing our crude militia upon a war footing were in constant demand, while his personal magnetism with the native French population aroused their military ardor. When Jackson reached New Orleans in December to assume supreme command, the panic—or rather, the feeling of disquietude that had at one time prevailed—had ceased to exist. Every man was at his post, and though few in numbers, when compared with the surging hosts about to be massed against them, the spirit of loyalty could not be mistaken.

The bold Tennessean, with quick and piercing eyes, soon discerned the eminent qualities of the giant Frenchman, and at once assigned him to duty on his personal staff with the rank of Brigadier General. This appointment was no sinecure or idle compliment. Of his manifold duties, one was the direction of the mounted scouts, a special corps of observation that did yeoman service in checking the two near approaches of the enemy's advanced pickets. Characteristic anecdotes are told of his dash and recklessness while engaged in this dangerous duty, his detestation of the English being frequently evinced by his mad-cap forays into their ranks and challenges to personal combat. He assisted in constructing the terrible redoubts so ably defended by Dominique You and Beluche on the right of the line, and in mounting the siege guns that did such havoc to Packenham's veteran troops in their final assault. A strict disciplinarian, he never shirked any part of the work he imposed on others. Thus it was that, on the day of the decisive battle, Jackson found himself surrounded by as brave, disciplined and enthusiastic a little army as was ever led to victory.

While the battle was raging hot and fast on the plains of Chalmette, and the enemy, after the loss of their leaders, were giving way before the fierce and murderous fire of our riflemen and artillerists, the alarming intelligence reached the camp that our troops, Louisianians and Western men, posted, on the opposite bank of the river, had suddenly ran away before the advance of the enemy, abandoning their arms, ammunition and guns. The turn which this shameful flight had given to the situation was very critical, for a road leading to the easy capture of New Orleans had thereby been thrown wide open.

Speaking of this unexpected success, achieved by British dash and gallantry, an American writer says: "Soldiers there have been, who would have seen in Thornton's triumph the means of turning the tide of disaster and snatching victory from the jaws of defeat."

Jackson at once apprehended the danger, and with his ready intelligence selected without hesitation the man who was to blot out the disgrace.

"This success," says Roosevelt in his history of the naval war of 1812, "though a brilliant one and a disgrace to the American arms, had no effect on the battle. Jackson at once sent over reinforcements under the famous French General Humbert, and preparations were forthwith made to retake the lost position."

There is no gainsaying the fact that the menace to our city's safety was a dangerous one. Had Col. Thornton, as Stonewall Jackson or Phil. Sheridan would have

ORLEANS THEATRE, BUILT IN 1813
As per plan in City Library.

CHARITY HOSPITAL, 1815
Canal Street, between Baronne and Dryades (Hevia).
From design in City Library.

MILITARY HOSPITAL AND BARRACKS IN 1752. As per plan in City Library.

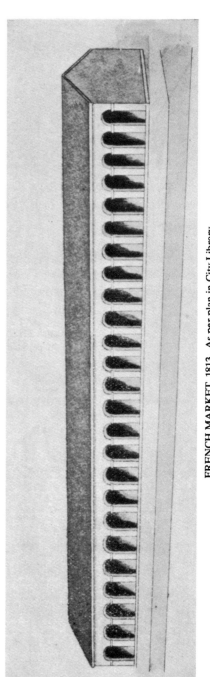

FRENCH MARKET, 1813. As per plan in City Library.

done under similar circumstances, availed himself of the general panic, and hastened his forces a couple of miles further up the river, he could easily, by crossing over by means of the numerous barge ferries then existing, have placed Jackson's army between two fires and thus imperiled his line of defence. Fortunately, the event proved otherwise. Parton, in his life of Jackson thus narrates the sequel:

"General Jackson, meanwhile, was intent upon dispatching his reinforcements. It never for one moment occurred to his warlike mind that the British General would relinquish so vital an advantage without a desperate struggle. Organizing promptly a strong body of troops, he placed it under the command of Gen. Humbert, a refugee officer of distinction who had led the French revolutionary expedition into Ireland in 1798, and was then serving in the line as a volunteer. Humbert, besides being the only General officer that Jackson could spare from his own position, was a soldier of high repute and known courage, a martinet in displine and a man versed in the arts of European warfare. About 11 o'clock, the reinforcements left the camp, with orders to hasten across the river by the ferry of New Orleans and march down toward the enemy, and after effecting a junction with Gen. Morgan's troops, to attack him, and drive him from the lines. Before noon, Humbert was well on his way."

From conversations I have had with parties who formed part of this command, I learned that the march was made with unusual celerity and order. In less than an hour after their departure, the men had reached the city and were hastening to the scene of danger. Here they were joined by groups of "home guards," who helped to swell the number to an imposing force. When they arrived at the spot, now a little village known as

'Tunisburg,' they met the discomfited and worried Creoles and Kentuckians, rallied them into good order and restored courage and confidence. The word to advance was given, and with fixed bayonets—Humbert's favorite weapon—the march was promptly resumed. On their approach, Gen. Lambert, the ranking General, alarmed at the changed condition of affairs, directed Col. Cubbins to abandon the captured works and recross the river with his whole command. "The order was not obeyed without difficulty," says Parton, "for by this time the Louisianians, urged by a desire to retrieve the fortunes of the day and their own honor, began to approach the last red coats in considerable bodies."

General Jackson recognized his services, in General Orders, to the following effect:

"Gen. Humbert, who offered his services as a volunteer, has constantly exposed himself to the greatest dangers with his characteristic bravery."

Gen. Jackson's subsequent measures have been the occasion of much criticism and considerable censure. It will be remembered that for some time after the treaty of peace had been signed at Ghent, the General refused to disband his volunteers under the plea that their term of service had not expired, and that they might at any time be needed to repel the enemy, who were still hovering in the vicinity of our coasts. Among those to whom this order was made to apply were a large number of French subjects, who, having loyally performed all the duties required of them during the times of emergency, deemed themselves unjustly treated by their enforced subjection to the inconveniences and diseases incident to camp life, after every prospect of danger was over. Besides, they complained of the sufferings of their families, whose sole supports they were. To these remonstrances the old hero turned a deaf ear, and abused them as secret traitors. It is evident that on this occasion, the General's usually equitable judgment had lost its balance. Their cause was, therefore, championed by the best men of the State, among whom were Louallier, a distinguished member of the Legislature, and the French Consul, the Chevalier de Touzac, a maimed soldier of the American Revolution, who had fought under Baron Steuben. This brought about a clash in public opinion, and Jackson determined to cut the Gordian knot by outlawing these parties and their adherents, imprisoning some and banishing others to Baton Rouge. Humbert, firing with indignation at the manifest injustice done to his countrymen, notwithstanding the loving admiration in which he had always held the Chief, boldly protested against this usurpation of authority, and matters looked as if serious trouble were brewing. But, with the official proclamation of the ratification of the treaty, calm counsels prevailed and the storm subsided. Thus ended an episode, which forms one of the most interesting epochs in Louisiana's history.

It is to be presumed that, after the events above narrated, Humbert, amid the congratulations of friends and proud of the laurels he had so richly won, must have relapsed into his old habits of conviviality and his deepseated affection for "*le petit gouave.*" And so matters drifted for a time, until one day he was induced by Mexican emissaries to once more don his armor in defense of liberty and independence. This was in the year 1816. Mexico was then in the throes of a bloody revolution, led by insurgents against the authority of Spain. The achievements of Hidalgo and Morelos are too familiar, in connection with the story of their political regeneration and final emancipation fron the rule of their Viceroys, to require here any extended notice. The tragic death of the former, the patriot-priest, is kept in holy remembrance in every town and hamlet in Mexico even to this day, while the memory of Morelos is held in equal veneration.

Determined to attach himself to this band of Patriots and to link his fortunes with theirs, Humbert enlisted in New Orleans about one thousand men, of all nationalities, and proceeded to the scene of action. This was the first and largest expedition of a filibustering character that ever departed from this city. When he reached Mexico, he found the condition of things entirely different from what he had been led to expect. Morelos, who had succeeded Hidalgo to the supreme command, had been captured and shot, and his forces dispersed. Balked in his hopes, he determined, however, to advance, and was joined by the formidable Indian Chief, Toledo, with a number of his dusky warriors. Thus reinforced, he fought his way into the very heart of the country, and succeeded in reaching El Puente del Rey, between Jalapa and Vera Cruz. But the back bone of the revolution had been broken before his arrival, and although he obtained several partial advantages over the Spanish forces, yielding to the inevitable, he disbanded his army and, in the spring of 1817, returned once more to his old home in New Orleans.

All that we know of him after this event is that "he taught in a French College"—the "Orleans" presumably—until the time of his death, which occurred in February, 1823.

As I had occasion to remark in the initial paragraphs of this sketch, nothing is positively known of this great man's last days on earth, and even his grave is unknown and unmarked. If this humble contribution to the history of Louisiana will serve to rescue from oblivion the memory of a patriot who loved our native State with more than filial devotion, who risked his life in her defense, and who died with a blessing upon his lips on American institutions, my aim, then, shall have been more than fulfilled.

CHAPTER IV.

A TALE OF SLAVERY TIMES.

It was on the morning of the 10th of April, 1834, that from the corner of Royal and Hospital streets, crepitating flames were seen to burst forth, threatening the entire destruction of a spacious brick mansion that adorned that locality. It was an imposing family residence, three stories in height, and the resort of the best society of New Orleans. Within its walls, European notabilities, including the Marquis of Lafayette, had been housed and entertained with that munificence, easy grace and cheerful hospitality peculiar to a Creole generation, now so rapidly disappearing. Its furniture and appointments—exquisite and costly gems of Parisian workmanship—were cited as *"chefs-d'œuvres"* in a city where objects of *"vertu"* and princely elegance were by no means rare. (It is a mistake to say that the Orleans princes were ever guests in that residence, as their visit to our city had occurred long before its construction. The Marignys were their hosts.)

Around this house were congregated a dense and excited throng, apparently feasting their eyes on the lambent and circling streams of fire that with forked tongues were rapidly enveloping the upper portions of the aristocratic abode. Their frowning brows and fiercely glistening eyes bespoke the terrible passions that raged within their breasts, for, that house, according to common tradition, was a hot-bed of cruelty and crime, and bore upon its frontispiece the curse of God.

The entire width of Hospital street was literally wedged in by a compact, surging tide, overflowing even adjacent thoroughfares. The pent-up blaze had burst forth from the kitchen above the basement, and from thence was rapidly ascending the story occupied by the family. The firemen, with their inadequate hand engines and equipments, were manning their brakes with might and main against the devouring element with only partial success, and were finally compelled to cut their way through the roof. On penetrating into the attic, and while ranging through the apartments, their blood curdled by the horrid spectacle which struck their view—seven slaves, more or less mutilated, slowly perishing from hunger, deep lacerations and festering wounds. In describing this appalling sight, Jerome Bayon, the proprietor of the New Orleans "*Bee*," wrote: "We saw where the collar and manacles had cut their way into their quivering flesh. For several months they had been confined in those dismal dungeons, with no other nutriment than a handful of gruel and an insufficient quantity of water, suffering the tortures of the damned and longingly awaiting death, as a relief to their sufferings. We saw Judge Canonge, Mr. Montreuil and others, making for some time fruitless efforts to rescue those poor unfortunates, whom the infamous woman, Lalaurie, had doomed to certain death and hoping that the devouring element might thus obliterate the last traces of her nefarious deeds."

When every door had been forced open, the victims were carried off and escorted by an immense crowd to the Mayor's office, where their irons were immediately struck off. Among those piteous blacks, was an octogenarian whose tottering limbs barely supported his emaciated frame. Among them, a woman confessed to the Mayor that she had purposely set fire to the house, as the only means of putting an end to her sufferings and those of her fellow captives. From nine o'clock in the morning until six in the evening, the jail yard was a scene of unusual commotion. Two thousand persons, at least, convinced themselves during that eventful day by ocular inspection of the martyrdom to which those poor, degraded people had been subjected, while the ravenous appetite with which they devoured the food placed before them fully attested their sufferings from hunger. None of them, however, died from surfeit, as it has been erroneously alleged. Numberless instruments of torture, not the least noticeable of which were iron collars, '' carcans,'' with sharp cutting edges, were spread out upon a long deal table, as evidences of guilt.

While these prison scenes were being enacted, supplying aliment to public curiosity, the excitement around the doomed building was increasing in intensity. As soon as the fact became generally known that Mrs. Lalaurie, with the connivance of the Mayor, had eluded arrest and effected her escape to a secure place of concealment, the howling mob, composed of every class, became ungovernable. They demanded justice in no uncertain tones, and had the hated woman fallen into their hands at that particular moment, it is impossible to say what would have been her fate. Actæon-like, she in all probability would have been torn to pieces, not by a pack of ravenous hounds, but by men whom rage had converted into tigers. During the whole of that exciting period, the populace awaited with anxiety, but without violence, the action of the authorities. It was the lull that precedes the coming storm. It was said that Étienne Mazureau, the Attorney General, had expressed his determination to wreak upon the guilty parties the extreme vengeance of the law. But when the shadows of night fell upon the city, and it was ascertained beyond a doubt that no steps in that direction had been taken and that powerful influences were at work to shield the culprits, their fury then knew no bounds and assumed at once an active form. At eight o'clock that night, the multitude having swollen to immense dimensions, a systematic attack upon the building was organized and begun. Their first act was the demolition of one of her carriages, which happened to be standing in front of Hospital street, and the same, it was said, that had borne her away. The sidewalk was literally strewn with its "débris." Next came the onslaught on the main entrance on Royal street, the portals of which had been previously barred and fastened and seemed to bid defiance to the shower of stones and rocks hurled against it. Abandoning this attempt, they obtained axes and battered down the window shutters, through which a wild horde of humanity poured in. No earthly power at that moment could have restrained the phrenzy of the mob—people resolved on exercising their reserved rights. Their work was no child's play. Everything was demolished; nothing respected. Antique and rare furniture, valued at more than ten thousand dollars, was mercilessly shivered to atoms. The cellars were emptied of their precious contents, and wines of choicest vintage flowed in copious streams, even into the gutters. Gilt panels, carved wainscots, floorings, carpets, oil paintings, objects of statuary, exquisite moldings, staircases with their mahogany banisters and even the iron balconies were detached from their fastenings and hurled upon the pavements. As crash succeeded crash, yells of delight rent the air. When Royal and Hospital streets became obstructed

with the accumulating wrecks, the latter were heaped
together in monticules and set on fire, which, together
with the glare of the blazing torches, offered a
sad and weird-like appearance. This first outburst of
popular retribution, notwithstanding the efforts of our local magistrates, continued not only during the entire
night—"*noche triste*"—but long after sunrise on the following morning. Then came a calm, a deceitful calm.
The fire had only partially destroyed the building, and
to obliterate the last vestiges of this infamous haunt became now the object of the rabble. The work of
demolition lasted four days, and only the charred partition walls remained standing, as a solemn memorial of a
people's anger. Tacitus says: "*Solitudinem faciunt,
pacem vocant.*" In the instant case, the work of destruction only ceased when there was nothing more to de-
stroy. The story that human bones, and among others
those of a child who had committed self-destruction to
escape the merciless lash, had been found in a well, is
not correct, for the papers of the day report that, acting
under that belief, the mob had made diligent search,
even to the extent of excavating the whole yard, and
had found nothing. When, on the subsidence of this
unwonted spirit of effervescence, reason had had time to
resume her sway, the local troops, with U. S. Regulars
to support them, were called out, headed by Sheriff
John Holland, who proceeded to the scene of disturbance and read the "riot act" to the crowd of curiosity
mongers who were loitering in the neighborhood.
Slowly and peaceably the people dispersed. Their
anger was allayed and their verdict carried into effect.
They now determined to wait and see what the constituted officers would do in furtherance of public justice.

In the meantime, thousands had been repairing to the
police station to witness the condition of the slaves, and

as the sickening sight only excited and increased their
resentment, our denizens were not slow in expressing
their contempt at the apathy and inaction of their municipal worthies. Judge Canonge, a man of strict integrity, and sound judgment, had not escaped the insults of
the enraged populace on the night of the first attack, and
while in the act of expostulating with them upon the
impropriety of their course several pistols had been
leveled at his head. Much, therefore, was yet to be
feared from the general discontent, as it was reported
that bodies of men had banded together for the purpose
of looting several residences, where similar barbarities
were said to have been commonly practiced. In fact,
this report proved no idle rumor, for a gentleman's
house in close proximity to Mrs. Lalaurie's was partially sacked, for which act the city subsequently was
mulcted in damages.

To repeat what I have previously mentioned, nearly
the entire edifice was demolished, the bare walls only
standing to indicate the spot where the God accursed
habitation had stood—walls upon which had been
placarded inscriptions in different languages, conveying
anathemas in words more forcible than elegant. The
loss of property was estimated at nearly forty-thousand
dollars. Says a contemporary·

"This is the first act of the kind that our people have
ever engaged in, and although the provocation pleads
much in favor of the excesses committed, yet we dread
the consequences of the precedent. To say the least, it
may be excused, but can't be justified. Summary punishment, the result of popular excitement in a government of laws, can never admit of justification, let the circumstances be ever so aggravated."

At last the wheels of justice were set in motion and
Judge Canonge proceeded to the office of Gallien Préval,

a justice of the peace, and furnished under oath the following information. The facts therein stated may,
therefore, be relied upon as strictly true, and furnish
data of a reliable character, of which some future historian of Louisiana may avail himself.

"Deponent (J. F. Canonge) declares that on the 10th
inst. a fire having broken out at the residence of Mrs. Lalaurie, he repaired thither, as a citizen, to afford assistance. When he reached the place, he was informed that
a number of manacled slaves were in the building and liable to perish in the flames. At first he felt disinclined to
speak to Mr. Lalaurie on the subject and contented himself with imparting the fact only to several friends of the
family. But when he became aware that this act of barbarity was becoming a subject of general comment, he
made up his mind to speak himself to Mr. and Mrs. Lalaurie, who flatly answered that the charge was a base calumny. Thereupon, deponent asked the aid of the by-
standers to make a thorough search and ascertain with
certainty the truth or falsity of the rumor. As Messrs.
Montreuil and Fernandez happened to be near him, he requested those gentlemen to climb to the garret and see for
themselves, adding, that having attempted to do so himself, he had been almost blinded and smothered by the
smoke. These gentlemen returned after a while and reported that they had looked around diligently and had
failed to discover anything. A few moments after, some
one, whom he thinks to be Mr. Felix Lefebvre, came to
inform him that, having broken a pane of glass in a
window of one of the rooms, he had perceived some slaves
and could show the place. Deponent hurried on, in
company with several others. Having found the door
locked, he caused it to be forced open and entered with
the citizens who had followed him. He found two negro
women, whom he ordered to be taken out of the room.

Then some one cried out that there were others in the kitchen. He went there, but found no one. One of the above negresses was wearing an iron collar, extremely wide and heavy, besides weighty chains attached to her feet. She walked only with the greatest difficulty; the other, he had no time to see, as she was standing behind some one whom he believes to be Mr. Guillotte. This latter person told him he could point out a place where another one could be found. Together they went into another apartment, at the moment when some one was raising a mosquito bar. Stretched out upon a bed, he perceived an old negro woman who had received a very deep wound on the head. She seemed too weak to be able to walk. Deponent begged the bystanders to lift her up with her mattress and to carry her in that position to the Mayor's office, whither the other women had been already conveyed. At the time that he asked Mr. Lalaurie if it were true that he had some slaves in his garret, the latter replied in an insolent manner that some people had better stay at home rather than come to others' houses to dictate laws and meddle with other people's business."

In support of the above statement, which is merely the recital of the discoveries made by the Judge personally and does not purport to include the result of the investigations of others, the names of Messrs. Gottschalk and Fouché were appended as witnesses.

What was the final issue of the affair? the reader will naturally ask. Nothing, absolutely nothing. From the 10th to the 15th of April, the day on which the riot was finaly quelled by the intervention of the Sheriff, the inactivity of the government officials had been glaring. The criminals, wife and husband, had been deftly smuggled through the unsuspecting throng, driven up Chartres street in a close carriage which I saw speeding at a furious gait and, after remaining in concealment some

time hurriedly departed for New York. From that
point they had continued their flight to Paris, which
they made their permanent residence. There I shall
not follow them, nor relate the effects of the ban under
which refined society placed them, nor of the hissing and
hooting with which the ''parterre'' assailed her once
at the theatre when their misdeeds became known.
The woman, it was currently reported in New Orleans
circles, finding every door closed against her, had subsequently adopted a strictly pious life and, spending her
time in works of practical charity, was fast relieving
her character from the odium that attached to it. A
characteristic trait in this singular woman's history is, I
am positively assured by persons who lived in her intimacy, that, at the very time when she was engaged in
those atrocious acts, her religious duties, in external
forms at least, were never neglected and her purse was
ever open to the hungry, the afflicted and the sick.
Like Doctor Jekyl's, her nature was duplex, her heart
at one time softening to excess at the sight of human
suffering, while at another it turned obdurate and hard
as adamant. In manners, language and ideas, she was
refined—a thorough society woman. Her reunions were
recherché affairs, and during the lifetime of her former
husband, Mr. Jean Blanque, who figures so conspicuously in Louisiana's legislative history, and whose important services to the State during a long series of years
should be gratefully remembered, her home was the resort of every dignitary in the infancy of our state. There
the politicians of the period met on neutral ground, es-
chewing for the nonce their petty jealousies, cabals and
intrigues, to join in scenes of enjoyment and refinement;
among whom I may cite Claiborne, the Governor; Wilkinson, the military commander; Trudeau, the Surveyor
General; Bosque, Marigny, Destréhan, Sauvé, Derbigny,

Macarty, de la Ronde, Villeré and others, all representatives of the "ancien régime;" Daniel Clarke, our first
delegate to Congress; Judge Hall, Gravier, Girod, Milne
and McDonough, destined to become millionaires, and
hundreds of others whose names now escape my
memory.

But "revenons á nos moutons." There is a class of
females, few in numbers it is true, the idiosyncrasies of
whose natures are at times so strange and illogical as to
defy the test of close analyzation, and to that class Mrs.
Lalaurie, with her sudden contrasts of levity and sternness, melting love and ferocity, formed no exception.
Whence proceeded this morbid spirit of cruelty? we ask
ourselves. Was it a general detestation of the African
race? No, for, of her large retinue of familiar servants,
many were devotedly attached to her, and the affection
seems to have been as warmly returned. All the theories, therefore, that have been built upon this particular
case, from which deductions have been drawn ascribing
exclusively the wrongs which I have just narrated to the
baneful and pernicious influence of the institution of
slavery, as some writers will have it, rest upon no better
foundation than mere speculation. Slavery was a social
device, replete, it is true, with inherent defects, but by
no means conducive to crime. The system was patriarchal in its character, not essentially tyrannical. The
master was not unlike the "pater familias" of the Roman
Commonwealth, but more restricted in power and dominion. Hence, it is more rational to suppose, and such is
the belief of many, that looking into the nature or "in-
doles," as the Latins had it, of the woman from its different points of view, she was undoubtedly insane upon
one peculiar subject—a morbid, insatiate thirst for revenge on those who had incurred her enmity. Our
lunatic asylums, it is said, are filled with similar cases,
all traceable to similar causes.

Upon the site of the old building, a fine structure, entirely new, was erected, noticeable in its design and architectural proportions.   A belvedere was added to it.   It has been named by some the " Haunted House."   There is no reason for the appellation, and if several of its occupants, with whom I have often conversed, are to be believed, there is nothing therein to haunt its inhabitants save ghastly memories of a by-gone generation.   No spirits wander through its wide halls and open corridors, but in lieu thereof there rests a curse—a malediction—that follows every one who has ever attempted to make it a permanent habitation.   As a school house for young ladies; as a private boarding house; as a private residence; as a factory; as a commercial house and place of traffic, all these have been tried, but every venture has proved a ruinous failure.   A year or two ago, it was the receptacle of the scum of Sicilian immigrants, and the fumes of the malodorous filth which emanated from its interior proclaimed it what it really is,

A HOUSE ACCURSED.

CHAPTER V.

ODD CHARACTERS AND CELEBRITIES.

THE CHEVALIER.

Toward the close of the last, and during the first decade of the present century, New Orleans society presented, like the hues of a kaleidoscope, varied and scintillating aspects. The bloody Revolution, which had been inaugurated by the taking of the Bastille and the excesses of the Jacobinical government which resulted therefrom, had produced in France an upheaval so terrible as to throw upon our shores a large number of political refugees. Many of these belonged to the old "noblesse." At a later period, on the accession of Napoleon to the Imperial throne, a large number of the dissatisfied and dangerous opponents of the new régime were compelled also to seek an asylum in our midst, preferring exile to persecution. Among the latter may be cited Gen. Humbert and Jean Victor Moreau, the hero of Hohenlinden and the hated rival of Bonaparte.

It was some time in 1795 that an *émigré* of the *ancien régime*, who, for convenience sake, I shall call the "Chevalier," made his appearance in our city. His intense hatred to everything savoring of social equality and his attachment to the flag of the " fleur de lys," un-

der which his ancestors had carved for themselves name,
fame and estate, had compelled him under his oath of
fealty to his liege and sovereign, to follow the royal
princes into foreign countries.   After sojourning a short
time in London, and eking out in that capital a meagre
subsistance by teaching French to the young scions of
its aristocracy, he had resolved to seek among our people a home, until such a time as the fortunes of war
should restore his idolized France to her lawful sovereign.

He was a quaint, odd-looking and singular old gentleman—the type of a gentleman, however.   He held in
holy horror the popular innovations of the *sans culottes*,
and reverently adhered to his powdered wig and queue,
his knee breeches, silken stockings, silver buckles and
frizzled shirt front and cuffs.   He was kindly received
by Baron Carondelet, and the residents greeted him with
a hearty welcome, deeming him a valuable accession to
the colony.

Although singular in manner, the worthy man was
an admirable philosopher.   Too proud to depend on
strangers for a living, he was not afraid or ashamed to
work, and with this object in view he opened a little shop
on Condé street, near Dumaine, which he pompously
dubbed a "confectionery."   The articles, and the only
ones, by the way, entitling the establishment to this
high-sounding name, were a stock of "*pralines*," red,
white and brown, by which we must understand the
kernels of pecans, ground nuts or peach stones, inclosed
in an envelope of burnt sugar.   Pralines, the necessary
adjunct of ginger cakes, "estomacs mulâtres," and
spruce beer, once so common upon the little stands kept
by colored women, were, as he claimed, his exclusive in-
vention, and, be the case or not as it may, he became by
this new industry the most popular man in the little com-

munity in his "quartier," particularly among boys. Besides this attraction, he had a monkey that possessed surprising qualities, and a pointer named "Sultan" that, like the dog in the Arabian Nights, could detect counterfeit money. At least, the honest folks who supplied the little market in his vicinity with chickens, butter and country produce thought so, and that was the same thing. It was amusing to hear the master of the shop calling his two familiars to aid him in picking out the good from the bad picayunes and 'leven penny bits. "*Allons*, Sultan, tell dose good ladie de good monay from le conterfait." Upon which, a seemingly important consultation would ensue between the dog and the chattering monkey. Pug would grin and scratch his side. Sultan would pretend to smell, and then with magisterial gravity would scrape the coin into the drawer. As there were no counterfeit "picayunes" or "bits" in circulation in those days, Sultan was never known to fail. " Madame," would the Chevalier say to the wondering, blowzing country lass, "Sultan is like de Pap; he is infallib; he nevaire make erreur." No wonder that Sultan and Bijou laid the foundation of this excellent man's fortune. They attracted crowds of custom, and, in two or three years he was enabled to expand his little business into a handsomer and more stylish store.

Later on, another attraction was added to his establishment—an attraction that at once diverted a portion of public admiration from Sultan and the monkey. It was a Dutch clock, heavily plated with gold, with two or three white and red figures in front. Before striking the hour, it played a waltz, whereupon the puppets were seen to whirl in the mazes of the dance. It was a decided hit. Such music had never before been heard in Louisiana, and the mechanism that produced such pleasing effects was a puzzle to their wondering eyes.

In those days, every unique piece of furniture or rare toy was believed to have formed part of the "spolia opima" of the French tornado, and, as a general rule, they were set down as the property of the unfortunate Marie Antoinette. The rumor, therefore, spread that the Chevalier's "horloge" was one of the rare objects of *vertu* that had at one time ornamented the boudoir of the murdered Queen. Whenever he was asked how much the supposed relic had cost him, or by what means he had become possessed of it, he would evade the questions with admirable dexterity. "Ah, *mon ami*," he would say mournfully, "ze Franch Revolution, it produce terrib effects. It was *grand* sacrifice. It is wort fifteen hondred Franch ginny." That clock, and the dog, and the monkey became the foundation of a fortune of fifteen thousand dollars from a beginning of a few pounds of sugar and a peck of pecans.

Such was the Chevalier in his *magasin*—a not inapt illustration of the French character of that period, adapting itself to every situation and exigency in life.

This pen picture of the Chevalier in his store bears no resemblance to that of the Chevalier after business hours. Then he would suddenly become once more the courtly and elegant man of the world. Society sought him and made him a favorite within its charmed circle, for the seller of *pralines* became transformed into a *roué* of the old court of Versailles. His conversational powers were brilliant and entertaining, and in narrating some of the horrid scenes he had witnessed during the Reign of Terror, he would hold his hearers for hours spell-bound by his manner and fervid declamation. Some of his *bon mots* and anecdotes, though savoring of that freedom which was the peculiar feature of the epoch, were full of piquancy and humor.

One of the princely habitations of New Orleans, in

which he always found a cordial welcome, was the mansion of Marigny, one of the magnates of the colony. An officer during the period of the French occupation of Louisiana, he had occupied important positions both in the civil and military service of the country. Sprung from a doughty, proud and noble race, the Marignys, from the famous d'Enguerrand, the prime minister and coadjutor of a King, and whose deeds and mournful death upon a gibbet fill many a page in medieval history, down to that branch, which settled and swayed in Canada, and from whom those of Louisiana are descended, were always noted for their chivalry in the field, and hospitality in their halls.

Thus it was that when, in 1798, Louis Philippe, then Duke of Orleans, accompanied by his brothers, the Duke of Montpensier and the Count de Baujolais, visited our city, the Marigny mansion became their home. Exiles, and wayfarers in necessitous circumstances, they were generously entertained, their wants supplied and their depleted purses well filled. Louis Philippe never forgot those acts of kindness, for, in after years, when an unexpected turn in the wheel of fortune placed him in power, he sent for Bernard, the son of his benefactor, entertained him with royal munificence in the Tuileries, and appointed his son, Mandeville, after he had completed his studies at St. Cyr, a lieutenant of cavalry. Had the latter continued in the service, it is impossible to say what high honors he might not have reached, with such a protector at his back, but love and yearning for his old Louisiana home compelled him to throw up his commission.

But I am digressing.

As soon as it became known in society circles that the Orleans princes had accepted the hospitality of the Marigny family, the Chevalier's ordinary habits under-

went a manifest change. He became taciturn, restless
and morose. The Marigny building knew him no
more. All the places of entertainment or amusement to
which the Duke was usually invited were studiously
shunned. His very nature seems to have suffered a
complete transformation.

One morning, Marigny called at the Chevalier's store.
"What has become of you, Chevalier, since the last ten
days? We see you no more. You have forsaken your
old friends. Come, come, cheer up, and spend this
evening with us. Moreover, the Duke is anxious to
know you, and, I am sure, you will be pleased with
his acquaintance." At the mention of the Duke's name,
the Chevalier cast upon his friend a look full of
reproach. "What you ask is impossible. You forget,
Pierre, that his father was one of my King's murderers. They are all dastards to their race and rec-
reants to their God. Mark my word! These Orleans
fellows will betray the Bourbon branch. Ah! *mon
ami*, they are all vipers of the same brood." Thus
speaking, the Chevalier gravely shook his head. It
seemed as if the spirit of divination had entered his
soul and laid bare to his mental view that policy of
state-craft and duplicity which eventuated in the utter
annihilation of the elder dynasty. Firm in his resolve,
he continued to avoid the distinguished exiles, and not
until after their departure for Havana did he emerge
from his enforced retreat and resume his habitual course
of life.

Toward the latter part of the year 1814, tidings were
received in New Orleans of the successful muzzling of
that dreaded lion, whose ravages had spread terror
through two continents, and of his captivity in the isl-
and of Elba. To the Chevalier this was gladsome news.
It meant not only the return to the throne of France of

her legitimate rulers, but also the restoration, as he supposed, of those wide, ancestral acres which the hand of spoliation had clutched. Whereupon, hastily converting into money his valuable effects, he set sail on a bleak December morning for Havre, amid the deep regrets of those who had learned to appreciate his kind heart, his fidelity to duty, and his fealty to King.

LAKANAL.

Several years after the departure of the Chevalier toward his *France cherie*, there came to Louisiana from the same shores a personage whose name had acquired extensive celebrity in Europe, and whose political character stood in striking opposition to the reverential nature of our friend, the Chevalier. That man was Joseph Lakanal, the Regicide. His life had been a series of startling contrasts. A man of science, an apostate priest, an agitator in Jacobin clubs, a stalwart in socialistic ideas, he had, by turns, exhibited talents of an exalted order.

Lakanal was in holy orders at the time when the flames of the French Revolution first burst forth. Burning with patriotic ardor, he left the church and was elected to a seat in the Convention, in which body he became one of the most enterprising managers of that faction which, by its energetic measures, prepared the triumphs of the Republican armies. On the trial of Louis XVI, he voted for the death of that monarch, as a matter of public necessity. He organized the institute and the military college, which, as '*l' ecole Polytechnique*, became so famous and useful under the Imperial government. His influence, invariably exercised in favor of men of letters, saved Bernardin de St. Pierre, the author of *Paul et Virginie*, and many other distinguished men from the rage of the Revolutionary Committee. He was a member of the body of the " Five Hundred."

On the return of the Bourbons, Lakanal's name, together with that of Carnot, Sieyès, Martin and Lucien Bonaparte, was struck from the rolls of membership of the Institute. During his long exile in the United States, Lakanal resided a good part of the time on the Spring Hill road, near Mobile, where, it is said, he cultivated a small garden and raised vegetables for the market. Previous to that, however, he had been appointed President of the College d'Orleans on the recommendation of Edward Livingston, but, notwithstanding his transcendent acquirements, both as a scholar and a teacher, he resigned his position soon after, as it became evident that his plans were not in accord with those of the Regency. Very few of his scholars are still living.

A revolution, which again drove away the elder branch of the Bourbons from Paris, put an end to the banishment of the aged patriot by the elevation to power as " *Roi des Français* " of that same Louis Philippe, son of Philip Egalité, whom we have already seen in New Orleans, as the guest of the Marignys. Lakanal, on reaching home, was feted by the Court, and was restored to his seat in the Institute, together with Martin and others. Thus was a regicide restored to his civic rights by the son of another regicide—a literal fulfilment of the prophecy of our eccentric but honest Chevalier.

Of Lakanal's early life in New Orleans but little is known. His scholarly habits, it seems, had made him somewhat of a recluse, and in the companionship of his favorite authors, it is said, he spent most of his leisure moments. His writings, found after his death, have never been published, and contain interesting memoirs connected with our early history. He was a kind and pure man, withal, but, unfortunately carried his theories to excess.

GEN. VICTOR MOREAU.

This hero, the enemy and popular rival of Napoleon Bonaparte, came to New Orleans in the first decade of the present century. He was originally a lawyer, but, on the declaration of war against France by Austria and other powers, he was elected, in 1791, chief of battalion of the volunteers of Rennes, his native town. He was made a Lieutenant General in 1794, and led the army of Flanders in a successful campaign. In 1796, he took command of the army of the Rhine and Moselle, and defeated the Archduke Charles, of Austria, at Heydenheim and in many other engagements ; but his supplies having been cut off by the withdrawal of Jourdan, who was to co-operate with him, he effected a retreat of twenty-six miles through three attacking armies, without losing a man, and bringing back seven thousand prisoners. He defeated the Austrians again at Hunningen in the following year, commanded in Italy in 1799, and in Germany in 1800, defeating the Austrians at Hohenlinden.

Napoleon was jealous of him. His growing popularity excited apprehension. He, therefore, caused him to be accused of complicity with the Royalists, and he was sentenced to exile in 1804. Moreau embarked for the United States, and, in the course of his travels through the country, halted at New Orleans. His public reception was a grand affair. The Governor, the military and civic authorities, as well as the people themselves—the *vulgus profanum*—turned out *en masse* to make the solemnity imposing. Judging from the meagre accounts of that period, the ovation must have been highly flattering to his pride. In these gratifying testimonials, his wife had a full share. The ladies were lavish in such acts of hospitality as were peculiar to the Creoles of the period.

He mingled freely with the French people, and was not slow in giving the accolade to the few veterans here who had seen service, both in Egypt and on the Rhine, of whom there were several. He played piquet with Pitot, discussed law with Derbigny, talked of strategy with Bellechasse, sipped wine with Claiborne, played billiards with Marigny, and in every way made himself agreeable and grateful to our elated citizens. He was extremely fond of horseback exercise, and would improve his leisure moments by taking short excursions around the surrounding country. It was during one of these jaunts in the neighborhood of New Orleans that, while in company with Major St. Gême, a man that had seen service in Jamaica, he was struck by the peculiar fitness of a piece of ground, which formed a natural bulwark against an invading land force from below the river. Sitting erect upon his horse, he critically examined the spot, and descanted with warmth on the many advantages which the locality offered, if fortified as an intrenched camp. His companion never forgot this incident, and related it to Livingston, who, in turn, repeated it to "Old Hickory," on the memorable, freezing 24th of December, 1814. That spot was Rodriguez' Canal, and it was the same which, upon its banks, Jackson selected and immortalized by his heroic defense! This is a historical fact.

Moreau was very short in stature, and, from the plainness of his person and the simplicity of his manners, no one would have imagined that under such a frail tenement was encased the soul of one of the greatest generals of the age. He was affable and engaging in conversation, and left a deep and favorable impression.

LAFAYETTE.

In the beginning of April, 1825, whilst the spirit of money-making and speculation was slowly developing itself on 'Change and other financial marts, the Marquis of Lafayette, the "Hero of Two Continents," as his admirers were wont to style him, arrived in our midst, after having visited Washington, at the special invitation of Congress, and journeyed through the various States.

The State Legislature, through an usual committee, had made arrangements for his reception with the Municipality. The Hall of the City Council, as well as the offices of Mayor Roffignac, had been entirely refitted, and were admirably adorned and luxuriously furnished. Everywhere the hand of tasteful woman was to be seen, as was evidenced by the gay festoons and garlands of natural flowers that graced the silken draperies. The public ovation tendered him was, if the public prints are to be credited, one worthy of the occasion, after which a grand dinner, with its consequent speech making, wining and consequent indigestion and headache, was gone through. Then a general illumination of the city followed, every citizen vying with one another in suspending from their balconies and windows tri-colored *lampions* or small lamps. A fine suit of apartments was, arranged for him at the "Hôtel des Étrangers," on Chartres street, and a table with thirty covers was set daily during the General's stay, for the entertainment of such planters and friends as he might wish to entertain. It is needless to say that, in the list of festivities, visits to the theatres and attendance at balls and select reunions were not overlooked.

He was fond of exhibiting to his visitors the sword of honor presented to him, more than forty years before, by Franklin, in the name of Congress, and to which was attached a peculiar history. It was in every respect an exquisite work of art. Its hilt and scabbard, of pure massive gold, were richly ornamented with precious stones and embossed figures. It was the worthy offering of a grateful nation to a patriot benefactor. During the Reign of Terror, Mdme. de Lafayette, dreading the excesses to which the sanguinary mob were liable to be driven, had concealed her most valuable effects in various secret places, and among the former was the appreciated gift of our infant Republic. Digging a hole in her own garden, at the foot of a tree, she buried the relic within a wooden box. It was not long after this occurrence that the Austrians seized the person of the General, and, after one year's captivity at Magdeburg, conveyed him to the citadel of Olmutz. Immured within one of the dungeons of that State fortalice, loaded with chains, a victim upon whom the Emperor Francis II was venting his rage, in retaliation for the cruelty and indignities inflicted upon his kinswoman, Marie Antoinette, he was only set free after a detention of many years by the sword of Napoleon. This occurred in 1797, but it was not before the year 1800, after the overthrow of the Directory, that he returned to France. His wife and two daughters, who had been permitted to share his prison life, accompanied him, and together they proceeded to LaGrange, his country residence in Brie. There Lafayette sought his hidden treasure, but alas! time, rust and moisture had entirely destroyed the highly tempered blade. Nothing but the hilt and scabbard had remained. To repair this mishap, and with a delicacy honorable to his character, Bonaparte, then Consul, caused a new one to be made, the materials used being the hinges of the dungeon doors of the Bastille, with allegorical devices illustrating the fraternal union of America and France.

DR. ANTOMMARCHI.

This is the name of a man long forgotten, except by the historical student. He was one of Napoleon's physicians during his captivity at St. Helena, and attended him in his dying moments.   Inasmuch as he resided and practiced medicine among us at one time, an outline of his previous career may not be out of place.

Francois Antommarchi was born at Marsiglia, Corsica, on the 5th day of July, 1789.   He attended the schools of Leghorn, Pisa and Florence.   In the latter city he became the pupil and afterward the successor of Mascagni, the great anatomist.   His works and researches were attracting much attention from the scientific world, when, in 1818, he was called away from his labors to attend the Emperor, at St. Helena.

Dr. Antommarchi left Rome in 1819, receiving verbal instructions from *Madame* Mére, as Napoleon's mother was called, and other members of the family.   Obtaining permission from the English government, he sailed for the rock bound island from Gravesend on board of a leaky merchant ship.

On his return to Europe after the Emperor's death, he published Memoirs entitled "Last Moments of Napoleon," wherein are transcribed all the particulars of his voyage and residence on the island; the sayings of Napoleon, the daily occurences of his life, and observations on kindred subjects.   Like the "Memorial of St. Hélène," by Count Las Cazes, and the *Mémoires* of Montholon and Gourgaud, they are full of thrilling interest. They abound in expressions of condemnation at the inhuman conduct of the captive's jailers.

When Napoleon, after enduring the martyrdom of a long agony, finally breathed his last sigh, Antommarchi closed his eyes, embalmed his body, inclosed his heart within an urn, and inhumed his remains.   As no calcined plaster could be found at St. Helena, the Doctor obtained permission to proceed in a boat to a distant part of the island in quest of some sulphate of lime, which, he was informed, was to be found in small quantities there. As soon as he had obtained a sufficient supply, and subjected it to a chemical process, he hastened, in the presence of the Emperor's household and of the British officers, to take a cast of the hero's features. He was perfectly successful. No disfigurement, no contortion, nothwithstanding the sufferings of a protracted death struggle, was visible on the mould, which a collector of "curios" in London was offering for sale, about two years ago, at 5,000 pounds sterling. Despite the opinion of some physicians, the Emperor's head was one of the largest known in Europe, and as Antommarchi himself said, *"un de ces phénomènes dont la nature se montre avare, et qu'il faut des siècles pour que la science en remarque de semblables."*

After the expulsion of the Bourbons, Antommarchi, who was in necessitous circumstances, made vain and unsuccessful attempts to dispose of the mask. He offered it to the government of Louis Philippe, but his proposition was declined by the Ministry. He refused, in London, an immense sum, 40,000 pounds sterling, it is said, but this statement is extremely doubtful. Whereupon, a joint stock company was formed in France, headed by Marshals Clausel, Bertrand and other distinguished ex-Imperialists, the main features of which was the duplicating of the bust to an indefinite number, and, with the proceeds of the sale, to purchase the Doctor's proprietary right thereto and to donate the precious memento to the *Hôtel des Invalides*. But the last part of the programme was never accomplished.

On a Saturday morning, November 9, 1834, the ship Salem, from Havre, reached our port. Among her passengers was Antommarchi. His arrival here had been preceded by the following letter, which spoke for itself :

" Paris, September 2, 1834.

"Monsieur le Grand Maréchal Bertrand :

"On the eve of leaving France for the city of New Orleans, I deem it my duty to acquaint you with the cause of my departure.

"As you are aware, the Emperor Napoleon, in his last will, had made provisions for my future and my fortune. Unforeseen obstacles have prevented the accomplishment of his benevolent intentions. The conservative measures which I took to enforce their execution have been disregarded. My rights and just claims being entirely ignored, I see myself compelled at this late day to resort to the tribunals of my country for redress. To attend in person to these judicial debates will be to me painful in the extreme. I separate myself, therefore, with great regret from France, and I kindly hope you will not disapprove of the motives that lead me to this determination. I hope that you will continue to do justice to one who has had the high privilege of once being your fellow-exile, of witnessing the long hours of anguish of the greatest man of his age, and of finally closing his eyes in death. Accept, *Monsieur le Grand Maréchal, etc.*,

" DR. F. ANTOMMARCHI."

No words can describe the enthusiasm of our French residents when, on descending the companion ladder, Antommarchi strode upon the wharf and was received by a large deputation, headed by Judge Maurian. He was escorted to the " *Salle Davis*," on Orleans street, where Dr. Formento welcomed him in elegant and feeling language. He was lodged provisionally at Marti's Hotel, known to-day as " L'Hôtel des Etrangers," on Chartres street, below St. Louis, where a continuous levee was held, an increasing stream of struggling humanity, and, at night, a serenade given him by the artists of the French theatre. These manifestations of respect and honor were prolonged during several days, at which time the effervescence having somewhat subsided, the Doctor was left a little more to himself and to repose. In response to inquiries, he said that his intention was to make New Orleans his permanent home, and by his industry and professional pursuits to earn the livelihood and position which had been denied him at home.

On the fourth day after his arrival, he addressed the following letter to Denis Prieur, the then mayor of the city.

" New Orleans, November 12, 1834.
"*To Monsieur the Mayor of New Orleans:*

" Deeply moved by the generous sentiments and the kind reception I have met at the hands of the sons of Louisiana, I have the honor to offer this city a bronze mask of the Emperor Napoleon, cast by me at St Helena, after his death, together with its base, made of bronze also.

"This gift is destined to perpetuate among your free people the memory of the greatest man of the world, and I am proud on this occasion of the opportunity which it offers to associate my name with the commemoration of those grand and glorious souvenirs which this illustrious and majestic head recalls to all brave Louisianians, as well as to the rest of mankind.

"Awaiting your orders in this matter, Monsieur the Mayor, I have the honor to be with high consideration,
" F. Antommarchi."

The communication was submitted to the City Council, and it was resolved that the *souvenir* should be accepted and placed in the Council Chamber. No sooner had this action become known, than the French residents determined to make it the occasion of a public jubilee. The Legion was called out on the "Place d' Armes," with flags flying and drums beating. French societies, in holiday attire, and thousands of the "unattached," preceded by numerous bands playing "*Partant pour la Syrie*" and the "*Marseillaise*," paraded Chartres, Royal and Bourbon streets, with Dr. Antommarchi at their head, until they finally halted in front of the old "*Cabildo*" (now the rooms occupied by the Supreme Court and offices), where the presentation took place in due form. I shall not go into the details of the affair, but the reader may picture to himself, as his fancy may lead, the speeches, the wine bibbing and the toasts that usually prevailed at such public convivialities.

Some years ago, while chatting with my regretted old friend, Mandeville Marigny, on old-time subjects, he reminded me of this incident, and, while the subject was still fresh in my mind, I went to the City Hall to see again this relic of a past generation. Together with an autograph letter of Louis Napoleon, the city's property also, it had disappeared. I remember that the "Evening States" called public attention to the fact at that time, but no information as to its whereabouts was ever elicited. This act of piracy occurred during the period of Reconstruction, of which our people had so much cause to complain.

A few days after the ceremony of presentation, he opened an office at Mr. Trudeau's residence, 13 Royal street, and another at the domicile of Nicholas Girod, one of the surviving mayors of the city, at the corner of St. Louis and Chartres. At this latter place, the poor were attended without remuneration.

It was not long after he had opened a practice among us that several persons whom he had offended, perhaps, by his garrulous habits, began to circulate reports that he was nothing but an arrant humbug—a *grand faiseur d'embarras*—and his popularity from that moment assumed a downward tendency. Several of our distinguished practitioners took umbrage at his empiric mode of advertisement in the daily papers, and looked upon him, if not checked in time, as a formidable competitor. Whether from motives of jealousy or in strict pursuance of their code of ethics, or from both causes combined, their persecution led to an angry controversy the result of which eventuated in disgusting him with the city and in his return to fatherland.

MARIQUITA.

Who is the man, woman or child that having lived in New Orleans, some fifty years ago, has not heard of poor "*Mariquita la Calentura?*" Her name was a household word, and her memory still evokes a smile. A poor, old, half-witted, tramp, she was once the terror of children, the martyr of boys and the sport of adults. Poor Mariquita! Though half a century has passed away since she left this world's harsh scenes, methinks I still see her as I saw her in boyhood's days, an incarnated Meg Merrillies, wildly gliding about the streets, her gray disheveled locks streaming in the wind, and the skirts of her dress bedraggled with mud.

Her appearance in public was the signal for the gibes and taunts of unruly urchins of every class and color, among whom she was always a special favorite. Then, like some ancient pythoness, agitating her lank, wiry form into every possible contortion, she would vent all the anathemas known to the Spanish vocabulary (whose language, by the way, is passably rich in billingsgate) upon their guilty heads. After which her pretended anger having somewhat subsided, she would usually close her tirade with a begging request. "*Donne moin picayon, papa? Qui ça to oulé fait avec? Acheté café.*" (Give me a picayune, papa? What do you want with it? Buy coffee.)

A life of strife and turmoil was her normal condition. She loved and wallowed in it. To be pelted with mud and clods was her supreme delight. If unnoticed, or allowed to pass along the street without a cat-call or a coarse joke, she would resent the slight without delay, and work herself into a passion. Then, her language, a strange *pot-pourri* of Spanish and Creole, became more forcible than polite, and chaste ears were rudely shocked. She was so well known about town, and was deemed such a privileged character, that the police and the public authorities never molested her. In fact, she was frequently to be seen around the Mayor's office, whom she would amuse with her sprightly sallies. She looked upon him as her natural protector. "*Ma vas dit Prieur, si to pas laissé moin tranquille,*" was her constant threat, whenever goaded beyond endurance. (I'll tell Prieur on you, if you don't leave me alone.")

Her origin and parentage were always a mystery—even the place of her birth. Upon those subjects she was determinedly reticent. Some said she was born in Cuba, others in the Phillipine Islands, and others again among the Islènos of St. Bernard, but, there can be no doubt that she first saw the light under the Spanish flag. My grandmother once told me that she remembered Mariquita in her younger days. Mariquita was married at that time to a middle-aged man, who peddled flints and spunk among cigar smokers (loco-foco matches being then an uninvented luxury), around the markets and the levee front. She was, at that period, a tidy, strikingly beautiful brunette, with dark lustrous eyes; fond of dress, and rather inclined to flirting and gallantry, a propensity which the snows of age seemed never to have checked.

Nothwithstanding her well-known disinclination to satisfy public curiosity as to her past history, I succeeded, on one occasion, to draw from her the fact that she had once passionately loved a Spanish officer. I concluded from her broken, disjointed sentences that grief for the loss of her lover had affected her brain. With a sweet smile irradiating her parchment-colored visage, she would exclaim : "*Ah! lité si joli, avec so beau riban rouge su so potrine.*" (Oh! he was so handsome, with his pretty red scarf around his breast.) Then, as if fearing she had said too much, she would resume with croning voice her usual refrain : "*Donne moin picayon, papa.*"

Poor Mariquita died some time in 1845, on Barracks street, under a shed in a woodyard. When found in the morning, she was arrayed in her usual tatters and rags. But, as soon as the boys, who had teased her so much in life, became aware of her sudden taking off, they purchased by a subscription among themselves, the neat coffin in which she was buried, and followed her remains to the ditch, which was to be her last resting place.

It is conjectured that nearly five hundred striplings— the sole mourners on the occasion—accompanied her funeral, a spectacle never witnessed before in New Orleans. They had lost their early, though demented friend, and God, who reads into the hearts of his creatures, smiled upon the affectionate scene.

It may not be amiss to give the origin of the name, by which she was universally known. Mariquita is the diminutive of Maria, and "*la calentura,*" which signifies "fever" in Spanish, was a *soubriquet* given her, on account of her constant suffering, as she claimed, from that ailment—the result probably of her disordered brain. One of the finest works of art in New Orleans was painted by an eminent local artist, and represents her in the attitude of stooping over a fireplace, watching her coffee pot and warming her hands. The resemblance is realistic, and, as a finished piece of work, it deserves to be preserved in an art gallery.

THE OLD MAN OF THE CATHEDRAL.

Keeping ward and vigil over the venerable pile erected by the erstwhile roysterer, Don Almonester, in expiation and atonement for many youthful indiscretions and peccadilloes, was wont to be seen, many years ago, from early morn to late sunset, a familiar figure, bent with age, flowing grizzly locks, unkempt beard and compact, heavy build. Slowly pacing up and down the pavement between the old Cabildo and St. Anthony's Alley, muttering prayers and soliloquies in words that no one could comprehend, and occasionally casting his eyes heavenward with expressions of fervor, as if wrapt in the ecstacy and contemplation of some holy vision, this pious octogenarian became the cynosure of every regard and the wonder of passing strangers. Strongly did he remind me of the words of the bard :

" His brain is wrecked—
For, ever in the pauses of his speech,
His lips doth work with inward mutterings,
And his fixed eye is riveted fearfully
On something that no other sight can spy."

His garb was uncouth and worn threadbare, of woolen fabric. A heavy winter overcoat, of a drab color, incased his muscular frame, which vestment he was never known to discard, not even in the midst of summer's solstitial heat. Poor Pietro! His life had no doubt been a checkered one, and his history an unsolved mystery. He never spoke to anyone. He never asked for alms, though occasionally, and only when want pressed upon him, he would accept a small piece of silver or a bit of food from the Catholic worshippers.

From early boyhood, I became deeply interested in this strange, reticent and harmless old man. As I grew in years, I endeavored several times by trivial acts of kindness to win his confidence, and in his native language to lead him into conversation. But my efforts proved fruitless; with a grateful look, but a sigh of bitter anguish, he would abruptly turn away, mumble a few incoherent words, and resume his patient vigil around the consecrated ground. It was evident that he would not speak, and that his secret, whatever it might be, was securely locked within his breast. Nor did my inquiries among the educated classes of the Italian colony, the Valettis, the Natilis, the Gabiccis, the Lanatas and other equally representative men, elicit more satisfactory information. Further than the facts that the mysterious " old man of the Cathedral" was a Genoese by birth, an erstwhile merchant prince, and the victim of a shipwreck on the coast of Yucatan, the horrors of which had bereft him of reason, while the angry waves, lashed into fury, had engulfed his worldly goods and hoarded wealth, nothing else could be learned. With the sinking of this precious argosy, all traces of his former self had forever disappeared. His physical appearance was peculiarly interesting. Despite his dirt-begrimed face, his matted beard, his shaggy, streaming white locks, his neck deeply sunk between huge stooping shoulders, yet his piercing eyes, commanding look and self-possessed demeanor bespoke a man of gentle lineage and good education. No one knew where he slept, or took his meals. He was sometimes seen munching a biscuit or cake, given him by some good natured youngster, but otherwise his retreat and mode of living was an impenetrable secret. With the deepening of night's shadows, he would suddenly disappear, while, with the punctuality of the sun's rise, he was to be seen at his post at the church door, intent on his devotions and the recitation of his beads. Then, his orisons concluded, he would rise from his kneeling posture and renew, like a faithful sentry, his usual rounds. When driven away by the intense heat, mopping his forehead dripping with beads of perspiration, he would hie himself to the rear of the structure and seek shelter under the grateful shades of the magnolias. Often and often, while on my way to the court building, have I watched his every motion, and noticed, not without surprise, the clock-work regularity of his daily movements and actions.

Unlike crazy Mariquita, the plaything and buffoon of the whole community, poor Pietro, though a victim to the same sad infirmity, had won the love and respect of every one. Never was a complaint, an oath or an obscene expression known to escape his lips. His sufferings he bore with meek resignation, and in the abodes of peace and rest to which his long suffering soul has sped, it is to be hoped that he still continues in his former occupation of " guardian of the church."

The following lines from the pen of Geo. W. Christy, a Louisianian as talented as he was modest, are worthy of reproduction.

THE WIZARD OF THE CATHEDRAL.

" When the vesper bell doth toll,
Calling on the weary soul,
                To tell a prayer;
And the dim old arches ring,
    As the full voicéd choir sing
                A solemn air;

Up and down, as in a spell,
　Treads that ancient sentinel,
Day and night, and night and day,
　Ever seemeth he a prey
　　　　To black despair.
Wan in feature, bent in form,
　Through the sunshine, through the storm
Round that ancient building going,
　Upward glances often throwing,
Never weary, in a spell,
　Treads that aged sentinel.
People say that he is crazed,
　Strangers passing seem amazed,
　　　　As they ask—
Where he lives, and what his name,
　Where he goes, and whence he came,
　　　　Idle task;
Whence he came, or whither goes,
　None may tell, for no one knows,
'Tis a simple tale to tell
　Why he plays the sentinel.
Dreaming ever in his mind,
　That by searching he will find
　　　　A treasure,
Lost to him long years before
　Near that old Cathedral door;
That the measure of his joys will come again
　If the treasure he regain.
Wan in feature, bent in form,
　Through the sunshine and the storm,
　　　　For that treasure
Looks he here, and looks he there,
　Round the building, every where,

That the measure of his joys may come again
  To relieve his fevered brain.
Sentinel! thy vigils keep
  Round that ancient building still
Near its sacred threshold sleep!
  There await thy Master's will.
'Tis the treasure of thy soul,
  Which thy dreaming Fancy sees.
List! again that Vesper toll!
  Enter, crawling on thy knees.
Ashes cast upon thy head,
  Bending meekly to the ground.
Now arise! thy dream hath fled,
  Lo! the treasure lost is found!

DOMINIQUE YOU.

After a residence in our midst, covering a period of
nearly twenty two years, there died in this city, on the
15th of November, 1830, a man who, despite the criminal record of his early career, and the obloquy once
attached to his reputation, achieved glory for himself,
nobly redeemed a tainted name, and at his death received public obsequies due only to heroes and public
benefactors.   This man was Dominique You, the Corsair
of the Gulf, the terror of the Caribbean Sea.

His life was a romance—a series of daring deeds.   He
was born in the Island of St. Domingo, in the town of
Port au Prince, and from boyhood was a rover on the
sea.   Finding himself in France at the time of the
Revolution, he took part in the several engagements
that preceded the establishment of the Consulate, and,
being an expert artillerist, accompanied Leclerc, Napoleon's brother-in-law, in his ill-fated expedition
against the revolted negroes of Hayti, in 1802.

After the return of the discomfited army to France, he engaged in privateering on his own account, but, finding this occupation unprofitable and expensive, he came to this city, where he soon found employment under Jean and Pierre Lafitte, the world-known reputed pirates, whose favorite lieutenant he soon became. He was nicknamed *Capitaine Dominique* by the French, though *Joannot* was the *nom de guerre* he had assumed. This *alias* is usually affixed to his name in court records. His courage was proverbial. At the time Venezuela declared her independence, You was granted letters of marque from the insurgent patriots, and inflicted terrible damage on Spanish commerce. His name became one of terror to the proud Dons, and it is more than likely that, in his newborn zeal for the infant Republic, he occasionally mistook neutrals for enemies. For several years he took part in the unlawful operations of the brothers Lafitte, such as the importation of slaves from the West Indies and the introduction of contraband goods unlawfully obtained, until in July, 1814, he was indicted by a United States Grand Jury for piracies committed in the Gulf. He succeeded in evading arrest. When Commodore Patterson afterwards made his successful raid on the establishment of the Baratarians, scattered their clans to the winds and seized all of their warships. You found a refuge in the swamps of the interior; but, when the English invaded the soil of Louisiana, after spurning their seductive offers, he at once proffered his services to the Government, which were accepted after some hesitation. His daring in that memorable campaign constitutes one of the most glorious pages of our State history.

Pardoned by a special proclamation of President Madison, he turned away from the path of crime, and engaged in peaceful pursuits. His example was imitated by many of his former companions, who forsook their predatory habits and became useful and honorable members of society. Several took wives among us, having left descendants who are now living in our midst. You was never wedded. In later years he occasionally drifted into politics, and, from the fact that he was always a staunch supporter of his veteran chief, I must suppose he was a "Jackson Democrat."

He died at his residence, at the corner of Love and Mandeville streets, at the age of fifty-five years, in a state of poverty bordering on penury. Too proud to ask for assistance from any of the friends who would have promptly and cheerfully relieved his pressing wants, he bore his adverse fate with a resigned spirit. It was only when death had seized him in its relentless grasp that his old comrades and the public generally became aware of his straitened circumstances. The members of the City Council, upon being apprized of the fact, resolved to pay the sacred debt of gratitude which the country owed him, and ordered, in the name of the corporation of New Orleans, extensive preparations for his interment. In this testimonial of honor the whole Legion, a model military organization of uniformed companies, to the success of which the deceased had greatly contributed during his lifetime, turned out to a man and made an imposing pageant. On the day set apart for the funeral, every bank and business house was closed, the flags of our shipping and public buildings, even those of the foreign consuls, were displayed at half-mast, while the salvos of the Orleans Artillery, of whom he was one of the original founders, rang out a last requiem over his memory.

He was buried in the old St. Louis cemetery in the centre aisle of which, near the gate, is now to be seen his well-kept tomb, upon which an epitaph in French commemorates his virtues and valor—

"Sur la terre et sur l'onde."

CHAPTER VI.

THE VOUDOUS.

THEIR HISTORY, MYSTERIES AND PRACTICES.

Who has not heard, in connection with the local history of New Orleans, of that mysterious and religious sect of fanatics, imported from the jungles of Africa and implanted in our midst, so well known under the appellation of *Voudous?* St. John's Day—the 24th of June—is the day consecrated by them to their peculiar idolatry. Drifting into this country and the West India Islands with the constant influx of the Slave Trade, this disgusting organization or order, with its stupid creed and bestial rites, made considerable progress among the low and ignorant of our population in the early period of the present century, and extended its ramifications among the servile classes through most of our Creole parishes.

Their dances are original, partaking somewhat of the character of the " *Calinda* " and " *Bamboula,*" now made world-famous by the genius of our fellow-townsman, Edward Gottschalk, who has set them to most exquisite music.   But it is not for these dances alone that the study of Voudouism deserves to be considered, but for the further reason that they are accompanied by cir cumstances so odd, strange, and, I may say, atrocious, as to deserve particular notice.

According to the Africans of the Arada nation, who claim to have preserved unsullied the faith and ceremonies of their religion, the word "Voudou" signifies an all-powerful and supernatural Being, from whom all events derive their origin. And what or who is that Being? A serpent, a harmless snake, under whose auspices these religionists gather. The attributes of prescience and knowledge of the past are ascribed to it, and these he manifests through the medium of a High Priest selected by the sect, and most frequently through the lips of the black wench, whom the love of the former has elevated to the post of a consort.

These two ministers of the God-Serpent, claiming to act under its inspiration, assume the pompous names of King and Queen; at other times the despotic titles of Master and Mistress, and sometimes those of a more affectionate nature, Pápa and Mamma. They hold office by a life tenure, and exact unbounded confidence from their adepts. They communicate the will of the Serpent in all matters appertaining to the admission or rejection of candidates. They prescribe the duties and obligations incumbent upon them. They receive the gifts and presents, which the God expects as a tribute to his power. To disobey or resist means offence to the Deity, and subjects the recalcitrant to great penalties.

As soon as this system of domination, on the one hand, and of blind submission on the other, has been well established, they hold meetings at stated periods, at which the King and Queen preside, in accordance with traditions borrowed from Africa, and varied at times by creole customs and others of European origin, as, for instance, in matters of dress and ornament. These reunions, whenever they are conducted in their primitive purity,

are always strictly *secret*, are held in the night time, and
in a place so secluded as to escape the gaze of any pro-
fane eye.   There, every member, after divesting himself of his usual raiment, puts on a pair of sandals and
girds his loins with a number of red handkerchiefs.
The Voudou King is distinguished from his subjects by a
greater number, and of a finer quality, of those coverings,
always using some crimson stuff, wrapped around his
kinky head, in lieu of a diadem.   A cord, usually blue,
encircles his waist.   The Queen is dressed with more
simplicity, affects red garments and adorns her person
with a sash of the same hue.

The King and Queen take their positions at one end
of the room, near a species of altar, on which is placed a
box, wherein the serpent is imprisoned, and where the
affiliated can view it outside the bars.   As soon as a strict
inspection assures them that no intruder is within hearing or sight, the ceremony begins by the adoration of
his Snakeship, by protestations of fidelity to his cult,
and of submission to his behests.   They renew into the
hands of the King and Queen the oath of secrecy, which
is the corner stone of their order, and, while this part of
the ritual is being accomplished, horrible and delirious
scenes follow.

The worshippers being thus prepared to receive the
impressions which the Sovereigns seem to infuse into
them, the latter, assuming the benign tones of a fond
father and mother, extol the happiness which is in store
for every faithful Voudou, exhort them to confidence,
and urge them to always seek their advice, whatever the
emergency may be.

The group then breaks up, and each one, according
to his wants or right of precedence, comes forward to
implore the Voudou God.   As the majority were slaves,
they would ask for the gift of domination over the minds

of their masters. One would solicit money, another success in love, while a third would crave the return of some faithless swain, or a speedy cure or the blessings of a long life. While a withered hag would be conjuring the God for a youthful admirer, a young one would hurl maledictions upon a successful rival. There is not a passion, to which human nature may be prone that is not incarnated or typified in these motley assemblies, while crime itself is frequently invoked by those carried away by malice.

To every one of these petitions or invocations, the Voudou King lends a heedful ear. The spirit begins to move him. He suddenly seizes the precious box, lays it on the floor, and places the Queen upon the lid. No sooner has her foot touched the sacred receptacie, than she becomes possessed, like a new Pythoness. Her frame quivers, her whole body is convulsed, and the oracle pronounces its edicts through her inspired lips. On some she bestows flattery and promises of success, at others she thunders forth bitter invectives. Following the trend either of her own wishes, of her personal interest, or of her capricious mood, she dictates irrevocable laws, in the name of the serpent, to a set of idiots, who gulp down every absurdity with stupendous credulity, and whose rule is blind obedience to every mandate.

As soon as the oracle has answered every question propounded, a circle is formed and the serpent is put back upon the unholy fane. Then each one presents his offering, and places it in a hat impervious to prying curiosity. These tributes, the King and Queen assure them, are acceptable to their Divine protector. From these oblations a fund is raised which enables them to defray the expenses of the meetings, to provide help for the needy, and to reward those from whom the society

expects some important service. Plans are next proposed, and lines of action prescribed under the direction, as the Queen always affirms, of the God, "Voudou." Of these many are contrary to morality and to
the maintenance of law and order. An oath is again
administered, which binds not only every one to secrecy, but to assist in carrying out the work agreed
upon. Sometimes, a bowl, dripping with the still warm
blood of a kid, seals upon the lips of the assistants the
promise to suffer death rather than reveal the secret,
and even to murder a traitor to this obligation.

And now the Voudou dance begins.

If there be a candidate present, his initiation inau-
gurates this part of the ceremony. The Voudou King
traces a large circle in the centre of the room with a
piece of charcoal, and places within it the sable neo-
phite. He now thrusts into his hand a package of
herbs, horse hair, rancid tallow, waxen effigies, broken bits of horn, and other substances equally nau-
seating. Then lightly striking him on the head with
a small wooden paddle, he launches forth into the
following African chaunt!

> "Eh! eh! Bomba, hen, hen!
> Canga bafio te,
> Canga moune de le,
> Canga do ki la
> Canga li."

As these words are repeated in chorus by the onlook-
ers, the candidate begins to "squirm" and to dance.
This is called " *monter voudou.*" If, unfortunately, he
should in the excess of his frenzy, happen to step
out of the line enclosing the mystic circle, the song
ceases at once, and the King and Queen turn their
backs upon him, in order to neutralize the bad omen.

When the dancer recovers his self-possession, he re-enters the ring, becomes convulsed again, drinks some stimulant and relapses into a hysteric fit. To put a stop to these symptoms, the King sometimes hits him smartly with his wooden paddle, and, if needs be, uses a cowhide. He is then led to the altar to take the oath, and from that moment he is a full-fledged member of the Order.

On the termination of the ceremony, the King places his hand or foot on the box where the snake is ensconced, and experiences a shock. He communicates by contact this impulsion to his Queen, and through her the commotion is conveyed to every one in the circle. Every one then begins to experience convulsions through the upper portion of the body, the head and shoulders. A work of dislocation of the bones seems to be going on. The Queen particularly appears to be most violently affected. She goes from time to time to the voudou serpent, to gather a new supply of magnetic influence. She shakes the box, and the tinkling bells, that are usually suspended from its sides, increase the general delirium. Add to this copious draughts of spirituous liquors. Then is pandemonium let loose. Fainting fits and choking spells succeed one another. A nervous tremor possesses everybody. No one escapes its power. They spin around with incredible velocity, whilst some, in the midst of these bacchanalian orgies, tear their vestments, and even lacerate their flesh with their gnashing teeth. Others, entirely deprived of reason, fall down to the ground from sheer lassitude, and are carried, still panting and gyrating into the open air.

What is undoubtedly true and is a remarkable phenomenon among these people, is the existence of that species of electric fluid which urges these people to dance, until bereft of sense through complete exhaustion. They are not unlike the Shakers in this respect.

These singular details are gleaned from a work entitled "*Souvenirs d'Amérique*," written by a talented Creole lady of New Orleans, who seems to have made a special study of the subject.

The greater portion of these people came to Louisiana at the period of the St. Domingo Revolution, when thousands of whites and blacks repaired to our shores in quest of an asylum from impending massacre. They brought with them the peculiar dialect of their unfortunate and doomed island home, and, among other customs which their slaves introduced, they domesticated in our midst the lascivious saturnalia, the horrid orgies and the dangerous, and, in many cases, criminal practices that constitute the ritual of this African institution.

A brief historical sketch of their existence and leaders in New Orleans may prove of interest to the general reader.

In the foreground of the Kings and Queens who wielded here their sceptres with despotic power, was a fellow, named John, better known as "DR JOHN," who lived out on the Bayou Road, near its intersection with Esplanade street. He was a negro of the purest African type. His ebony face was horribly tattoed, in conformity with the usages of the Congo tribe. He was glib of tongue, neat in his apparel, always wore a frilled shirt front and claimed miraculous powers for the cure of diseases. His room or office was packed with all sorts of herbs, lizards, toads and phials of strange compounds. Thousands visited him. As an Indian doctor, he was a great success.

In addition to this industry, he cumulated the functions of an astrologer, a mind-reader and professed cartomancy and divination also by means of pebbles and shells. His control over the credulous and super-

stitious element of society was incredible. He pretended ability to read the past, to know the present and
to forecast the future. Charms and amulets were special objects of traffic in his shop, and realized very
high prices. One would stand aghast were he to be
told the names of the high city dames, who were wont
to drive in their own carriages, with thickly veiled
faces, to this sooty black Cagliostro's abode, to consult him upon domestic affairs. As he was well informed of many family secrets, through the connivance
of the hundreds of negro servants attached to the
cause of Voudouism, his powers of vaticination cease
to be a subject of wonder.

He exercised the functions of voudou royalty for upward of forty years, and was most strict in the observ-
ance of the African ritual. He was a negro to the
core—in color, origin and principle. A mulatto was
his special aversion. " Too black to be white," he was
wont to say, " and too white to be black, he is nothing
but a mule." He was well off, having accumulated
some property. He died shortly after the war, at a very
advanced age, but such were his vitality and powers of
endurance that his body ever remained erect and his
hair jet black.

Not unlike " Doctor John " in many respects, *Marie
Laveau*, deserves mention. In her youth, she was a
woman of fine physique and a noted procuress. Introducing herself into families as a hair dresser, she would
assist in the clandestine correspondent of sweethearts,
and aid youthful lovers—and old coquettes as well—in
their amours. She was an essentially bad woman.
Though queen of the Voudous, she excised the ritual
of the original creed, so as to make it conform to the
worship of the Virgin and of other saints. To idolatry
she added blasphemy. She was the first to popularize

—I should say, vulgarize—voudouism in New Orleans. She would invite the reporters of the press, the magnates of the police force, the swells of the sporting fraternity to their public dances and drinking bouts, where a snake in a box, a beheaded white rooster and other emblems of their religious belief were conspicuously exposed. These festivals occurred yearly on St. John's eve, at some convenient spot not far from the bayou which bears that name. But this was a mere device to hoodwink the unwary. Her secret conclaves were usually held in a retired spot upon the lake shore known as the "*figuiers*"—once a big orchard,—beyond which she had constructed a frame cabin, that she used as a summer resort.

Her house, situated on St. Anne street, between Rampart and Burgundy, is said to be one of the most ancient frame residences of the city. It is a rickety concern today, and is retired from the street.

She also dealt in charms against malefices, and pretended to cure many ailments, particularly those produced by "*gris-gris*" and other criminal devices. Such was the superstition of our people in her palmy days, that her apartments were often thronged with visitors from every class and section, in search of aid from her supposed supernatural powers. Ladies of high social position would frequently pay her high prices for amulets supposed to bring good luck. Politicians and candidates for office were known to purchase what we would call "mascots" today at her shop of Fortune, and sports would wear, attached to their watch chains, pieces of bone or wood dug from the graveyard. Some of these were curiously and fantastically carved. Is it needless to say that she was an arrant fraud? Yet, money poured into her purse.

A fellow by the name of DR. ALEXANDER succeeded her in this profession of dupery. He had for sometime a large following in the suburbs, but frequent arrests by the police hampered his business. He died a few years ago, I believe.

The prince of the occult science, styling himself *Don Pedro* is now the recognized head of the sect, and his adepts, I am told, are legion. The police have, however, nearly broken up his business, having compelled him to go in hiding. He is heard of sometimes through the medium of the press, as he advertises occasionally as a healing medium. As long as charlatans are not put down by the strong arm of the law, there will ever be a host of believers.

The organization of the voudous, as an organization, has been suppressed in a great measure by the efforts of our municipal authorities. I remember a raid, made by Captain Mazerat, of the Third District, some forty years ago, which was accompanied by circumstances of such a startling nature, as to give the association a deadly blow. Many of the old residents remember the "Racket Green," along the St. Bernard Canal, where thousands were in the habit of congregating to witness the battles of the "Bayous" with the "La Villes," in the games of *Raquettes*. The field was an immense one, extending from Claiborne as far back as Broad. In the centre stood an old pottery, apparently untenanted. While the game was progressing, the Captain aided by a strong corps, advanced unobserved upon the dilapidated tenement and arrested the whole concern—Voudous and paraphernalia—while engaged in one of the wildest orgies which the most prurient imagination can conceive. The women, having cast off their every day apparel, had put on white *camisoles*—called today "mother hubbards"—and were all found clad in this

uniform attire.   Blacks and whites were circling round
promiscuously, writhing in muscular contractions, panting, raving and frothing at the mouth.   But the most
degrading and infamous feature of this scene was the
presence of a very large number of ladies (?), moving in
the highest walks of society, rich and hitherto supposed
respectable, that were caught in the drag net.   Two of
them, through consideration for the feelings of their relatives and connections, so unexpectedly brought to
shame, were permitted to escape, while the husband of a
third, unable to survive the disgrace of his wife, deliberately took his life on the following day.   These facts are
beyond controversy, and the scandal, attested by thousands, was made the subject of town gossip for many a
year.

Besides the potent incantations which they claim the
power to perform, it is an admitted fact that they use
philters, drugs and poisonous substances in their wicked
operations.   These they call "*gris-gris.*"   One of the favorite ingredients used is a decoction of the " *concombre
zombi,*"—Jamestown weed—which they mix in coffee.
It is the plant from which that rank toxicant, known as
stramonium, is extracted.   They use dirt taken from
graveyards.   They employ certain powders, which they
scatter around such places as they suppose their victims
are apt to touch with their hands or feet, and the effect
of these powders is to produce inflammation, pain and
fever.   Even feather pillows are impregnated with dele-
terious substances, in the guise of poisoned crosses, coffins, images etc., but how they contrive to introduce
these objects therein without detection, is as yet an unsolved mystery.   Perhaps, some one may answer: "By
the black servants, of course."   But I and hundreds of
others have heard of various well authenticated cases in
families where no menials were engaged, and every

household duty was performed by the inmates themselves. I am no believer in supernaturalism, but I am
free to confess that the mystery appears at this present
day as far from explanation as ever.

The tribe of Voudous, as a tribe or a class, deserves to
be stamped out of existence, and with the advances of
our superior civilization it is to be hoped that the hour
is not far distant when the last vestige of its degrading
and dangerous influence will be forever wiped out of
existence.

CHAPTER VII.

THE OLD PARISH PRISON.

EPISODES IN ITS EVENTFUL HISTORY.

No edifice in this city recalls more tragical or dramatic reminiscences than those evoked by the scenes once enacted within the gloomy walls and narrow cells of the old Parish Prison. There, is to be found the criminal calendar of our metropolis, including, outside of revolting executions, sad scenes of suicide and murder committed inside of its iron bars. To detail them at length would require volumes. To depict them with the pen of a Zola would provoke disgust and nausea. In this path I am not disposed to tread. I shall content myself with merely reviewing some old-time recollections connected with its sixty year old existence. Like the Tower of London, the Tombs of New York or the Conciergerie of Paris, the Parish Prison of New Orleans is rich in legendary lore, in unique traditions and in startling facts.

The foundations of this quaint old structure were originally laid in 1832, during Mayor Prieur's administration, upon a parallelogram bounded by Marais, Trémé, St. Anne and Orleans streets. The grounds, measuring 240 feet front by 131 feet in depth, were

acquired for the sum of fifteen thousand dollars by the
city from a thrifty and enterprising Frenchman, named
Olivier Blineau, on which a soap factory had been erected, that had become a common nuisance to the neighborhood. It was situated on the inner edge of the
swamp, called *marais*, about the period that the latter
was being slowly reclaimed and made fit for human
habitation. The buildings in the vicinity were few and
far between, of a poor and lowly character. In the winter season, the crack of the rifle or the report of the
double barreled shot gun was not an unusual sound, as
the enterprising sportsman slowly plodded his way
through the dangerous morass, in search of game. It
was not only a favorite retreat for runaway negroes, but
for truant school boys, of whom, I may say, *magna
pars fui*. The woods were full of *senelles, gomme copale*
and a variety of wild berries, not to speak of water
moccasins, rattle snakes and even alligators.

The jail was not completed until the year 1834.

The first prison built in New Orleans was under the
Spanish *régime*, and was a fortress in itself, if one may
judge from its solid construction and massive walls. It
was situated on St. Peter street, and extended from
Chartres to within ninety feet of Royal street, at which
point there was a guardhouse. It included not only
the offices occupied by the present Recorder, but the
rooms and space now constituting the Supreme Court.

With the constant increase of our population, the
building was found insufficient to hold with safety and
hygienic comfort the unfortunate inmates. The germs
of pestilence and disease were rife among them. Escapes were matters of daily occurrence, for it was not
only a place of detention for criminals awaiting trial,
but a penitentiary or penal institution for convicts of
every class. It was only after State prisoners were or-

dered to be transferred to Baton Rouge, that relief was afforded to every parish, which, under the previous system, had been compelled to maintain at its own expense the charges of keeping its own malefactors. Under these circumstances, Denis Prieur, a man of energy and action, then Mayor of the city of New Orleans, induced the City Council to appropriate a sufficient amount of money for the construction, outside of the limits of the "*carré de la ville*," of a spacious structure adequate to the needs of the community. Thus it is, that the stately and gloomy old pile that now looms up on Orleans street, with one of its old turrets truncated and shivered by a stroke of lightning, was erected in one of the dreariest spots then known to our people.

As far as my memory serves me, the first dramatic incident connected with this venerable edifice was the tragic death of PAULINE, the negress, who expiated her crime upon the gallows. The offense, with which she was charged, was the beating and maltreating of her half-demented mistress, a white woman, which, under the provisions of the "Black Code," was made punishable by death. The poor, unfortunate wretch died penitent, reciting her beads to the very last moment, acknowledging the justice of her punishment, and eliciting by her meek demeanor the sympathies of the gathered throng. It was the first public execution of a woman that our people had ever witnessed, and the unusual scene had attracted thousands. She was hurled into eternity from a trap overhanging the low wall, whioh encloses the passage that divides the prison from the old Parish Jail, now the Fourth Precinct Police Station.

From the same spot and from a similar platform, I recall the execution (so horrid in its details, that the impression will never fade from my memory,) of DELILLE and ADAM, charged with the murder of a slave. The date of this shocking occurrence, so far as my memory serves me, was in the year 1852. The history of their crime reads more like a romance than stern reality, and so revolting are the incidents connected with the affair that the heart shudders at their contemplation.

Delille and Adam, with both of whom I was acquainted, were painters by profession, and had been engaged by a grocer, named Chevillon, who resided at the corner of Craps and Clouet streets, to paint the exterior as well as the interior of his house. While thus engaged, they found no difficulty in making themselves thoroughly acquainted with the habits of the inmates, and what, to them was far more important, in locating the spot where their wealth was hoarded. They noticed that it was the invarible habit of the old lady (the grocer's wife), to attend Vespers every Sunday afternoon, and to leave the house and store in charge of her colored servant, while the husband, during her short absence, would cross over to Clouet street to a neighbor's residence, where, seated upon the gallery and in full view of the front of his establishment, he would spend an hour or two in pleasant chat. To plan the robbery was, therefore, no difficult matter. Taking Delille's younger brother as a confederate, they proceeded to consummate their enterprise. Concealing themselves behind the corner, they espied the aged lady repairing to her church, not far distant, and saw old man Chevillon walking off leisurely toward his opposite neighbor. The coast was clear. Leaving his brother to watch on the outside, Delille, who besides the ferocity possessed the lithesomeness and suppleness of a panther, leaped over, unobserved, the picket fence in the rear, opened the gate and admitted his accomplice. They had no time to lose. They hurried to the armoir, possessed themselves of the bag which, besides a considerable sum of money in gold and silver, contained trinkets of value, and were about effecting their escape, when they were unexpectedly confronted by the appearance of the faithful servant, who barred their passage. With the rapidity of lightning and with muttered curses, Delille grappled the woman around the body, while Adam, throwing back the unfortunate victim's head coolly severed her neck from ear to ear. A stream of blood gushed forth from the severed artery and stained Adam's shirt front. Here, a peculiar whistle from the street warned them to hurry, and they sallied forth, unseen and unsuspected. The treasure was committed to the care of the younger Delille, who went off in one direction, while the murderous pair hastily proceeded up town, towards the cathedral. When they arrived there, they stopped awhile at the police station, and engaged in conversation with the commanding officer. They several times referred to the time of day by the Cathedral clock. This was done, no doubt, with the view of establishing possibly an alibi, should any arrest ensue.

The police were soon apprised of the fact. Capt. Eugene Mazerat, a born detective, within whose bailiwick the crime had been committed, got scent of the affair and was soon on the trail with the eagerness of a sleuth-hound. He knew the Delille's intimately. He had been their neighbor for a number of years, and as soon as he learned the fact that young Delille had been seen prowling in the vicinity of the grocery, and knowing his previous shady reputation, he arrested him without delay. When he learned further that the elder Delille had been employed by Couvillon, the whole truth flashed upon his mind, and he, too, soon followed his brother. Adam was the last apprehended.

Mazerat had the culprits, but the proof was wanting. There was the rub. The fertile brain of the gallant officer soon furnished an expedient. A rough sailor, apparently in the last stages of intoxication, was thrust into Adam's cell. Gathering himself up as well as he could, the helpless inebriate fell in a heap, as it were, in a corner, where, soon after, his stertorous breathing and unearthly snores proclaimed him oblivious of all surrounding objects. Nothing unusual occurred in the cell until about midnight, when a pebble flung at the grated window announced the fact that a friend was on the watch outside. Such proved the fact. A hurried interview ensued, and was still progressing when a cry of anguish escaped the lips of the pretended drunkard, who in piteous tones began to crave for water. It was the signal agreed upon. The spy had played his part to the life.

A few seconds had not elapsed before the emissary was in the Captain's grasp, and, frightened to death, he made an abject confession. That night, Mazerat had recovered the stolen jewelry and money, and had every accomplice in safe custody. The sequel may be briefly summarized. They confessed their crime and were sentenced to die.

Their execution took place, as I have stated before, on the same spot where Pauline had forfeited her life. Thousands, if not tens of thousands, attracted by a morbid curiosity not unusual at such spectacles, attended. It was a pleasant summer day, and no disturbance in the atmosphere gave token of the terrific storm that was soon to burst forth. During the entire period of their confinement in the Parish Prison, their conduct had offered a strange contrast. . Adam was reticent and maintained a stoic attitude. He was a Frenchman by birth, slow in speech, slow in gait, but endowed with herculean strength. Delille, on the other hand, was small in stature, restless, talkative and an inveterate grumbler.

Passionately fond of drink, he would, while under its influence, indulge in dire threats against his enemies, of whom every prison official, he thought, was one, thus making life disagreeable at times to those who were intrusted with his keeping. He was a Creole of St. Domingo.

When led to the scaffold,in the presence of the largest assemblage that hadever gathered in the neighborhood of the Trémé Market. each betrayed the salient points of his nature. Theyhad both spurned the consolations of the church. Adam was pale, collected, and evidently bracing himself for a supreme effort. He refused to make a speech,when offered the privilege. He would occasionally turn round to his fellow convict, and admonish him to be quiet. Delille, on the other hand, was apparently intoxicated. It was evident that he was afraid to die, and had indulged too liberally in the ardent spirits that had been furnished him to steady his nerves and tremulous frame. He was more than voluble. At times he ranted, like a stage-struck maniac. His eyes were livid with fury, and he called upon the French Consul and the home Government to avenge his death and to exact reparation from the United States.

At this point, the hangman appeared upon the scene. The prisoners were soon fettered, blindfolded and the noose adjusted around their necks. A sharp click rang out upon the air, and the trap fell. It was mid-day. The chimes of the Cathedral bells were just announcing the hour of twelve, when a sheet of lightning—a sheet so blinding, so dazzling, so stunning as to partake of the unnatural—illuminated the scene and rent the skies in twain. Nothing so weirdly, so terrifically grand, so indicative of the power of an offended Deity had ever before been heard. Simultaneously with this dreaded cataclysm of warring elements, a torrent of rain descended from the heavens and compelled most of the obstinate curiosity mongers to seek shelter under the eaves of the neighboring houses, and under the covering of the Market. Meanwhile, the two dangling bodies had disengaged themselves from the ropes, and were seen falling to the pavement below. A cry of horror broke forth from the crowd. The surging mass, eager to relieve the criminals, beat in vain against the police cordon that encircled the gallows. Adam lay insensible. Delille's right arm was fractured above the wrist, the same arm, it was said by a bystander, that had once struck a mother in the face. He was crawling away on his hands and feet.

The sheriffs at once hurried the doomed men through the Orleans street entrance into the reception room. The Sheriff was perplexed. He knew of no precedent that governed the case. The mob outside were growing excited and were clamoring for a reprieve, there being a great many who honestly believed that it was unlawful to hang them a second time. At this juncture, the Governor was appealed to for instructions, and pending the arrival of an answer, another singular affair occurred. As Adam and Delille, it was found, had been stunned into a state of insensibility, a dispute arose between the City Physician and the Coroner as to the advisability of restoring them to life by bleeding. Although one of them protested, the operation was performed. Immediately thereafter came an order from the Executive to proceed with the sentence. Limp and pallid, the two men were bodily carried upon the platform, in the midst of the tempestuous rain fall. Commiseration, was depicted upon every countenance. The fierce mood of the populace had given way to pity. Again was the fatal knot adjusted around their necks.

Again was the click of the executioner's ax heard. Again was the trap seen to yield under its own weight, and the victims were suspended in mid-air. The contortions of their limbs and the heaving of their chests indicated death by suffocation. In the efforts occasioned by these muscular contractions their veins swelled and distended, and, bursting from the bandages which had compressed them, ejected copious streams of blood over their light-colored clothes. The blood, thoroughly diluted by the drenching rain, gradually spread over their vestments, and imparted to them a crimson hue. Not unlike two ghastly spectres, images of Milton's wildest conceptions, that haunt men's memories through a lifetime, stood out in bold relief, clearly limned against the frowning skies, the dangling, writhing forms of the murderers. From this heart-sickening scene men averted their eyes in disgust, and women fainted. The strongest minded men, not excepting even the stern ministers of the law, lost their self-possession. It was a sight, once seen, never to be forgotten.

This horrid execution shocked the conscience of the community by reason of its demoralizing effects. The Legislature was appealed to for a change in the law, and public hanging became henceforth a thing of the past.

Another memorable event that occurred within the walls of the grim old dungeon was the suicide or, rather as I am led to believe, the felonious poisoning of AN-TOINE CAMBRE, convicted of murder, on the eve of the day set for his death. This tragedy occurred during the bloody Saturnalia of crimes, known as "Know-Nothing" times. He was a resident and native of this city. He belonged to an old and highly respectable family, and, though imperfectly educated, had succeeded in obtaining several responsible positions. He was a bitter and

uncompromising hater of Loco-focoism, and his aversion
to foreigners was very pronounced. Hence, upon the
disruption of the Whig party, he espoused with ardor
and bigotry the cause of native Americanism, and together with the Guérins, the Lockwoods, the Legetts,
the Johnsons and the Duprats of the period, became one
of the leaders of the crime-accursed "Red Warriors."

At the time of his arrest, he was one of the commis-
saries of the notorious "Louisiana Ball Room," one of
the numerous dens of iniquity which once infested the
Third Municipality, where debauchery, gambling and
intoxication held high carnival. To regulate the tough
and dangerous element that usually thronged this noted
den required a man of unflinching courage, and Cambre
proved himself equal to the task. But his unfortunate
fondness for liquor not infrequently led him into trouble, and as the supply was never stinted there, it is needless to say that he made a frequent abuse of it. With
this preface, I shall now proceed to relate the history of
his crime.

It was about 4 o'clock in the morning, after the ball
with its gambling hells had closed, that Cambre, in a
semi-inebriated condition, left the place and repaired
downtown toward his home. The morning was just
breaking, and the street lamps were being put out. On
his way, he happened to stumble against the ladder of a
lamp lighter, who was just in the act of extinguishing a
light. Hurt by the sudden blow, he cursed the innocent offender and a war of words ensued. Enraged by
this altercation, he hurriedly left the scene in search of
a weapon. In the meanwhile, the lamp lighter had
gone off about his business. Cambre returned soon after, and hurrying to the corner of Louisa and Greatmen
streets, saw another lamp lighter approaching him with
a ladder, whom he mistook at once for his assailant.

Acting upon this suspicion, without a word of premonition, he deliberately placed his pistol to the poor German's breast and shot him through the heart.   It was a clear case of mistaken identity, but it was a clear case of brutal and wanton murder.

Cambre was arrested and immured within the Parish Prison.   All the influences, which the powerful secret association with which he was connected could command, were brought to bear in his behalf, but every effort proved futile.   He was furnished with able counsel, renowned both for lore and eloquence.   But the facts were too stubborn, and could be neither palliated nor explained.   Under the administration of justice dispensed by such a firm man as Judge Robertson, whom hired bullies could not intimidate, the result could not long be doubtful, and the doom of Cambre was sealed.

The verdict was a crushing blow.   Still he had hopes. He could not realize the fact that the thousands of oathbound brothers, leagued together with him for mutual protection, would ever abandon him to his fate.   He looked to the Supreme Court for relief.   That tribunal decided against him.   His eyes were now turned toward the Executive.   But Governor Wickliffe was inflexible.   The Hercules that had strangled the hydra of Know-Nothingism in Louisiana two years before, lent an obdurate ear to every pleading for life. Society demanded a fearful example.

Cambre was afraid to die.   Friends flocked to the condemned cell in which he was confined, and proffered poison.   They urged upon him, inasmuch as his execution was inevitable, the necessity of self-destruction, as the only means of rescuing his family from disgrace. But this he flatly refused to do, as he still had hopes of the Governor's favorable interposition.

On the day preceding that fixed for his execution, he

was found dead in his dungeon, and here lurks a mystery, which, like many other mysteries connected with the now celebrated penal institution during that eventful period of its administration, has never been satisfactorily solved. I refer to the "*causa mortis.*" Was it the effect of nature, or of suicide, or of preconcerted action on the part of his friends?

It was generally rumored at the time, that he had succumbed to an attack of malarial fever, but the suddenness of the demise excluded the hypothesis, and hence the assertion was not believed. The autopsy revealed the existence of poison in the stomach and intestines. Hence, the question, "by whom administered?" was frequently asked. The trepidation displayed by him during the last days of his life, and his deep-rooted aversion to the crime of *felo de se*, set at naught the theory of suicide. Who, then, had conveyed the poison?

The following is the story related to me by an old and faithful officer of the Parish Prison, and, I believe it to be truthful in every essential particular.

Who has not heard of Marie Laveau, the whilom Queen of the Voudous and infamous bawd, who, blending African mysteries and superstitions with the worship of the Blessed Virgin, posed for so many years as a character of importance, when, in very truth, she was naught else but an arrant and consummate impostor? It was usual in those days, and the custom still prevails, to allow prisoners about to suffer death to receive the last consolations of religion, and, if a Catholic, to erect an altar for the celebration of mass in the chapel. This altar was always placed in the charge of a female, and Marie Laveau, who, from her previous acquaintance and intimacy with Cambre, was thought to be a proper person, was selected for the purpose. She had, therefore, ready access at all times to Cambre's cell, and would cheer him for hours with her sprightly talk.　As the time for his execution was fast approaching—it was on the eve, I believe—Marie approached him, and in her usual Creole dialect said :

"*Ti moun, avant to mouri, si to dois mouri demain, dis moin ça to oulé mangé.　Ma fé toi bon diné.*"　(My young one, before you die, if you have to die to-morrow, tell me what you would like to eat.　I'll make you a good dinner.

At this proposal Cambre, it is said, mournfully shook his head.

"*Ma fé toi gombo filé comme jamais to mangé dans to la vie,*" said the temptress.　(I'll make you a *gombo filé* such as you have never eaten in your whole life.)

These were prophetic words !　Cambre assented, and a few hours thereafter was writhing in the agonies of death.

Such is the story related to me many years ago, and I give it for what it is worth　Many are the secrets of the Old Parish Prison, and this is one of them.

The mysterious death of Antoine Cambre brings to my mind the suicide of CÉLESTIN LÉONARD.　He was a man of color, born free, and a great favorite with the people of the Seventh Ward.　He had been condemned to die on the scaffold by Judge McHenry for killing another colored man in an alleged affair of honor.　The facts elicited on the trial of the cause do not appear to have been very clearly established, and the benefit of the doubt, I fear, was cast against him.　I have a slight recollection of the facts, the affair having occurred some forty years ago.

It seems that his adversary had forced a quarrel upon him, the result of which was an agreement to fight a duel on the following morning with fowling pieces, both being professional hunters.　A place was selected in the rear of the fishermen's village on the Bayou St. John, near the lake shore. On reaching the ground, the quarrel was renewed, and Leonard, heedless of all previous arrangements, rushed upon his adversary with the frenzy of a mad bull and slew him. It was evident that he had been laboring under the influence of liquor and anger combined. Having dispatched his enemy, he leaped over the intervening hedges and hurriedly made his way to the city, closely pursued by the dead man's friends. His arrest immediately followed. He was defended by Cyprien Dufour, Esq., and the writer, who was just entering the practice of the law ; and, notwithstanding the ingenuity, tact and fervid eloquence of his senior counsel, the jury found him guilty of murder. The evidence, if believed, was too strong to admit even of mitigating circumstances.

As one of his counsel, I had become interested in him and had occasion to visit him at times in his solitary cell. I always found him penitent, polite and docile. " I am not afraid to die," he would frequently say, " for I have already faced death without a quiver. But under circumstances so full of shame as these, I confess that I tremble. Let me confide to you a secret ; it is one which eats like a canker into my heart. It is this. I have no children, but, when I am gone away, I shall leave behind me a child, a young girl, whose godfather I am, and whom I love with passionate tenderness. Now, to think that as she grows up to womanhood, she will be pointed at in the streets as the goddaughter of Célestin Léonard, *le pendu*, the man that was hanged for murder, and will be made the target for every enemy's sarcasm and raillery, is more torture than I can endure. I pray God every night to deliver me from this world, and should He deny me this boon, well ''—here he hysterically grasped me by the arm,—"well, remember I shall never die by the hangman's hand." Such was the look of despair and resolution that accompanied these last words that I became convinced that he had revolved in his mind a settled plan of self-destruction.

As the days flew by, and the time set for his execution was fast approaching, no change in his demeanor attracted attention. Always cheerful and communicative, though not loquacious, to visitors, a gloomy, despondent cloud would overhang his visage when left alone. Brooding is the most graphic expression I can find to describe his mental condition.

One morning, just as dawn was breaking upon the yawning and sleepy city, one of the wardens of the jail, in making one of his early rounds, was astounded at the sight of a pool of coagulated blood on the flagging of the court-yard, just immediately under the eaves of the condemned cells. Astounded at this ghastly find, the officials were soon scurrying through the hall in the direction of the convict's room. There the inanimate, nude and bloodless corpse of poor Leonard was seen stretched out upon a mattress on the floor, with arms and thighs firmly compressed with thongs, and long gashes across the brachial and femoral arteries. He had bled himself to death. It must have come as a relief to him, for a sweet smile was still playing upon his lips.

Now, how shall we qualify this act? Heroism, Duty, Dementia or Crime? God, who reads the hearts and motives of man, alone can tell.

Celestin was the son of a white man, named Antonio, who, for many years, occupied the humble post of Town crier, an office which supplied the place of the special advertising columns of the modern press. Accompanied by a boy beating a drum, he would stop at every street corner, and make known to the people the escape of a runaway slave, the loss of a child, of a pocket-book or a stray mule, or the finding of some object of value. These functions originated in the period of the Spanish occupation, when, even the edicts of the magistrates were proclaimed by beat of drum.

One of the narrowest escapes from the gallows that I have heard related was that of a slave, named *Caliste*, sentenced to be publicly hanged at the time that Capt. Jos. Gros was the captain of the Parish Prison. The crime with which he was charged was striking a white person, and drawing blood therefrom, an offense which, under the provisions of the Black Code, was made punishable with death. He was tried under that law by a Justice of the Peace and six slaveholders, and was to have been executed from the very spot on which Pauline, and Adam and Delille had expiated their crimes, on the 25th of April, 1862. Every preparation had been made for carrying out the mandate of the law. The scaffold had been erected in public on this occasion, as was the custom when slaves were to die. The executioner was awaiting orders in the sheriff's office, and the officers themselves were anxiously expecting the summons to proceed with their disagreeable duty. Just at that moment the cannon ot the Federal fleet, that had just forced the passage of the forts, was heard reverberating through space, the drums began beating to arms, the military were marching away in their hurried exit, the torch was being applied to the millions of dollars' worth of produce on the levee, and the Confederate States government, as far as New Orleans was concerned, had become a thing of the past.

"Bofill," said Capt. Gros to his chief deputy, "what shall we do? Must we hang that nigger?"

"Hang, be blanked!" was the prompt reply. "Where is now our authority?" And thus was the problem solved.

A few days after, Caliste was set free by the provost marshal.

Caliste, now an old man, is frequently seen passing along Burgundy street on his way to work. Since his miraculous escape, he has had, I am told, two boys whom, in commemoration of the event, in *rei perpetuam memoriam*, as it were, he has christened "Farragut" and "Ben Butler." I will not vouch for the story, but "*si non è vero, è ben trovato.*"

Later on, in the course of time, comes the recollection of the dramatic incidents that attended the deaths of Pedro Abril and Vicente Bayona, two Spaniards, convicted of the murder and robbery of a Malay cook. The crime was a horrid one, evincing premeditation and cruelty. To secure the sum of forty dollars, they had hacked their unoffending victim to pieces, and then flung his ghastly body into the river. They never manifested the least sign of repentance for their dastardly deed, and received their sentence of death with a smile of defiance. While in the condemned cell they were very insolent to visitors, particularly to those attracted thither by curiosity, but toward their keepers they were generally obedient and submissive.

The Spanish Consul, aided by several Spanish merchants, made every effort in their behalf, with a view of securing a commutation of their sentence, but, owing to the temporary absence of Gov. Warmoth from the State, Lieut. Gov. Dunn refused to interfere. His reply to the committee that waited upon him at his office in the Mechanics' Institute was characteristic: "Were I a white man, I would consider myself free to act, but as I am a negro, no end of abuse will be thrown upon me. The Governor has left the State, I believe, for St. Louis, to throw this responsibility upon me. I will not assume it." With this firm and decided answer, the committee took their leave.

On the eve of their execution, I was requested by the consul to visit them and to convey them a message. I found them cheerful, and ready to die. They were both communicative, particularly Vicente Bayona, who was small in stature and very talkative. He was one of the most restless men I ever saw, constantly rolling cigarette after cigarette, and puffing away at the fragrant weed. Pedro Abril, on the other hand, was phlegmatic and spoke to the purpose. It was evident that they both possessed undoubted courage, although manifested in different ways. They complained bitterly, not of the severity, but of the partial and corrupt administration of justice in New Orleans. Money, they claimed, was the lever which had overturned law and decency in our courts, for juries were mercenary institutions.

" Had we had rich and influential friends, we would not be in the strait in which we find ourselves. Just look," said Bayona, "to that red-handed murderer who was acquitted some days ago, not because he was innocent, but because he was the officer of a bank, had wealthy connections and bought the jury with ready cash. And you call this American justice? It is true we are poor, but to-morrow we shall show these accursed *Americanos* how Spaniards die." In this rambling, disconnected and nervous way did Bayona continue his harangue, sandwiching each sentence with a whiff from his cigarette.

On the following day they were led to the scaffold within the flagged court-yard. The condemned cell, as well as the narrow gallery in its front, was crowded with officials, members of the press and a few privileged visitors, while the unfortunate actors in that day's drama were busily attending to the operation of the toilet. They were neatly attired in immaculate linen and white pants. Stepping out of his dungeon, Bayona gazed intently through the bars at the buzzing, laughing and somewhat disorderly crowd in the yard below, and his eyes flashed with anger, and his lips curled with scorn.

" The cowards," he cried out in Spanish, " the low curs, they come to gloat over our blood, but we shall show them what we are," and, with a look of supreme contempt, he deliberately and repeatedly spat upon their upturned faces. Abril went up to him with dignity and began to expostulate, but his urgent admonitions, "*quedate quieto*" (keep quiet) fell upon heedless ears. All the curses, English and Spanish, that he had ever learned, and of these he seemed to possess an abundant fund, he excitedly flung àt their heads, in tones that thundered through the echoing corridors.

When they were placed upon the fatal platform, their demeanor underwent no change. When Deputy Sheriff James Houston approached to bid them good-by, Abril accepted the proffered hand, but Bayona angrily refused.

"Me no shek 'an wid you; you no fren'." Then turning to a warden, " Bofill, gibby me *cigarillo*."

Gazing wildly at the immense multitude: "Sanababiches," he yelled out, " *canallas de Americanos*, cowards, dogs, may God curse you as you deserve." In this strain he continued, until the trap was sprung and his agony began. His last word was a blasphemy. Abril, on the contrary, faced death with the cynicism of a Stoic. The holy priest, who stood by his side, found his heart steeled against every religious belief. No Indian, ever led to the blazing fagots, confronted fate with such a serene countenance. His only care seemed to be directed to the restraining of the angry and undignified behavior of his confederate in crime.

Their remains, on the demand of responsible parties, were placed in neat coffins and conveyed, not to the Potter's Field, but to Pepe Llulla's cemetery, where they were privately buried in the ground.

Such was the termination of one of the most impressive events ever recorded in the annals of the Parish Prison.

So many and varied are the reminiscences that occur to my mind that I can not omit a reference to the records of *Bertin* and *Capdeville*, those two daring and expert burglars who, for many years, had baffled the ingenuity of our whole detective force and laughed all their efforts to scorn. They were masters in their craft. No lock or safe, however secure, had ever resisted their skill, and for daring, coolness and murderous courage, they were undoubtedly unsurpassed. Capdeville, having betrayed his partner, was permitted to go free and was subsequently killed in St. Louis. Bertin, after undergoing imprisonment for many months in the Parish Prison, was finally sent to the Penitentiary to expiate his numberless crimes. He is still there, I believe, under a second sentence.

One of the boldest and best matured plans ever executed by this essentially wicked man was the one whereby the store of Rochereau, the banker, was entered in the night-time. The affair created a wide-spread sensation. In that case, ex-Chief Justice Bermudez appeared for the prosecution, as associate counsel with the writer. It was his maiden effort at the criminal bar, and his pure diction, coupled with his varied and thorough knowledge of the intricacies of law, deeply impressed the court and contributed not a little to the conviction of the culprits.   The money, bonds and jewelry deposited in the coffers of the Rochereaus, who were the trustees for a large class of French non-residents, approximated in value, as far as my memory now serves me, to nearly two hundred thousand dollars, and with the exception of a large number of bonds that were discovered in the hands of a lawyer, as he was in the very act of assorting them and of passing upon their commercial value, the bulk of the treasure was never recovered.   The lawyer was arrested as an accessory after the fact, but was subsequently released from custody.   He had been a few years before a District Attorney.

My first recollection of Paul Bertin was at the time when he was employed with the late Mr. Forget, the successor of Galpin, at his fashionable restaurant on Royal street, near Customhouse.   He was the butler of the establishment, and was considered a good *connoisseur* in wines.   His address was genial, polite and pleasant, and no one would have then suspected that, under such a gentle exterior, lurked the venom of a serpent and the spirit of a demon.

The first charge that brought him to the attention of the police was in connection with the robbery of a respectable old citizen, named Menendez, who kept a barroom opposite the French Opera House.   There was absolutely no direct evidence against him and, therefore, his previous good character served him in good stead.   The District Attorney refused to prosecute him, but Bertin, insisting on his legal right to an acquittal by jury trial, was persistent in his demand, and posed as a martyr in the eyes of his friends, who really believed him innocent.   After events showed that he was undoubtedly guilty.

A few months after this incident, Forget's establishment went into insolvency, and Bertin was appointed a sheriff's keeper. As such, he lived and slept on the premises. Adjoining, was the cigar store of Fernandez & Villa. On a Monday morning, these merchants, on repairing to their place of business, were astounded by the discovery that their safe had been blown open during the night-time and rifled of its valuable contents, amounting to several thousand dollars. An entrance had been effected through a hole cut in the partition wall, sufficiently large to admit of a person's body. Bertin was, of course, suspected of the crime, but, for want of evidence, he was again released. Bertin subsequently confessed his guilt.

Some months later, another daring burglary was committed at the corner of Elysian Fields, directly opposite the head of the late Port Market. This time it was a coffee house that he and his confederates had invaded. The proprietor was the banker of the principal butchers, and always kept their money locked in a rear room. It is affirmed that, while they were in the act of operating upon the iron chest, a night watchman, attracted by the noise, stopped before one of the doors to listen. One of the "pals" began to betray some trepidation, whereupon Bertin, placing the muzzle of his revolver to the man's head, threatened him with instant death. The work done, they secured the plunder and made their escape without detection. Fortune again favored the criminal, who, as usual, succeeded in freeing himself from the meshes of the law and of the detectives.

Such is the outline of one of the most dangerous outlaws that ever infested this city.

Before proceeding further with this retrospect of the

various episodes that have illustrated in the past the character of this celebrated penal institution, a few words in relation to its internal police and discipline may not be inappropriate.

As soon as a criminal has received the sentence of death, no matter whether a suspensive appeal has been taken or not, he is at once segregated from the body of the prisoners at large, and is immediately transferred to one of the condemned cells. Of these there are four: Nos. 1 and 2, on the third gallery, and Nos. 3 and 4, on the second. All these overlook the spacious court-yard below. These rooms, which so many never leave until the final death march to the gallows is ordered, measure about ten by twelve feet, the walls being covered with rude drawings, inscriptions, expressive of the feelings or bent of mind of the forlorn wretches who once tenanted them. The prisoner is allowed no knife or fork. His meat is previously cut up into small pieces by an attendant. He must eat with a spoon only. He is permitted no furniture save a mattress on the bare floor, a mosquito bar, a pillow and necessary bed clothes. During the day his door is left open and, as he is permitted access to the gallery in front, he is enabled to take some exercise and to hold converse at times with the prisoners in the yard. He partakes of the same fare furnished at the officers' table. At sundown he is locked up for the night.

As soon as the Governor has signed and transmitted the death warrant, the prisoner is placed under stricter surveillance. The eye of his keeper never leaves him. He is frequently searched. Every object calculated to effect self-destruction, either by poison, strangulation or any other mode of violence, is removed. No visitor is admitted to his quarters, save in the presence of a trusted warden. Such is the discipline enforced under what is known as the "death watch."

On the eve of his execution the convict is attended by the members of the society of St. Vincent de Paul, by the Sisters of Mercy and by a priest or minister of the Gospel. In one of the apartments fronting Orleans street, formerly known as the "department for fraudulent debtors," is to be found the "Chapel," where a temporary altar has been erected, and it is within that improvised temple of God that he spends his last night on earth in meditation, prayer and even sleep. All his proper wants are gratified. Dr. Deschamps, it is said, is the only prisoner who ever refused to enter the portals of that curious little place of prayer, or to converse with the holy sisters, or to accept the least ministrations of religion. He was an unbeliever to the last. As he was being led to the fatal platform, he reconsidered, however, his previous determination, and held, in cell No. 8, a protracted interview with the Nuns; but this action, it is uncharitably asserted, was due solely to his desire to prolong life, in the hope that some unexpected contingency might come to his relief.

After leaving the chapel in the morning, and receiving the sacraments or rites of his own church, the prisoner is again led back to his cell, where, after partaking of breakfast, he proceeds to his toilet. This is a ceremony which consumes a little time. A number of persons, usually friends and members of the press, gather around him and receive his last words. He is always furnished with new and decent clothes. When the time has arrived, he is conducted toward the gallows, through the gallery leading in the direction of St. Ann street, and is halted at the above referred cell, No. 8, by the hangman, who there takes him in charge. His arms are pinioned. The death-warrant is then read to

him by the Sheriff, who shakes his hand and bids him
"God-speed." The distance from that end of the gallery to the gallows is about three feet, and over the
chasm a gangway is thrown, and, as soon as the criminal reaches this temporary stage, the rope is placed
around his neck. This is done to prevent any attempt to
hurl himself into space. Stepping on the platform, which
is suspended in mid-air by means of ropes connected
with the hangman's room, the prisoner is led to a seat,
his feet are tightly bound, the noose carefully adjusted
and the cap drawn over his face. Immediately the executioner hastens back to his room, in the rear. A
short, sharp click is heard—the work of the axe that has
severed the cords—the platform gives way under its own
weight, a dull thud appals the heart of the spectator,
and a quivering body is seen dangling in the air, writhing and drawing itself up in the midst of the most sickening contortions. Society is avenged, and the hangman
has done his work well. Twenty minutes afterward
the body is partially lowered to permit the physician's
examination. The pulsations of the heart are stilled.
The body is placed upon the ground. The crowd dis-
perses. An autopsy is held. The bloody, mangled
carcass is thrust into a cypress coffin. The Potter's
Field receives it, and thus closes the last act of the terrible tragedy.

The post or stanchion to which the ropes of the
"trap," as the gallows is technically called, are attached, bears traces of twenty three indentations, this
being the number of human sacrifices offered to the
majesty of the law. Putty and paint have obliterated
those that had previously existed.

The hangman, disguised under the folds of a black
domino and a hideous mask, is a loathing object to look
at. Unlike *Monsieur* Deibler, the executioner of France,

who always on such occasions makes his appearance in public in kid gloves and a *costume de rigueur*, the uncouth form of our hangman lends such a character of grotesqueness to these dramatic scenes as to bewilder the reason of an onlooker. In former years there was no official *bourreau*. Sheriffs were frequently non-plussed in the performance of this revolting duty, and were at times compelled to solicit the pardon of such minor criminals as were willing, for that consideration, to undertake the job. Hence, the operation was often performed in a bungling manner. But now, *nous avons changé tout cela*. We now have a semi-official one. His name, though known to me, it is needless to give. He was once connected with the commissary depart-ment of the Parish Prison, under the administration of ex-Police Commissioner Thomas Agnew—one, by the way, of the most honest, progressive and laborious offi-cers the city ever possessed—and, since 1889, when Taylor—the name escapes me—undertook the task of hanging a negro in the town of Plaquemine, he has adhered to the "profession." His operations are not only confined to the city, but extend throughout the State. I am credibly informed that he has already executed more than twenty of the law's proscribed.

The "trap" is carefully laid aside in cell No. 8, in the negroes' quarters, until brought out again for ser-vice. It was borrowed from the prison in 1862 by the military authorities, and served to hurl into eternity the unfortunate Mumford from the portico of the United States Mint.

With these preliminary remarks, I proceed with my narrative.

The case of DR. DESCHAMPS is still fresh in the minds of our people. His crimes, his lame defence, his wayward conduct under prison discipline, his bungling attempts at suicide, his terrible atonement upon the gallows, and the mysterious disappearance of the judge who tried him, have invested this remarkable case with a degree of interest and mystery that reflects sombre hues upon the walls of his dreary dungeon.

To thoroughly understand this memorable case, the previous history of the man, as well as his peculiar idiosyncrasies, should have been conscientiously studied. In doing so, the question would have occurred : Was he a criminal, or was he insane? I unhesitatingly believe that he was both. His nature was essentially depraved. His instincts were bestial. Though his reasoning faculties were no doubt defective, he certainly deserved the degrading punishment which he underwent, for *offenses other* than that of which he was found guilty. But he was a victim of prejudice. That his conviction on the charge of *murder* was a judicial error, a blot upon the administration of criminal justice, a fatal mistake, is an opinion to which I have firmly clung, and my reasons therefore are very clear. Here are a few facts that speak for themselves.

Deschamps, many years ago, after practicing some time in this city, became an itinerant dentist, traveling particularly in the parishes of Lafourche and Terrebonne. He was far from being an educated man. Apart from some aptness and skill in the mechanical branch of his profession and a general dabbling in the principles of animal magnetism, in the mysteries of which he claimed to be a firm believer, his knowledge of chemistry and medicine was limited and insignificant In one of his rambles upon the islets and keys that intersect the gulf waters in those regions, once the habitations and hiding places of Lafitte's buccaneering followers, it happened that some old coins and trinkets were discovered, deeply buried in the sand. This "find" was sufficient to excite his cupidity and thirst for gold, and from that moment he became a monomaniac. He had no confidence in divining rods, but, in the science of clairvoyance or hypnotism, he believed he had discovered a solution to the problem of exhuming, like a second Monte Christo, the hidden treasures of the Baratarians. To attain this end, he imagined that all that was required was the instrumentality of a fully developed "subject," a slave to his will and mesmeric control.

Filled with this idea, he returned to New Orleans and became accidentally acquainted with his beautiful victim. To her father he communicated his plans, who, led captive by the seductive arguments of the fanatic, intrusted his elder daughter to his almost parental authority, unsuspicious of any danger to his child's honor or personal safety. Under the training of the scoundrel the poor girl was frequently put to sleep, and, while in an unconscious state, would, it is said, obey his every bidding * * *. Here, I must draw the curtain, for the post mortem examination of her body disclosed infamies at which the heart rebels, and which alone would have warranted a sentence of death under our criminal statutes.

But it is a fact that she died from an undue administration of chloroform, and from no other cause. She was given the subtle fluid in the presence of her younger sister. This circumstance alone tends to show there was no premeditation, no attempt at concealment in the commission of the act. The charge, therefore, should have been, under these circumstances, no other than that of manslaughter. Whoever reads the sworn statement of the sister, as recorded in her examination at the Coroner's inquest, with an unprejudiced eye, will

arrive at this conclusion, for I see therein related the
further fact that as soon as the Doctor realized that the
child had succumbed to the influence of the drug, he
threw himself in despair upon his knees and exclaimed :
Mon Dieu ! Mon Dieu ! Qu'ai-je fait. (My God !
My God ! What have I done?) Then immediately follows his double attempt at suicide. This part of the
evidence—the only direct evidence, by the way, ad-
duced—if handled with dexterity, would have proved a
complete bar to the accusation of wilful and deliberate
murder. But the plea of insanity was interjected, or,
rather, was made the sole basis of his defense, and, of
course, was properly discredited, as his mind was not so
diseased as to incapacitate him from distinguishing right
from wrong. Inasmuch as the unauthorized administration of drugs is made punishable by the common as well
as the statutory law, and its fatal results become a highly penal offense, I can not conceive what other verdict
could have been rendered, except one of manslaughter.
Moreover, a person whose intent is to murder another
will not likely use an anæsthetic, when the pharma-
copœia furnishes such a variety of deadly poisons.

But the question may be asked, what was the chloroform used for ? The answer is not a difficult one.

Specialists who have treated the subject of hypnotism,
and some of them are men of the highest erudition both
in Germany and France, recommend in their works the
use of this dangerous fluid as an aid to the development of latent magnetic forces. Its action, they assert,
hastens the production of the trance state, and perfects
the condition of the "subject." Be this as it may (for
I candidly confess my ignorance of the principles of
this wonderful mystery of nature), the theory is more
than probable that Deschamps, in his attempts to expand
the perceptive and occult faculties of his confiding

pupil, with the view of determining through her aid the exact localities wherein lay concealed untold riches, was merely but unskilfully putting into practice what he had been reading in some books.

Such has always been my belief about this celebrated affair, which gave rise to so much comment, and so little scientific discussion.

Deschamps was one of the most disagreeable prisoners that the Parish Prison ever held.   He was of a morose, fretful and dictatorial disposition.   Nothing pleased him.   He found fault with everybody—with his counsel, his keepers, the members of the press, and even with the few friends, who were attempting to assist him in his hours of trial.   He grumbled at his fare, growled at the strictness of the watch kept over him, and quarreled with his fellow prisoners, as, with shuffling and unsteady gait, he paced the narrow limits of his gallery.

Such is the concurrent testimony of the officials then in charge of the institution, and I have every reason to believe that, when he was finally hurled into eternity, they found themselves relieved of a terrible incubus.

In addition to the executions and attempts at suicide, some successful, that once occurred within those ancient walls, one singular homicide took place therein, after an interval of forty years, as far as I can remember.   I refer to the killing of George Deno, one of the keepers, by another keeper.   His death is another of the mysteries of the prison.   This happened a few years ago.   A quarrel, a scuffle, a shot, a victim, a plea of self-defense—this is about all that the public in general were allowed to learn.   Poor Deno! with all his faults he deserved a better fate.

I pass over the cases of Polydore, of Ford, of Lindsay

and of so many others, which present highly dramatic features, but the narrow limits of a chapter necessarily confine me to mere outlines.   But I can not pretermit the opportunity of incidentally reverting to the massacre of the Italians, now a world-wide known occurrence. We are all familiar with the history of the "Sicilian Vespers," and, in this instance, it was a repetition of the same scenes, except on a more limited scale. Hence, the uprising of the people on that eventful morning may not inaptly be styled the "Sicilian Matins."

This was the first time when a mob ever succeeded in forcing an entrance into the recesses of the prison.   An attempt had been once made, many years ago, at the time when young Reynolds committed suicide within its walls, and the firm and courageous attitude of Holland, the sheriff, backed by a handful of determined enemies, overcame the belligerent multitude and quelled the disturbance.

As is well known, ingress had been obtained through the battered door of the Captain's room, fronting on the Trémé street side.   A few seconds after the occurrence, I was permitted to enter and visit the scene.   Its ghastliness is indescribable.   The victims were stretched out in various positions, terror being the invariable expression depicted upon their features.   Proceeding up stairs, I saw one of the victims lying on the floor, with what seemed to me like an Indian war club firmly grasped in his hand.   It was the formidable weapon with which he had, but a few moments before, attempted to batter down the fastenings of a door.   A few paces from him, was another sufferer gasping in the agonies of death. He was utterly unconscious.

The history of the Parish Prison would be incomplete without any reference to the annex, formerly known as the "Negro Police Jail" and "Insane Asylum." The former, situated at the corner of Marais and Orleans streets, was used principally for the detention and punishment of slaves, under the regulations provided by the "Black Code." Flogging at the whipping-post, wearing an iron collar and dragging a ponderous ball and chain, while at work upon the public streets—such were the usual modes of castigation employed.

Lunatics were lodged in the apartments of the second story, and the unfortunates were huddled together in most uncomfortable quarters. They were, for a number of years, under the skilful treatment of Dr. Délery, a much regretted physician, who had made a special study of the subject of insanity. But the condition of these outcasts was a sad commentary upon the niggardly conduct of our city government, and furnished matter for severe diatribes at the hands of the editorial fraternity. In fact, if my memory does not deceive me, one of the correspondents of the London *Times* published in that journal, about the beginning of the Civil War, one of the most damning and terrible arraignments ever penned against New Orleans, for its neglect to improve the hygienic necessities required by this unhappy and irresponsible class of people.

I here close my narrative of the history, the traditions and principal events connected with the venerable edifice on Orleans street, which is about to be converted into a plant for a new system of city drainage. But as long as its weather-beaten walls stand in their massive grimness, and its grated windows continue to frown upon the surrounding world, so long will the memories that cluster around them live in the recollections of "ye" old inhabitants.

CHAPTER VIII.

NEW ORLEANS UNDER DENIS PRIEUR.

In the early part of 1828, Mr. Roffignac, being about to undertake a voyage to Europe, concluded to vacate the office of Mayor, which for eight long years he had honorably filled. He accordingly forwarded his resignation to the Council, which was accepted with regret. An election was thereupon ordered, and the 7th day of April selected for the same.

Parties at that time were nearly balanced. The members of the Press, forgetful of those amenities due to their profession were unstinted in their denunciations of one another, the Jackson partisans being championed by the redoubtable Peter K. Wagner, on the one hand, and the Adams Administration faction by the equally hot-headed John Gibson of the *Argus*. These two were in every respect representative men of party fury, and were, in some measure, imitated by writers of lesser note. As these people were always armed and prepared for trouble, the wonder is that personal rencounters were not of more frequent occuirence. Their vocabulary teemed with such expressions as "rogue," "coward," "scribbler," "turncoat," and "liar," for it seemed as if no other epithets or forms of speech were so appropriate for provocation or insult.

It was in this condition of the public mind that the name of Denis Prieur, who, during the outgoing administration had creditably performed the duties of City Recorder, an office second in dignity only to that of Mayor, was brought out by the Jacksonites as their standard-bearer.

From this election, it may be said, dates the organization of the Democratic party, under that political appellation, in the State of Louisiana.

Mr. Prieur was a man of chivalrous instincts—a noble type of his race. Popular with all classes of society, brave to a fault, charitable to the needy, and accessible to all, it is no wonder he became a formidable candidate.

His competitor in the race was another honored creole, A. Peychaud, whose lineal descendants are yet living among us. But, unfortunately for his chances of success, his claims happened to be urged by a small coterie of Adam's men—a ''ring,'' we call them now—of whom the members of the party were tiring. Hence, many people were found ''kicking in the traces,'' and refusing their support. Political conventions and ''regular'' nominations were unknown quantities in the science of electioneering. The usual practice was for every man looking for a local office to make the race upon his own individual merits, and partisan feeling was often laid aside in the general scramble. Hence, the one who had most friends was invariably the winner, and became, in fact, the choice of the community.

As was generally expected, the poll resulted in favor of Prieur, but not without a respectable opposition, the vote standing 888 for Prieur and 531 for Peychaud. The Jackson partisans made a great ado over this victory, claiming it as a crushing defeat to the administration forces, which was not really the case. The gladsome

news was heralded by them throughout the North and
West, as the precursor of assured success in the approaching campaign, for the country was again being
convulsed in the throes of a new Presidential election.

Upon the very threshold of his administration, a difficulty arose in the City Council, which came very nearly stopping the machinery of the municipal government.
It seems that, among the members elected, Mr. William
Harper, duly returned to represent the 6th Ward, offered himself in the Council Chamber to take his seat as
one of the Aldermen. The recognition of this claim
was at once opposed by some members on the ground that,
inasmuch as Mr. Harper was holding an office under the
Federal administration, his case came within the pur-
view of the clause of the State Constitution forbidding
any person from holding more than one office of profit
or trust at the same time. The objection being sustained, Mr. Harper was denied his seat. This was the first
skirmish between the Jacksonites and the Administration
people in the Council.

The discomfited Federalist determined to apply to
the law for redress, and, with that object in view,
applied for a writ of mandamus against the Mayor and
Council, in Judge Lewis' court, which, after argument,
was duly granted. The judgment authorized the rela-
tor to assume his seat as Alderman of said ward, and
required the Council to recognize him in that official
character.

But the Council were not to be balked in their settled
purpose. Assuming the ground that the court was
divested of all jurisdiction, inasmuch as the Council
were made by law the exclusive judges of the qualifications of their own members, they locked horns with
the civil tribunal, and refused obedience.

The judge met this act of insubordination by ordering the sheriff to sequester the revenues of the corporation.

As might have been expected, this judicial action brought matters to a crisis, and on the 1st of May, 1828, the outlook assumed a menacing aspect. The difficulty was one which admitted of no delay. Hence, an appeal was forthwith taken to the Supreme Court, which three weeks afterward, opined in favor of the city. It held that the law, giving to city courts the right of deciding on the eligibility of members, was unconstitutional; that the article of the Code of Practice interdicting courts of justice from passing upon the validity of elections was unconstitutional; that the sheriff was bound to inquire into the legality of an order of court addressed to him, and was responsible for the execution of illegal orders; that the mandamus, ordering the City Council to admit Mr. Harper to his seat, as well as the writ of *distringas*, were both *ultra vires*, and, finally, that the sheriff was guilty of trespass in executing the latter writ.

Thus, under the cover of legal authority, did the Jacksonites succeed in ridding themselves of one of their most obnoxious opponents!

Another unexpected difficulty presented itself. In the hurry and confusion incident to the great fire, which had completely consumed the State House, toward the close of Roffignac's administration, the Legislature and Governor were guilty of a most extraordinary oversight, the former in passing and the latter in approving a law entitled "An Act further amending several articles of the Civil Code and Code of Practice." By the 25th section of that enactment, the whole State was thrown into confusion, inasmuch as it repealed all acts anterior to the promulgation of the New Civil Code. Consequently, the charters of every corporation were an-

nulled, our courts of justice became inoperative, and no
other laws remained in force, except such as were contained in the New Civil Code, the Code of Practice and
the statutes enacted since 1824. The evil was, however, remedied, by a new convocation of the General
Assembly.

A few months before the induction of Prieur into
office, a disastrous fire had occurred at the corner of
Toulouse and Levee streets, destroying, among other
buildings of value, the State House—*la Maison du Gouv-
ernement*—with many of its historical contents. There
is no doubt that, at that period, the city was infested by
a band of organized incendiaries, and the origin of this
conflagration was naturally attributed to them, for,
three days after the event, some citizens arrested two of
them in the act of applying the torch to several buildings in the faubourgs back of town. Lynching was an
unknown factor in those days. Labor in the streets,
with ball and chain—exposure at the pillory on the public square—the lash applied on the bare back—these
were the usual punitive measures.

In the early days of his administration, the demon of
crime seems to have been set loose upon the thoroughly
affrighted community. Notwithstanding the vigilance
of the city guard, incendiarism continued to brandish
its hellish torch, and robberies of a daring character became almost nightly occurrences.

To check these growing evils, the Council adopted a
resolution requiring the Mayor to organize regular patrols for each and every square, thus superseding the
necessity of maintaining a force of armed men, who had
long been in the habit of stopping and even insulting
belated and respectable citizens without the shadow of
any excuse.

The fire department, if the system which then existed

can be dignified by such a name, was somewhat improved by the restrictions thrown around the *personnel* of the company of colored firemen, to whom the corporation, in its prodigality, had awarded the sum of three hundred dollars for meritorious services rendered at the State House fire. Some of them were, no doubt, honest and deserving, but many, and, perhaps, the greater number, were perfectly worthless. It was not an uncommon occurrence to see them, during and after fires, stretched about the streets, dead drunk.

The following items, selected at random from a large number of others in the local periodicals of the day, are illustrative of the spirit of lawlessness then rampant in our poorly guarded city.

"ROBBERIES.—The lock of the Postoffice door, on Bienville street, was forced open on Saturday night (May 19, 1828) and the Postoffice entered and robbed by thieves, who carried off one letter containing some fifty or sixty dollars, visited another, and took some small change from the front compartment, leaving ten or fifteen dollars in the back of the drawer. A sack containing empty mail bags was opened, but nothing else in the office appeared to have been touched. The thieves very kindly left an axe behind in pay for what they took."

And again :

" The office of the Register of Conveyances was broken open on Saturday night and robbed of a small amount of money, the papers thrown about the office, and some of them probably carried off. The same night, one or two stores were broken open and robbed, and attempts made to get into others. As it was a cool, pleasant night, and but few mosquitoes buzzing about, it is

probable our city guard, so long oppressed with the suf-
focating heat of July, had seized upon the agreeable
change of the atmosphere to take a comfortable nap.''

And again :

" ROBBERY.—On Tuesday night last (April 24, 1828)
the store of Messrs. Robinson & Booth, on Chartres
street, was broken open, and a large quantity of valuable goods stolen. The villains, with the greatest impudence, made their entry in the rear, boring a hole
through it sufficiently large to admit an arm and undo the
fastenings. George Buchanan and Louis Goodly were
arrested. They were apprehended on a flatboat lying
in the river. A large part of the goods stolen was recovered. In their possession, about fifty keys of all
sorts and sizes were found, a fine steel saw, and a number of arms of all descriptions. George Buchanan is
supposed to be the man who lately robbed the Mobile
Bank. Louis Goodly has turned State's evidence, and
given away other accomplices.''

And so on, *ad infinitum*, were I disposed to chronicle
every instance of daily recurring crime. When we take
into consideration the fact that the whole population of
New Orleans did not greatly exceed 40,000 inhabitants,
including slaves and colored denizens, and that the
mercantile portion of the community was mainly confined to the space embraced from the river to Bourbon,
and from Customhouse street to St. Philip, it becomes
self-evident that the proportion of criminal offences was
abnormal. This sad condition of society was mainly
due to the same causes that had given Roffignac's administration so much reason for discontent and tribula-
tion. These were licensed gambling, and its concomi-
tant horde of villainous black-legs from every part of
the country. Prieur's predecessor, notwithstanding

honest and energetic efforts, had failed completely to cauterize the ulcerous sore, and as long as the gaming evil was tolerated—nay, legalized by State authority—measures more coercive than those within his reach were alone adequate to ward off the impending menace to society.   To this end the Mayor devoted his energies with varying success, during the whole term of his office.

In 1828, Gen. Jackson, then a candidate for the Presidency, was formally invited by the General Assembly to visit New Orleans as the guest of Louisiana. In the resolutions adopted by that body, all reference or allusion to political issues was carefully avoided, but terms of gratitude for his noble defence of the country, on the banks of Counselor and ex-Alderman Rodriguez' old canal, were kindly expressed.   This course had been adopted in imitation of similar action taken by other States, and was merely intended as a compliment, without political significance or other ulterior design.   But different was the construction placed upon the matter by the hot-headed partisans of President Adams.   They had serious misgivings as to the ultimate object.   They looked askance at the Trojan horse.   They determined, therefore, to act on the defensive and with proper reserve.

Jackson had accepted the invitation, and in due course of time reached the city.   He was received by the State and municipal authorities with flattering ceremonies. He was fêted, wined and banqueted, as is usual on such occasions.   He was paraded through the streets in a carriage of State, drawn by six milk-white steeds, and acclaimed with loud huzzas by the gaping multitudes. But hardly had these official manifestations of honor,

which lasted several days, ended, than the leading
politicians of the Democratic party—the Livingstons,
the Marignys, the Wagners, the Davezacs, and a host of
admiring friends, took hold of the unsuspecting General,
and began to hold levees and receptions at their private
residences, calculated to arouse the ire and jealousy of
their opponents.   This circumstance proved regrettable
in every respect ; for the old hero, who had consented to
the visit in the expectation only of reviving forgotten
memories, and of quietly enjoying his corn-cob pipe in
the company of old-time acquaintances, suddenly found
himself in an unenviable predicament.   He became the
target of abuse and slander at the hands of the Opposition press, particularly of the *Argus*, which began the
publication of a serial biography of the General's public
and *private* life, so exaggerated and infamous that the
wrathy Tennesseean swore by the Eternal that he would
shake from his feet the dust of a city where, expecting
to be treated as a guest, he had found insult, ingratitude
and inhospitality.

His departure did not seem to have appeased the vindictive Federalists, for when the bill of expenses was
presented for payment, it found strong opposition in the
Legislature, and was only finally settled after much
haggling and curtailing.   To such extremes was party
spirit then carried !

From these reminiscences I shall proceed to describe
the city, as it then existed.

The town proper was a parallelogram, about seventy-
eight arpents in front and fourteen in depth.   This is
to-day the dimension of a moderate sugar plantation.
Under the régime of Baron Caronlelet, and during the
early part of Governor Claiborne's administration, it

had been defended from outside attack by a line of
fortifications and a ditch, the vestiges of which were yet
visible many years thereafter. The works had been
dismantled, and the ditches, which had become nurseries of disease, had been filled in at the time that
Denis Prieur assumed the reins of municipal government. In the centre, and directly fronting the river,
was a public park, or, more properly speaking, a Place
d'Armes, surrounded by an iron railing erected on a
granite coping. The enclosure originally consisted of a
fancy wooden fence, the gates being flanked by imita-
tions of cannon, cut out or carved from the same material. This was the Jackson Square of to-day. A
triple row of sycamores encircled the grounds, and the
weeds were allowed to grow rank and tall, except where
wide swaths had been cut by pedestrians on their way
to the markets, the church or the public buildings. Immediately in the rear, occupying the whole space from
St. Peter to St. Ann, stood the City Hall—the *Cabildo*
of the Spaniards—the Court House, once the habitation
of jolly old monks, and the Cathedral. The two first
structures retain their original appearance, but the
Cathedral the gift of Almonester, was of Gothic architecture. Sixty years after its construction, it was discovered that, notwithstanding the solidity with which
the edifice had been originally put up, the walls were
becoming insecure—it was supposed—from the shocks
of frequent artillery discharges in its vicinity. Large
fissures had made their appearance on the front and
sides, and, in consequence, the upper portion was torn
down, and a new design was suggested by Louis Pilié,
a city surveyor. and adopted by the wardens. It is a
fact worthy of note and known only to a few, that in
the work of excavation which these repairs required, the

masons were compelled to disinter the remains of the
priests interred at the foot of the altar of St. Francis,
whence they were carried in wheelbarrows to the cart
destined to convey them to the cemetery. Among these
relics are the bones of the sainted friar, Père Antoine,
now resting in the "Priests' Tomb," on Basin street.
Those, therefore, and there are thousands, who repair to
the Cathedral, and kneel at his supposed crypt in prayer
and repentance, are victims of a deceit, which has been
kept secret and for which there is no excuse.

The *façade* of the square—that toward the river—was
perfectly open, there being no railroads in those times to
obstruct the view or breezes from the Mississippi with
their unsightly freight depots. Each of the lateral
streets, St. Peter on the upper and St. Ann on the lower
sides, was covered by a block of buildings, built of
bricks between posts, uniform in size and construction,
two stories in height, with small projecting balconies.
These buildings were used as stores, the families of the
occupants usually living up stairs. They were in a
great measure used for the sale of tropical fruits, the
trade being mostly controlled by hardy Austrians and
Sclavonians—a thrifty and peaceable race. At the corner of St. Ann and Chartres, was a popular *café*, where,
besides all the paraphernalia of a modern bar-room, coffee, chocolate or tea, steaming hot, were served on small
tables to customers immersed in the mysteries of dominoes. The name was the *Café del Aguila.* Across the
street was the low-roofed, Spanish tiled building kept
by Benito Duran, surnamed *Valiente*, where the purest
Mayorca was always to be had. There were also, here and
there among these houses, now called the Pontalba
Buildings, the establishment of an ingenious watch-
maker, named Labarre, who manufactured a one-year

running clock for the use of the Cathedral tower; a hardware store, a restaurant, a gunsmith's store, and a bar-
ber shop; but fruit seemed to be the staple commodity
in that quarter.

Along the iron railings, on the opposite side, were to
be seen booths for the sale of oranges, bananas, ice-
cream, peanuts, ginger beer (*bière douce*), cooled in
large tubs, and the inevitable *estomac mulâtre* (ginger
cake), as highly prized by the urchins of that generation as they are at present.   Lining the river, small
huts were erected along the water front for the sale of
oysters by the wholesale or on the half-shell.   These establishments were well patronized by families and respectable society, for the luggers engaged in the trade
were wont to tie to the posts opposite the markets with
their daily loads of fresh and luscious bivalves.

On Sunday afternoons, the scene around the square
was more than picturesque.   Greek ice cream vendors
in tasseled fez; Choctaws reeling drunk in Father
Adam's costume, a well worn, diaphanous blanket being
substituted for the historical fig leaf; mulatresses
decked with gaudy colored tignons; children in holiday
attire romping over the weeds in innocent glee; specta-
cled gentlemen, sporting their gold-headed walking
sticks and dainty gold snuff-boxes; groups of City
Guards in gala uniforms and with formidable cutlasses;
fashionable loungers—the dudes of the period—discuss-
ing the rival claims of Calvé or Bamberger, the favorite
brima donnas of the Opera—all these commingled together and in incessant motion, offered the ever varying
and dissolving views of the kaleidoscope.   Without being charged as a "*laudator temporis acti*," I can assure
my readers that those days were happier far than ours,
in this particular, at least, that citizens could gather

together in social entertainments and exchange the amenities of life in peace and amity, free from the intrusion of drunken hoodlums or Workhouse rowdies.

Not less animated or amusing was the once famous French Market, a central point for sight-seers and Northern tourists. Sundays and holidays were the times in which she would don, like a pretty coquette, her most variegated attire. There, every conceivable language, from Choctaw to Greek or Maltese, not to omit our sweet, euphonious Creole French, was spoken. A constant ebb and flow of human streams would often obstruct locomotion, and this annoyance, increased by the interlocking of baskets, was often a source of merriment to the visitor. Strange, indeed, were the scenes to be witnessed within its gay precincts and around its massive pillars. Here Aglaé, stately and gracious, with her turbaned head and ebony features wreathed in smiles, dispensed her steaming coffee to *mo ti moun*, as she patronizingly called her younger visitors, nor was the *calas tout chaud* ever omitted. Here also was to be seen the tidy little quadroon, offering her lilliputian bouquets of Spanish jessamines, carnations and violets, as *boutonnières* for the old beaux, who, before proceeding to their usual morning avocations, were in the habit of taking a stroll through its crowded walks. Here the demure dame, accompanied by her sable-hued *domestique*, and the comely damsel, on her way from church, usually chaperoned by some elder relative, were wont to make *la tournée*. A trysting place for lovers, many a *billet doux* was furtively exchanged, and many a side glance spoke a mysterious language. Many were the Indian squaws, squatting on the side pavements and vending their wares of ingeniously worked baskets, sassafras roots, genuine *gombo filé* and leaves of *plan-*

tain; while the braves of the Nation, a set of dirty and inebriated rascals, stood around them, disposed of their *sarbacanes* or blow-guns, with their furze-tipped arrows, at a picayune apiece. Nor must I omit to mention the politicians of the day. These frequently held their little reunions in this market, on Sunday mornings, where they discussed the leading topics of the week, laid out their little programmes, and, not unlike two celebrated Governors, would frequently adjourn to a neighboring *café* during the intervals of discussion.

The city was intersected by seven parallel and twelve perpendicular streets, but its suburbs, above and below, extended about three miles. Below Esplanade street was the *faubourg* Marigny; above Canal street, *faubourg Ste. Marie;* and back of Rampart street began the *faubourg* Trémé. Beyond these named suburbs there were others, but the above formed the boundaries proper of the corporation. The depth of the habitable territory in the rear of New Orleans extended no further than *Rue* Marais (Swamp street), and all the rest, as far back as the lake, was what was called *la Cyprière*, a trackless and almost impenetrable morass.

Old Levee, Chartres and Royal, and most of the perpendicular streets, as far as they were intersected by these three streets, were considered the commercial and principal portion of the city, and possessed a respectable number of elegant brick buildings, some of them three stories in height. Of the latter, the oldest one is the quaint and old-fashioned structure at the corner of St. Peter and Royal streets, once the residence of Dr. Yves LeMonnier, whose monogram is still to be seen on the balconies. The late General John L. Lewis was wont to relate how, while the building was progressing, hundreds of people would gather at the corner diagonally opposite and predict the failure of the undertaking. They expected to see it topple down at every moment, grounding their conjectures upon the yielding nature of the soil !

The same well-informed authority pointed out to the writer the building No. 124 Chartres street, near the corner of St. Louis, as having been erected by some enthusiastic Frenchman as a future residence for Napoleon Bonaparte, then confined at St. Helena, whom they had sworn to rescue by a *coup de main* from his prison island. Visionary as this scheme may appear to us at this day, the expedition was actually planned, and only fell through by the unexpected announcement of the death of the martyr-emperor. Of this project there can be no doubt. Nicholas Girod, the millionaire and ex-mayor of New Orleans, was the furnisher of the required sums, and Dominique You, with a select crew of desperate Baratarians, was to have been the leader. Of this daring officer General Jackson once said, when elated with the prowess of the " hellish banditti,'' ''Were I ordered to storm the gates of Hell, with Captain Dominick as my lieutenant, I would have no misgivings of the result.''

On the same side of the street, and at the corner of St. Louis, stood the comfortable and well known residence of Mr. Girod, of whom I have spoken. He was not only a philanthropist, but a man of character and great public spirit, who contributed, while an executive officer of our city, in materially aiding Jackson in his memorable defence.

Diagonally opposite was the *Bourse* or Exchange, kept by Maspero and afterward by Hewlett, a great auction mart and place of public entertainment, and the forerunner of the St. Louis Exchange. This was a favorite resort. It was here that public meetings were usually held ; that Jackson was triumphantly carried after paying his fine to Judge Hall's marshal, and that all important commercial transactions were carried on.

The rest of the *carré de la ville* was made up of small frame houses, one story high, some very mean ; and Judge Martin, a contemporary, says that the proportion of the latter was much greater than in any other city of the Union.

In addition to the public buildings, fronting the square, already mentioned, there were two nunneries, the older of which was the Ursulines Convent, occupied now as the official residence of Archbishp Janssens. The other was established on the space of ground bounded by Nuns or Religious street, in the upper part of the city.

There were also a Presbyterian and an Episcopal church. One known as Christ Church was situated at the corner of Dauphine and Canal.

The jail was located on the site of the lower Recorder's Court and Arsenal, until a penitentiary was built in Baton Rouge. There, the convicts—*les forcats*—were detained and manacled together, white and black alike, and were made to labor upon our public streets. The practice of forcing white criminals into the chain-gang with negroes was continued for several years, but, in 1829, Gov. Derbigny put a summmary end to it, for causes and under circumstances which form one of the most dramatic episodes in the history of Louisiana. The action of the executive was much commented upon at the time, and gave rise to a sharp correspondence between Prieur and Derbigny, but the latter, backed by law and supreme authority, maintained his fiat, and from that moment the system was broken up.

There was a dilapidated concern, called the Custom House, at the foot of the river, close to the spot where is now situated the Canal street ferry.

The United States Court then stood in the centre of the area now occupied by the Custom House. A spacious walk, shaded by a few stunted trees, led to it. It was a dingy, two-story brick building, facing Canal street, and was demolished in 1848. Alongside of it stood a Bethel. On the same side of the street, between Royal and Bourbon, was the residence and place of business of Judah Touro, the philanthropist, and close to it a synagogue, a low structure put up with his own funds. In the centre of the road was a canal, which, together with Gravier's, a little higher up, on Poydras street, was utilized for drainage purposes.

There were three theatres, one on St. Philip street, where the public school of that name is now being conducted; another, subsequently the French Opera House, was managed by Mr. John Davis, and is now a convent on Orleans street, between Royal and Bourbon; and the third was the Camp Street Theatre, opposite Natchez alley, afterward converted into an armory hall, and to-day the site of the hardware stores of Rice & Born. To repair to this place of amusement, flatboat gunwales or planked sidewalks had been constructed, and lanterns had to be used by the belated patrons to avoid falling into the bordering ditches.

There were also three banks, not to speak of several offices of discount and deposit. Of the former, the Louisiana State Bank was the oldest, being the first bank established under the American system, in the early portion of the first decade of this century. The building is still to be seen on Royal street, between St. Louis and Conti streets, the initial letters L. S. B. being conspicuous on the original projecting balcony. The first cashier was Mr. Zacharie (as is attested by the epitaph on his honored grave), who resided on the premises, in the upper story—a man of wit, humor and thorough business habits. His grandchildren still live among us, and are justly proud of their ancestry.

Two orphan asylums provided for the necessitous and helpless young unfortunates.

In the rear of the city, starting from its centre, was a basin or port for small schooners ; a canal of about two miles in length led from it to Bayou St. John, and thence to Lake Pontchartrain.   Another canal, in suburb Marigny, on Elysian Fields street, afforded also easy communication with the lakes.   It began within a few yards of the Mississippi (where Bernard Marigny's grandfather had years before put up a saw-mill), and discharged itself into the Bayou St. John, at a short distance from its junction with the Carondelet canal. Along the river margin, the levee or bank was twenty feet in width, and afforded ample space for walking.

Another, but a natural, outlet to the sea was Bayou Sauvage, which, flowing directly in the rear of the Bretonne or Indian Market, on the Bayou Road, took its course through the Gentilly to Bayou Bienvenu, and thence to the Gulf.   This water-course was navigable for small boats only, and was frequented by hunters and men of predatory habits.   When too hotly pursued by the American authorities, it was claimed that Lafitte and his motley crew were wont to bring through its sinuous passages their ill-gotten gains to this city.   It is a well established fact that Daniel Clark was one of their merchants and secret agents here, and having his bachelor home and depot—at least, one of his depots—on the convenient banks of the stream, near the junction of Esplanade and Bayou Road streets, no more suitable place could have been selected for the illicit traffic. This statement rests not only on tradition, but is supported by the well known reputation for acquisitiveness of our first delegate to Congress.

Our streets were narrow (thirty feet in width), and were made purposely so, with a view of furnishing ventilation and shade, while their gutters, whenever the rise of the river would permit, were copiously flushed every evening by means of sluices ingeniously inserted through the levees, not unlike our discarded system of rice flumes. Boys used to float tiny boats in the swift current, and to watch their erratic course as they sped away toward the swamp, where the turbid waters lost themselves, depositing their fertilizing sands upon the marsh. Much of the *cyprière* behind the town, was thus slowly and gradually reclaimed.

The houses, in general, as I have already said, were low frame structures, bricked between posts, *briquetées entre poteaux*, roofed with shingles, although, in buildings of a more pretentious appearance, bricks were used and Spanish tiles substituted, some flat, others convex. Remains of this style of architecture are yet to be seen in the Second District. Flat tiles were used on terraces, with which several buildings were embellished after the style of Mexico and Havana, where members of the family were in the habit, after sundown, of inhaling the cool breezes wafted from the river and lake. No house of aristocratic pretensions was without its court-yard or *patio*, the centre of which was ornamented with a fountain and enlivened by tropical plants. The main entrance was through a wide gate or *porte cochère*, in the interior of which was kept the cumbersome family carriage, and beyond, a wide staircase led to the upper apartments. The windows, those of Spanish construction, I mean, were very wide and always *arched*. This was a distinctive feature. They opened upon the *patio*. The sills were covered with pots of aromatic plants, chief of which was the fragrant rosemary, which was believed, besides its medicinal properties, to possess the virtue of good luck. Few residences, therefore, were without their *matas de romero*. Iron balconies, objects of hygienic necessity in this hot climate, were attached to every building more than one story high, and became matters not only of comfort, but of beauty, with their burnished brass knobs placed at short intervals from each other.

Royal street, between Conti and St. Philip, notwithstanding the inroads of time, still retains some well preserved specimens of the architectural style of more than a century ago. The timber employed for building purposes under the Spanish régime, was under the control of police regulations, since it was forbidden to fell trees except at certain periods of the year and phases of the moon. The wood was, therefore, extremely well seasoned and entirely free from decay. As an illustration of this fact, I have now in my possession the section of a post, taken from the old country residence of Don Bernardo de Galvez, more than one hundred and twenty years old, in as perfect a state of preservation as when it was first adjusted into its present shape by the carpenter's adze. The cement in use was also a subject of government supervision, but the secret, like that of the Roman cement employed in the construction of the *Via Appia*, is, I fear, unfortunately lost. No Schillinger or any other process is comparable to what it was in hardness or durability. When, some years ago, a por-

tion of the old Cathedral walls was torn down, owing to
the fissures caused by the depression of the soil, the
mortar had become so firmly incrusted and blended with
the brickwork as to have formed a concrete mass, which
defied the repeated blows of the pick. Granite could
not have been harder.

Now, a few words as to the suburbs. There, the
frame buildings were more modest in appearance, nota-
bly in the faubourg Marigny. That portion of the city
extended from Esplanade street to a considerable distance below, covering the whole acreage of the old
Marigny plantation. At the foot of Elysian Fields, just
where the Morgan Railroad depot is now situated, stood
a saw-mill, propelled by water power supplied from the
river. It was a very thriving establishment, the raw
material being carried from the swamps through a canal,
running parallel with the present road-bed of the Pontchartrain Railway, and, continuing its course through
the Metairie ridge, connected its waters with Bayou St.
John and the lakes by means of the Carondelet canal,
into which it emptied. It was both deep and wide,
affording facilities for navigation to sloops and schooners
of a moderate size. Large rafts were daily hauled
through by mule power and *cordelles*, which kept the
mill busy, besides enhancing the value of the adjacent
property. This enterprise had originated with Bernard
Marigny's grandfather in the last quarter of the preceding century. In 1832 the mill was abandoned. The
new railroad had killed it. The cavity was then filled
up as far as Greatmen street, and, by degrees, as high
as Claiborne street, where its rapidly filling channel is
yet distinctly to be seen. I remember that, in the days
of my boyhood, the banks of the sluggish stream, as far

back as the Luzenberg Hospital, were lined on Sunday
mornings by Gascons who, with hound and gun, were
in the habit of hunting a species of very large bull-
frogs, named *wararons* by the French.

The limits of faubourg Marigny extended originally
only to Spain street, but in the course of time the thriving section had completely absorbed all the lesser suburbs below and behind it.   In the rear it reached a little
beyond Girod street, the *"ultima thule"* of civilization.
The inhabitants consisted chiefly of Europeans of Latin
extraction and of Creoles, white and black.   People of
the Saxon or Celtic race were few and far between.

" *Rari nantes in gurgito vasto.* "

The frame houses were mostly one-story high and
small.   Within its precincts the nomenclature of streets
underwent an entire change.   Thus, Chartres street,
which, below St. Peter street, was named *Condé*, became, below Esplanade, *Moreau* street, in honor of the exiled general of that name, who had paid New Orleans a
hasty visit a short time before; Old Levee, originally *"le
Chemin Public,"* was transformed into *Victory;* Royal into
Casacalvo; Dauphine into *Greatmen;* Burgundy into
Craps, so-called, tradition says, because the strip of land
through which it had been opened had been lost by old
Bernard Marigny at a game of "craps," a game of cards
then much in vogue; Rampart into *Love;* St. Claude,
named after Claude Trémé, the founder of the suburb of
that name, into *Goodchildren*, and so on.   Along the
lower side of Esplanade some nice residences were
occasionally to be seen, among others that of Judge
Canonge, at the corner of Casacalvo, but, as a general
rule, the buildings, though comfortably built for the
climate and temperature, were of rude and cheap structure.   Small flower gardens, teeming with clusters of

creeping Spanish jessamines, relieved the monotonous aspect of the *quartier*. Specimens of these old houses are still to be seen in a state of decay on Bagatelle, Union and St. Anthony streets.

In that part of New Orleans, style or etiquette was unknown, the women being clad in homespun and *in-diennes*, and the matrons, especially the *émigrées* from St. Domingo, sported picturesque *tignons*, a sort of head-gear, consisting of a fancy bandana handkerchief (Madras) tied around the upper part of the head—a fashion which some old Creoles follow even to this day. Though unpretending in dress and appearance, they lived in happy unity and commerce, except when, now and then, some thoughtless or mischievous gossip (and they were not a few) would throw a brand of discord into the com-munity. Then women's tongues were set loose, and bits of scandal rehearsed, as each took part with the contend-ing factions. Apart from these little mishaps, which the hand of time would effectually allay, it must be ad-mitted they were a cheerful, contented and industrious class. Their great luxury was coffee, for the pot was everlastingly simmering over the embers of the kitchen hearth. This beverage was the first thing offered to a visitor. They were frugal also. A plate of *gombo filé*, a dish of *jambalaya*, of *sagamité*, a peculiar preparation of corn, a chunk of salted meat, flanked by a salad, con-stituted their usual day's meal They were the most obliging people in the world, and as nurses could not be excelled. Whenever a neighbor got sick, or during seasons of epidemics, it was a noble sight to see these people engaged in their holy ministry, and vying with one another in preparing medicinal antidotes, of many of which they possessed the secret. They were adepts in the knowledge of the curative properties of certain

herbs and roots.   Not a cent would they ever charge or
accept for services of this nature.   Reciprocity of favors
was the only reward expected.

I have already spoken about the public park, known
as the *Place d'Armes*.   Perhaps my readers may wish to
know something about the once much talked of Congo
Square.   I shall describe it, such as I knew it and
saw it.

This piece of ground was, I believe, originally donated
to the corporation by Claude Trémé, out of the immense
reach of swamp lands he owned just beyond the rear
limits of the city.   In front of it were the remains of the
old fortifications erected by Carondelet, with their glacis
and partially filled trenches.   Its original name was
Circus Square, and was so designated from its destination and use.   For, here it was that the *Senor Cayetano*
held high revel with his menagerie of wondrous animals, and retinue of clowns and daring horsemen.   The
following Creole doggerel commemorates his popularity :

> '' Cést Michié Cayetane,
>   Qui sorti la Havane
> Avec so chouals et so macacs !
>   Le gagnin un homme qui dansé dans **sac;**
> Le gagnin qui dansé si yé la main ;
>   Li gagnin zant' à choual qui boi' di vin **;**
> Le gagnin oussi un zeine zoli mamzelle,
>   Qui monté choual sans bride et sans selle **;**
> Pou di tou ca mo pas cababe,'' etc.

Its popular name has always' been that of Congo
Square.   It was the favorite rendezvous of our African
slaves on Sunday afternoons.

There are hundreds yet living in our midst who
remember what a gala day for these people was the
Sabbath, and with what keen sense of relish and an-

xiety they awaited its coming. Attired in their picturesque and holiday dresses, they would gather by
thousands in the afternoon under the shade of the old
sycamores, and romp in African revelries to the accompaniment of the tam-tam and jaw-bones. Nothing
could be more interesting than to see their wild and
grotesque antics, their mimicry of courtly dames in the
act of making an obeisance, and the dances peculiar to
their country. In the midst of the ludicrous contortions
and gyrations of the Bamboula, not unlike those performed in the equally famous Voudou dance, they
would sing with a pleasing though somewhat monotonous rhythm strange Creole songs, the burden of one
of which, I remember, was:

"*Dansé Calinda*, bou doum, bou doum."

To these festivities *nègres 'Méricains* were not invited.
There was no affinity between them. Here the noted
characters of the race were to be seen, from "Lapin"
the chief of the Raquette players, to "Bras Coupé," the
Robin Hood of the Swamp. The victor of the "Pape-
gaud" prize, a tournament in which a wooden rooster,
decorated with floating ribbons, was the target, was
here also made the recipient of boisterous applause.
Everything was tumult, motion and hilarity. Children
romped over the grass plats, and nurses looked com-
placently on their gambols, while listening perhaps to
the honeyed words of some dusky swains. Taken
altogether, it was a scene well worth visiting and the
like of which we shall never see again.

As soon as the shadows of approaching night began to
deepen, the crowd would slowly disperse, singing in
chorus:

"*Bonsoir dance, soleil couché.*"

White people, from motives of curiosity or fun, invariably attended these innocent pastimes. Their presence alone was sufficient to repress any serious disorder—an occurrence extremely rare.

Along the edges of the sidewalks and of the iron in·closure, rude deal tables were set out, screened from the sun by overhanging cotton slips. From their tops long streamers fluttered in the breeze. Upon these improvised counters was to be seen an imposing array of tumblers, pies, roasted peanuts and cakes, the *estomac mulâtre* usually predominating among the latter. Nor was coffee wanting—pure, fragrant and steaming—such as the Creoles alone can prepare. Presiding over these rustic booths, colored women dispensed *la bierre du pays* from bottles plunged in buckets of cold water. This beverage, a compound of fermented apples, ginger root and mellow pines, furnished a palatable substitute for ale, and was an object of great demand by the little chaps of that generation. It was a source of considerable profit to the *marchandes*. *Li tout fini* (no more left) was not an infrequent reply to requests for more. As no strong liquors or wines were allowed to be sold on the grounds, and no "corner grocery" hoodlums were allowed to flourish and thrive in those old-fashioned and unprogressive days, breaches of the peace at places of public reunions were seldom witnessed. There was then a pillory and whipping-post, which did more toward maintaining good order than all the fines administered to-day in our so-called courts of justice.

Congo Square, as I shall continue to call it, was at one time used for public executions also. On its grounds several balloon ascensions took place, notwithstanding that the usual locality for such performances was within the yard of the present Archbishop's palace, or an empty lot at the corner of Condé and Barracks. Many people will remember how egregiously duped they were by one Petin, an aeronaut, in that very square. But to the circus man, with his side show of animals and monsters, this spot was always an object of preference. It was, in every respect, the chosen ground for popular exhibitions.

Speaking of places of amusement, I must not omit the Saturday night balls. Some of these were unique affairs. One was located in a long, dingy, frame building on Condé street, between Maine and St. Philip, at the extremity of which a public bathhouse was kept open during week days. The following advertisement, which I textually copy from one of our local papers, will give the reader a clear insight into their character :

"CONDÉ BALL ROOM.

"A Grand Ball.

"Admission one dollar. The ball will take place every Wednesday and Saturday.

"The subscriber having a small ball room, can not receive more people than what his apartment will contain, he has made a regulation for a sufficient number of ladies for his room. The ball is not public for the ladies ; they will not be admitted without the invitation of the subscriber, and where they will have a personal ticket that the subscriber will distribute himself, to be more secure. The ladies that will have a ticket of admittance are requested not to put themselves on the floor for the counter dance, and particularly those that have a handkerchief on their head. To avoid all inconveniences at the door, the gentlemen are requested not to forget their ticket on going out of the room. A particular place is made at the entrance of door to put their cloaks, hats, etc., for which the waiter will be responsible, after he will have delivered the number of the article to each one.

"Those who desire to subscribe for the balls can enter at the ball room from 9 o'clock in the morning until 9 in the evening.   ST. MARTIN."

"*Spectatum admissi, risum teneatis, amici?*"

I leave it to the reader's imagination to conjecture what lots of fun our youngsters must have had with damsels subjected to such primitive rules of social etiquette.

There was also another ball room on St. Philip street, between Royal and Bourbon, within the very walls of the school now bearing that name, where the managers advertised to "keep good harmony."

A more *recherché* affair was to be found at the corner of Bourbon and Orleans streets, where the young bloods were wont to resort, and which subsequently became the theatre of many a difficulty, culminating in bloody duels between the Creoles and *les Américains*. These were the celebrated quadroon balls.

The only place of this character up town was to be found in the faubourg St. Mary, at the corner of New Levee and Girod. If one may judge from the character of the location, it must have been the resort of flatboat-men and hoosiers from the Western country, who, at certain seasons of the year, carried on a profitable and extensive trade with our merchants. These strangers usually tarried with us only a few days. After disposing of their produce, which they had floated down in rafts from the Ohio, they would lavish their money in every conceivable manner, paint the town "red" see all the "sights," the "elephant" included, until, stranded at last, they found themselves in the calaboose.

Paying their small fines, they would go home satisfied.
They had been to "Orlins."

Such was the diversity of customs, religion and
language, not to speak of the jealousy and distrust that
separated the old settlers from the new comers of Saxon
and Celtic origin, that two hostile factions resolved
themselves into distinct camps, and it has required the
triturating influences of several decades to mould these
conflicting interests into a homogeneous mass. Some
curious letters addressed by Gov. Claiborne to his confidential correspondent, Gen. Wilkinson, throw floods
of light upon a certain period in our State history, and,
if published, would furnish interesting reading matter.

When the English was adopted as the official language of the country, it became a matter of serious
necessity for our people of Spanish and French ancestry
to adapt themselves to the new *régime* and to delve into
the mysteries of Anglo-Saxonism. The pronunciation
of its gutturals proved a serious drawback at first, and
provoked many a malediction; but, in the course of
time, they gradually acquired a sort of "*pot pourri*"
mod of expression, which, though not Chesterfieldian,
still enabled them to transact the ordinary affairs of
life with their more energetic neighbors. If not elegant
and refined, it had the merit, at least, of being intelligi-
ble, as the reader may have already seen from the
speeimen of St. Martin's style. As a pendant or companion to it, I can not resist the temptation of placing
on record the following advertisement. posted on Chartres street in my school-boy days, by a prominent auc-
tioneer :

NOTISE !

" These Estore Fort Sale."

Apart from the unique spelling of this short production, when it is borne in mind that the last two words "fort sale" mean, when translated into English, "very filthy," his abortive attempt at idiomatic composition was simply ridiculous.

The people residing at a distance from the public market were usually furnished with provisions by a class of females, generally colored, called "marchandes." Their supplies were varied and reasonably cheap. In addition to the choice cuts of meat which they purchased from the butcher stalls, they would select their vegetables direct from the gardens which girded the town. Hence, their stock was always fresh and abundant. They filled all orders given them, and came regularly every morning to their customers' doors. This system of daily delivery antedated the period of American occupation, and had its origin under the Spaniards of colonial days. They drove, no doubt, a profitable trade, for their commodities were far superior to those of some of our "private markets." This class of traders is now extinct. The Sicilians have crowded them out, as they have done our home folks in every department of industry in which they have engaged, substituting therefor a nondescript and offensive species of peddling and "dago" shops, not only in antagonism to traditional customs, but dangerous to public health. They are confessedly to-day nothing else but hot-beds of infection, disease and filth.

Of the police force I have already had occasion to speak. They were indistinctly called "gendarmes" or "City Guard." Taken as a whole they were a worthless, lazy set, uniformed somewhat after the fashion of

Falstaff's men in buckram. Sailors seem to have been their special aversion, for, on arriving in port, they never failed to have a set-to or scrimmage with them. Jack Tar, it is well known, must have his fun on shore, and, in resisting arrest, these hardy but rough fellows would unsheath the knives strapped to their belts and rush upon their tormentors. Hence, battles royal would ensue, and as the police used their sabres or cutlasses, these affrays would inevitably terminate in the infliction of severe gashes and sword thrusts. Many scenes of this kind have I witnessed in my childhood days.

Next to the performance of this duty, which they considered paramount and supreme, their occupation seemed to consist in loitering about town, in lounging around cabarets or in dozing away their time upon the benches of the guardhouse. The night watchmen were no better, although this branch of the service was occasionally supplemented by a citizen patrol. After sundown the streets became the property of footpads and garroters. Incendiary fires were matters of almost nightly occurrence, as well as burglaries. People ventured out of their houses after dark only at their peril and with great apprehension, and never without a lantern.

It is only since the consolidation of the different municipalities, some forty years ago, that our police organization assumed a better character, and, by laying aside the cutlass and rattle for a club and whistle, began its onward march toward that degree of perfection which it is far from having attained. In this general condemnation of the old system I must cite as notable exceptions Capts. Harper, Winter, Youennes and Mazerat. Here and there, a tolerable policeman might have been found, but these were exceptional cases, and as doctors would say, isolated from the prevailing infection.

During the period of Denis Prieur's administration, two deaths occurred which recalled to the old inhabitants saintly works of charity, and memorable deeds of war. One was that of Père Antoine, the other of Dominique You, whose record is outlined in these pages.

In the year 1829 there died in this city a holy friar, who, for fifty years, had been the guide and consoler of the afflicted, rich and poor alike. The lowly cabin or hut, thatched with palmetto leaves, which he had constructed with his own hands, stood at the corner of the vacant lot directly behind the Cathedral, and which forms now the angle of Royal and St. Anthony alley. I refer to Fra Antonio de Sedella, a capuchin of the Franciscan order, better known as Père Antoine. Though his death was not quite unexpected, its announcement proved a terrible blow to the entire community, for he was beloved by all, irrespective of creed or nationality.

His corpse was laid out during three days upon a gorgeously decked catafalque, in the centre aisle of the church, attended by a civic and military guard. The surging masses had to be restrained. Viewed as a saint, his parishioners, in their desire to retain some relic of their good pastor, had cut into small pieces his humble serge cassock, and would have proceeded to further extremities but for the exertions of Mayor Prieur, who, in person, promptly restored order in the house of God, and took measures to prevent their recurrence.

His death was looked upon as a public calamity. All the public buildings were draped in mourning, and the flags of foreign ships, of the various consulates, of the banks, etc., were hoisted at half mast. Crape was hung on the doors of hundreds and hundreds of private residences, for every family seemed to feel that it had lost a friend, a benefactor, a father.

The City Council, the Legislature, the bench, the learned professors, even the Masons (whom the Catholic Church excommunicates), adopted in their several places of meeting eulogistic resolutions, and signified their desire to attend the obsequies. Edward Livingston, though a free-thinker, pronounced a beautiful oration before the assembled barristers and judges. The funeral services were conducted with unusual pomp and magnificence. Three thousand wax tapers illuminated the sacred edifice. L'Abbé Maenhaut, who succeeded him afterward, delivered the funeral sermon. The whole military force of the city, including the far-famed Legion, were arrayed in front of the square. When the procession took up its line of march through the streets, every church bell tolled the sad, solemn parting knell, and few were the eyes unmoistened with tears. If we are to believe tradition and contemporaneous accounts, the pageant was one of the grandest manifestations of a people's grief ever witnessed in New Orleans.

CHAPTER IX.

THE EXECUTION OF PAULINE.

"Any slave who shall wilfully and maliciously strike his master or mistress, or his master's or mistress' child, or any white overseer appointed by his owner to superintend said owner's slaves, so as to cause a contusion or shedding of blood, shall be punished with death or imprisonment at hard labor for a term of not less than ten years."—*Black Code, Sec. 3.*

I am about to relate one of the most revolting crimes that ever startled the community of New Orleans. The details of the atrocities to which a white and respectable woman of this city was actually being subjected by her own slave, in her own house, when first unearthed; the fiendish barbarity with which this demon in human shape was discovered torturing and ill-treating her martyred mistress, was a crime so unprecedented even in the darkest days of African servitude that the public mind was literally appalled. And what added to the hideousness of the spectacle was the fact that the crime was shown to have been authorized, nay instigated, by the husband himself of the half-demented martyr. The facts present a remarkable pendant to the Lalaurie case, narrated in full in Chapter IV. Gleaned from contemporaneous sources, they furnish an authentic account both of the crime and of its expiation:

In the early part of January, 1845, Edgard Montégut, then Mayor of this city, received through the postoffice, an anonymous letter informing him that a white female was imprisoned in a house, No. 52 Bayou Road, a prisoner of her own slave. The same missive also apprised him that she, for some time past, had been treated in a most horrid manner. The Mayor, accompanied by Recorder Jos. Génois and some police officers, immediately repaired to the designated place, where they found a Mrs. Rabbaneck, the lady of the house, with three of her children, respectively aged seven, four and two years, confined in a back cabinet. Their clothing was worn to tatters and rags; they were covered with filth and ulcers, and their limbs were shrunken and emaciated. The body of Mrs. R. was covered with bruises from head to foot, and in many places with lacerations, indicating where the lash had entered the flesh. Her blackened eyes bore evidence of heavy blows, and her hair was clotted with blood. The three children presented nearly the same shocking appearance, the two eldest in particular. Upon being questioned by the Mayor as to the cause of her distress, Mrs. R., seeing that her slave, Pauline, was present, answered that her husband had beaten her. As she exhibited much trepidation whenever the eyes of her servant were bent upon her, the Mayor ordered the latter's removal from the room, whereupon the woman acknowledged that she was afraid to make statements in her presence, dreading death to herself and little ones. Her husband, she stated, had been absent on a visit for the last six weeks to St. Louis, since which time Pauline had taken possession of the house and its contents, and incarcerated her and children in a closet, where they had been beaten almost daily, sometimes with a cane, at others with a strap, and furnished with food barely sufficient to sustain life. Medical aid and attention were immediately given them at the Mayor's instance, and the negress was arrested and committed to prison. A few days after, a preliminary examination was held before Recorder Génois, and the above facts being fully substantiated she was ordered to be tried before the Criminal Court, under the provisions of the " Black Code."

It is needless to say that, on the day of trial, an immense concourse of people had swarmed in and around the avenues of the court house to listen to the dramatic details. To such a height had public excitement reached that we may well wonder now how the wretched culprit could have escaped, then and there, the fury of an angry and avenging mob. But to the honor of the city authorities be it said, and the exertions of Montégut, no serious outbreak occurred.

Everything being ready for trial, Judge Canonge appointed N. Z. Latour, Esq., to defend the prisoner. The members of the special tribunal, six in number, were called to the book and severally sworn by the judge, upon the oath prescribed by the Code, the judge being in turn also sworn in by one of the jurors as the presiding officer. The prisoner was then arraigned, entered a plea of " not guilty," and stated that she was ready for trial. The district attorney then read the indictment, and explained to the jury the law of 1814, under which the prosecution was instituted, and which inflicted the penalty of death upon any slave to strike his master, mistress or any of their children, so as to cause a contusion or shedding of blood ; also the amendment to the above act, passed in 1843, giving the jury the privilege to commute the punishment to imprisonment at hard labor for life.

The testimony elicited on the part of the prosecution went to show that the slave Pauline had been purchased by Peter Rabbeneck about two years previous from Mr. Francois Roubieu, who owned a plantation a short distance below Natchitoches, on which Rabbeneck had been for some years acting as overseer. Rabbeneck removed to the city and rented one-half of a double dwelling house, No. 52 Bayou Road, from Mr. Isenhart, who occupied the other half. About six weeks previous to the occurrence, Rabbeneck, who had business to transact in St. Louis, went up the river, leaving his wife, whom he had represented to Isenhart and his daughter to be crazy, and his children, together with upward of $200 in money, in charge of Pauline, who was proven to be his paramour, and claimed to be about to become a mother.

Immediately after Rabbeneck's departure, Pauline took possession of her mistress' apartments, and removed her and the three children to the back cabinet, which she had herself previously occupied. Mrs. Rabbeneck, who had sufficiently recovered to appear in court, testified that, since her husband's absence, she had been subjected to the most cruel and barbarous treatment from her slave, who had beaten her at times with a cane or leather strap, as well as with her fist, and had obtained such a mastery over her will that she was afraid, in case she disclosed to any one her sufferings, that her life would be taken. She also testified that she had a knowledge of her husband's intimacy with Pauline, which intimacy had caused much ill feeling between them, and had resulted on several occasions in her being struck by her husband. Mrs. R. also testified to the cruel manner in which her children had been beaten by Pauline.

This testimony was corroborated by a slave named Dinah, who, on or about Christmas, had been employed by Pauline to work by the day to wash clothes. She stated that on the second day after she had been employed, upon Pauline's returning from market, and discovering that a biscuit was missing from the breakfast table, she charged the taking of it on Constance, the oldest child, who, upon denying the theft, was dreadfully beaten with a leathern strap by Pauline, who also tied the child's clothes over her head and forced her for some time into a kneeling posture, with her knees resting upon the rough edges of small pieces of brick, which she had broken up for that cruel purpose. A few days after she heard Pauline abusing some one in the cabinet, and upon the latter leaving the house she entered the room, and for the first time discovered that there was a person confined there. She raised a mosquito bar and inquired if she could render Mrs. R. any assistance, but upon receiving no direct answer she paid no further attention to the matter. On another occasion she again heard Pauline in the cabinet cursing her mistress, calling her opprobrious names, and telling her if she did not get up and go to work she would whip her to death, Pauline at the same time dragging her mistress by the hair out of bed upon the floor and beating her in the face with her fist. Upon witness remonstrating with Pauline, she attempted to close the door of the cabinet upon her, and forced the child Constance to hand her a cane, with which she beat Mrs. R. in a most shocking and cruel manner. The witness on the same day informed a gentleman, by whom she was occasionally employed, of the above circumstances, who, on the next day, addressed an anonymous letter to the Mayor, which led to the arrest of Pauline and the release of the unfortunate family from their pitiful situation.

The testimony of the Mayor and of Dr. Beugnot, in relation to the condition of the sufferers, at the time of the discovery of the crime, confirmed the above statements in every particular.

Catherine Isenhart, who occupied with her father a part of the same dwelling with Mrs. Rabbeneck, testified that the only time she had seen Mrs. Rabbeneck was a day or two after she had first occupied the house. Mr. Rabbeneck told her, before leaving for St. Louis, that his wife was crazy, had permitted one of their children some years since to starve to death, and that he had been compelled to purchase Pauline to attend to his children on that account. He also told her that his wife would hardly ever speak to any person, not even to him. The witness also testified as to the beating of the child Constance on one occasion. She had frequently heard Pauline cursing her mistress, but as witness was frequently absent from the house, if she had inflicted blows upon her it must have been during her absence.

The case was submitted to the jury without argument, who, after being instructed by the court in regard to the law, returned the following verdict :

"We, the undersigned, freeholders, forming the special tribunal which was convoked and sworn to try the slave Pauline, belonging to Peter Rabbeneck, accused of striking her mistress so as to cause the shedding of blood, do unanimously find her guilty and agree to sentence, and do hereby sentence the said Pauline, belonging to Peter Rabbeneck, to death, and do hereby unanimously fix and appoint the 21st day of February, 1845, between the hours of 10 A. M. and 2 P. M., as the time when the said sentence of death shall be carried into effect, the place of execution to be opposite the Parish Prison. And inasmuch as we are given to understand that the said Pauline is now 'enceinte,' and this sentence can not be carried into execution while she is in that situation, we, in such a case, do further unanimously order that said sentence of death shall be executed at the same hour and place on the 28th day of March, 1846.''

During the whole course of the proceedings Pauline's attitude was entirely passive. She appeared to be about twenty-eight years of age, of middle size, and with a sulky, stubborn and revengeful look. It was bruited about that she was a Virginian by birth, and had at one time belonged to President Monroe. The throng in the evening was as great as that in the morning, and the police had to resort to adroit devices to take the prisoner back to jail, without passing through the crowds in waiting to see the wretch. A cab being in readiness, she was put into it and safely driven to her prison quarters.

A committee of physicians was appointed by Judge Cauenge to examine the condition of Pauline, and, upon their report, her execution was fixed for the 28th of March, of the ensuing year. During nearly the whole period of her incarceration she appeared indifferent to or unconscious of the fate that awaited her, and her statement as to her delicate condition was proven by time to have been fictitious, and made only with the view of extending her lease of life.

In the meantime some kind souls residing in the parish of Iberville, commiserating the condition and abandonment in which she had been left by the brutality and unfeeling conduct of her equally guilty husband, had provided for Mrs. Rabbeneck a home in the town of Plaquemine, where she was leading a life of usefulness and retirement. But the wretch who had blighted her life and sacrificed her love for the meretricious embraces of a slave-mistress, was not to be deprived of his prey, and, discovering her new place of abode, went in pursuit of her. But the people of that town, loath to have such a reptile in their midst, soon checked his infamous career, as I find in the following paragraph from the *Plaquemine Gazette:*

"The miscreant who ill-treated his wife so outrageously in New Orleans, last fall, and then left her and children to the tender mercies of the slave, Pauline (now under sentence of death for her barbarities toward her mistress and children), was found prowling about the premises of one of our citizens Thursday night, and was very properly arrested and put in jail. His object in hanging round the house in question was to see his wife, but whether with good or evil intent it is difficult to tell. He will hardly find a lawyer in this place who for the sake of a fee will undertake to shield him from justice."

Thus wandered the wretch through the paths of life, with the curse and brand of Cain upon his brow! Discharged from custody, he became an outcast, friendless and despised.

On Saturday, March 28, 1846, Pauline was hung pursuant to her sentence. Orleans street, in front of the prison, was blocked up by an immense crowd as early as 8 o'clock in the morning. At 11 o'clock she was robed for the execution, confessed and took the sacrament. At 12:15 she was taken from the cell and conducted to the scaffold, erected on a platform connecting the Parish Prison with the Police Jail. I have witnessed executions of different kinds, but I never saw such a perfect example of firmness as that which she displayed. Some would have called it indifference, but such was not the case. She died not only penitent and resigned, but exhibited great moral courage. When seated on the chair, the Abbé Louis said a prayer in which she joined with apparent eagerness and devotion. When asked whether she desired anything, she replied in the negative—nothing except a crucifix and a glass of water. The question was then put whether she was ready, and she calmly answered "Yes." The drop fell, and she suffered three or four minutes ere she expired. When her form was drawn back to the scaffold, it was found that her neck had not been dislocated, and she must have died from strangulation. There were no less than 4000 to 5000 persons to witness the execution, among whom serious and sorrowful faces strangely contrasted with the boisterous and merry. Bedizened courtesans flaunted their charms in open carriages; women of all descriptions were there on foot, young and old, of all colors. Loud was the laugh and merry the jokes which provoked mirth among the lookers-on, and as I contemplated the swinging and circling form of the expiatory victim and the stolid indifference of that heterogeneous crowd, I thought that a public execution was a beastly and barbarous exhibition—a brutal privilege of the law to satisfy the morbid appetite of those who delight in scenes of cruelty. The zealous offices and Christian-like attentions of the Abbé Louis and of Miss Madelaine Labertonnière to the condemned were assiduous, and received great commendation.

After hanging about twenty minutes, the culprit was pronounced dead, and the body lifted to the platform, whence it was taken back to the prison for interment.

The sheriff and officers under his direction performed their duties well, and the press gave them much credit for the dignified and orderly manner in which the stern but just mandate of the law had been obeyed.

Such was the ending of one of those phases of the institution of slavery which furnished such a prolific theme for heated discussions.

CHAPTER X.

LOUISIANA PLANTERS.

In this age of so-called advancement and progress, when the primary principles of political economy are being antagonized by speculations and theories of doubtful soundness, and under the specious and high-sounding phrases of "tariff reform," one of the staple productions of Louisiana, and the main source of her prosperity and wealth, is being threatened with utter ruin, a retrospective view of the sugar industry of our State, and of our plantations in ante-bellum times, may not prove to-day inappropriate or amiss.

A trip along the Mississippi coast never failed to prove a visit of delight and pleasure. The beautiful light-green foliage, the regular and uniform color and growth of the cane, extending in an unbroken sea of verdure as far as the eye could reach, rendered a cane field the most delightful sight which could greet the vision of one who loved scenes of rural and agricultural beauty. At certain seasons, so sturdy, so thick, tangled and towering seemed the stalks, that one could hardly refrain from pitying the poor blacks who had to cut them down. And yet this task was to them a labor of love, and they appeared to enjoy the fun. Although the necessities of the crop demanded almost incessant exertion, and allowed no time for rest or recreation, the slaves preferred it to any other employment, and always looked forward to the grinding season as a pleasant and exciting holiday.

Along the whole distance from New Orleans to Baton Rouge was a succession of most elegant villas, mostly in the French and Italian style of architecture, many of them on a scale of great magnificence. The residences were usually large, roomy and commodious, and a large space was always devoted to the duties of hospitality. A room or two for invited guests, or the strange wayfarer, was the not uncommon appendage of a planter's house. Their repasts were bounteous and *recherché*. Profusion seemed to be the rule. Their domestic circle was emphatically the lares at which these typical Creoles sat and worshiped. Surrounded usually by a large family, the planter felt an innate pride in the training of his children, in the purity of his stock, and in the culture of his flowers. His home was surely an ideal home.

A peculiarity of their plantation residences, and, by the way, one which proved of superior advantage over the homes of our Northern farmers, was the broad, airy and lofty galleries, that rested on massive stuccoed columns and encircled the four sides of the habitation, instead of the pretentious porches so frequently seen at the North. The rooms were, therefore, thoroughly ventilated and cool, freely admitting the summer breezes wafted from the lake and the Mississippi river, and afforded ample room to the little ones during the rainy season to romp and play. The basement, converted in summer into a spacious dining room, was oftentimes the coolest portion of the house, while hammocks, suspended here and there, attested the habits of the family and their fondness for the daily siesta.

At some distance in the rear, midway between the planter's residence and the edge of the swamp, was to be seen a huge, massive pile, over which towered an immense chimney. This was the sugar mill, the pride of the Louisiana planter. The cost of these structures, with their complete outfit of machinery, was in several instances enormous. They were built almost exclusively of brick, and as fire-proof as possible. The expenses for running these establishments were then much greater than they are at the present day. With our now improved system of granulating the juice of the cane, the yield of the saccharine matter is not only much greater, but the desiccated bagasse furnishes an excellent substitute for coal. Not so, in ante-bellum times. The planter had no other supply for fuel than in the swamp back of his plantation. This apparently worthless piece of land was his providence. It furnished him with timber of every description—good, bad and indifferent. But the trouble to hew, haul and store away the hundreds and sometimes thousands of cords necessary for the grinding season was very great and harassing, and the outlay became a matter of some consequence. This indispensable work was usually done after the cane had attained some degree of maturity.

Next to his sugar mill, the planter used to look with complacency upon the quarters of his field hands. These were unique, picturesque, and constituted in themselves thriving villages. They were regularly laid out in the form of a paralellogram, intersected by numerous streets, built generally of wood, freshly whitewashed, with a small plat of ground attached for cultivation by each occupant. The proceeds of this patch, as well as those resulting from the sale of chickens and eggs, were the property of the slaves, the policy of the master being to encourage in them habits of thrift and love for work.

The grounds surrounding the mansion house were always laid out with profuse and magnificent shrubbery. This was the spot which usually betrayed a woman's tender care. A spacious avenue, leading from the residence to the gate facing the public road, was the first feature to attract attention. Lined with stately magnolias, their umbrageous limbs diffused a cool temperature, without obstructing the course of any current of air. The walks were hedged with jessamines and little groves of myrtles and cedars, of arbor vitæ and arbor cali, with lines of rose and pomegranate bushes marking off the squares, while now and then a huge-stalked banana tree or a bristling cactus or Agave Americana would start up and betray our vicinity to the tropical zone. Towering above all this diversified shrubbery were various wide-spreading and well shaped pecan trees, or, perhaps, the jagged, twisted and gnarled limbs of that Spartan of the forest, the live-oak. Completely encircling the whole house, yard and garden was a rich dark hedge of orange trees, which, in the fall of the year, were nearly weighed down with the burden of their abundant fruit.

This is only but a brief outline of the river planter's habitation and environments during the period which preceded the war. But as to himself what pen can graphically describe his genial humor, his proverbial hospitality, his innate sense of justice and his affectionate treatment of his slaves? Who can enter the inner circle of his private life, and see without admiration his devotion to wife, his solicitude for his children, his temperate admonitions to his employés, his cheerful intercourse with his neighbors, his delight in taking the weary traveler by the hand and making him a welcome guest at his board? Alas! that proud race of nature's noblemen is, I fear, extinct forever.

The river planter was a worker. Though raised and nurtured in the lap of fortune, he had been made to acquire in early youth habits of activity and industry, which he retained through life. At early dawn, as soon as the plantation bell was summoning the laborers to their daily toil, he would be seen, mounted on his wiry horse, riding across the fields to see that his overseer was carrying out his orders. He was constantly busy ; here attending to a fallen fence, there to the deepening of a trench, or again to the repair of a dangerous bridge. Believing in the old adage that "the eye of the master fattens the horse," his time was much engrossed in superintending every detail. Thus it was that at some seasons he realized large profits. But there were periods, also, when he was made to undergo serious reverses. Those were the times when the crops failed, when premature frosts rendered abortive the labor of months of toil, or when financial depression hung over the country. During the continued crash of banks and other moneyed institutions which marked New Orleans' history in the '30s, no one suffered more severely and resisted the overwhelming tide with more courage and persistence than the Louisiana planter. Fortunes were swept away at one fell swoop, and heavy, oppressive mortgages were the result. As a general rule, the planter was a man of refinement and culture, educated in the best schools of Paris or America. The French Opera, during the gay season, was his special enjoyment. He delighted in convivial reunions, the pleasures of refined society, and, above all, in the attractions of the home circle. Taken all in all, he was emphatically one of the mainstays of the country's wealth and progress.

CHAPTER XI.

A STRANGE STORY OF THE SEA.

On the morning of the 8th of June, 1841, the citizens of New Orleans were startled by the appearance at one of the city wharves of the ship Charles, of Bath, Me., Captain Gorham, which had left the city for Bordeaux on the evening of the 1st previous with a cargo of 65,000 staves, 75,000 feet of lumber, and a lot of heading and wheel spokes. She was brought back to the city by the towboat Tiger. Her unexpected return was due to the following inexplicable circumstances :

The Charles had cleared on a Tuesday and gone down to the Balize the same evening, crossing the bar and getting well into the Gulf on the morning following. During the whole of Wednesday and Thursday the Charles, as well as the Louis Quatorze, which had gone out at the same time, was distinctly visible from the Balize, the weather being rather calm ; though it was observed that the Charles steered to the westward, while the Louis Quatorze headed to the east of the Southwest Pass. On Friday morning, at an early hour, the captain of the Tiger noticed a vessel apparently directing her course for the Southwest Pass, and seeming at that distance. as if her studding sails were set. Presuming that the vessel was in want of a pilot, he directed his boat toward her. On nearing her he discovered it was the ship Charles. Nearly all her sails had been set, and the jib, which was flying loosely, appeared to have been cut, probably to make an awning for one of the boats. Not a solitary being was on board.

On descending into the cabin several bottles, which had contained porter and had had their necks knocked off, were found on the table. Some of their contents had been spilled, and the froth looked quite fresh. Every particle of luggage had disappeared. Not a trunk, nor a mattress, nor any article of clothing, save an old pair of boots, was to be seen. The apparel and bedding of the captain, crew and passengers had evidently been carried off also. On examining the vessel's decks, spots of blood having the appearance of having being recently shed, together with eight or ten hend-spikes, were seen on the starboard side. On the larboard was a pool of blood running toward the scuppers, and on the same side on the outer part of the vessel were eight stains of blood also, which had apparently flowed from some wounded person being carried or forced over the ship's side.

It must be borne in mind that this appalling discovery was made at an early hour in the morning. After fully establishing the facts just recited, the Tiger very properly put to sea and cruised for some five or six hours. In the course of this search, at a distance of about ten miles from the Charles, a boat, identified as one belonging to that vessel, and in it a dog said to have been the property of one of the passengers, were picked up. The animal appeared by no means exhausted, and had evidently not been long adrift, as when offered water he did not lap very eagerly.

After cruising some time longer and finding nothing

whatever to clear up the mystery, Captain Crowell returned to the vessel, fastened her in tow and brought her to the city.

It is needless to state that this singular discovery gave rise to speculations of every kind. Horrid rumors of murder and piracy, mutiny and assassination, flew from mouth to mouth with incredible rapidity. The prevalent supposition—although about as vague as every other—was that the crew had rebelled, murdered the captain and passengers, seized the baggage and valuables on board and escaped in one of the yawls, which was found to be missing.

The city authorities on the receipt of this news assembled and counseled together. A meeting of the Council of the Second Municipality (now First District) was held, at which decisive measures were adopted for the elucidation of this dark and horrible enigma. The steamship Neptune was immediately chartered to cruise in the Gulf, and a crew of sixty able-bodied seamen were engaged, fully armed and equipped, the whole under the command of Captain Butler, harbor master of that section of the port. A large number of citizens offered their services to accompany this expedition, but as the Neptune had already her full complement of men, the proffer was declined. At her departure from our river front, the wharves were lined with eager spectators.

A further search of the Charles brought to light additional mystifying facts. In the steerage hatch of the now notorious craft, in a heap of rubbish and refuse stuff, were found several articles of female wearing apparel and a very good black coat. There was also the upper portion of a lady's dress; the skirt was missing. The inside portion of the right breast was stained with blood and revealed a small rent, as if it had been pierced by a poignard. Said a local paper: "Every additional circumstance appears to corroborate the belief that the helpless and unoffending victims on board this ill-fated vessel have met with a bloody and watery grave."

Immediately following the Neptune, the Merchant with sixty men, and a schooner carrying twenty-five others, set off upon the same errand. The first was a steamboat plying on Lake Pontchartrain, on board of which a number of volunteers had embarked under the command of General Persifor F. Smith, who took the lake route. After an absence of several days, she came back to port with a startling account of her operations. It was substantially as follows:

Shortly after the arrival of the Merchant in the Gulf, she met the United States brig Consort, with which she cruised some time in company, both of them scouring the coast from the mainland northward to the Balize. On Tuesday, the 8th of April, a heavy firing was heard by the Merchant and the Consort at the Balize. It was likewise heard by those on board the Neptune, but the noise sounded to them like that of distant thunder. On the Friday following, the Merchant left the Consort on her way to the westward of the Passes, and returned to the Balize for water. The expedition there heard of a marauding party encamped on Lime Kiln Bayou, in the vicinity of the Chandeleurs. The party immediately directed their course thither, and arrived at the bayou at night.

They made their way along the stream in boats, but as the water became narrower and shallower at every step, the boats were obliged to follow each other in single file, the first being commanded by General Smith in person, the second by Captain Hozey, and the third by Captain Thacker. After traveling some time in this fashion, the expedition came upon the encampment and, the night being dark, General Smith jumped ashore, followed by the men of his company. In front of a tent stood a sentinel with a musket. He was ordered to surrender. He did so, but was thrown to the ground in order that he might be pinioned. In the meantime General Smith had gone behind a tent to reconnoitre. At this moment an individual, said to have been the brother of the sentinel, hearing the noise, rushed out of the tent, armed with a bowie knife, and falling on the two men outside wounded them both severely. One of the party rushed back into the water, exclaiming: " I am stabbed," whereupon Captain Hozey's company stepped on shore, and one of them, putting his musket to the assailant's side, discharged its contents into his body. General Smith, hearing the tumult, sprang from the inside of the tent, which he was engaged in inspecting, sword in hand, and stumbling over the prostrate body of the dying man was stabbed by him on the forehead and on both sides of the body. Fortunately, none of the wounds proved dangerous. The survivors were immediately secured. They consisted in all of four men and a boy. They were conveyed to the Balize and left in charge of the authorities there.

This is the sum of the statement which the officers of this volunteer expeditionary force condescended to furnish the press on their arrival at New Orleans, and as people were conjecturing as to the cause of the attack and the character of the people attacked, a new surprise awaited them in the form of a judicial prosecution, instituted by the relatives of the camping party. When their names became known and their narrative given to the public, it was discovered that a terrible mistake had

CHURCH OF ST. LOUIS, 1794
As per plan in City Library.

LATROBE'S WATER WORKS, 1813
At the foot of the vegetable market.

H.C.C. JR. DEL.

ST. PHILIP STREET THEATRE, 1810
Copied from design in City Library.

STATE OR GOVERNMENT HOUSE, 1761
From design in City Library.

been committed and a deep and grievous wrong perpetrated. A warrant, signed by the mayor, was issued for
the arrest of Smith and Hozey.

Now arose another complication.

The facts, as related by the prosecuting parties, may be
thus summarized : The latter consisted of Messrs. Paul
Luscy, Elmire Luscy, a boy and two friends, who, acting
under medical advice, had repaired to the sea shore for
a change of air. They had stopped at first on "Bird
Island," but a fisherman having offered to convey them
to another island, where trees and game were more
abundant, they had accepted the proposition. They
had been living four days upon this spot, and had
erected thereon a camp tent, under which they habitually slept, when, toward 9 o'clock in the night-time, the
two Luscys were surprised at hearing the sound of oars.
Aware of what was being said about pirates, Elmire
Luscy took up his gun, and perceiving two boats coming toward their encampment, and suspecting that they
were revenue officers, he went directly to them, and
offered to give up his gun. The sequel is better related
by himself in the following communication, which appeared in the French columns of the *Bee:*

"I owe it to my family, my fellow-citizens and myself
to publish the result of the cruise of the steamer Merchant, Captain Griffin, which culminated in the assassination of my brother, Paul Luscy, who was the only
support of a numerous family.

"On the 3d instant, toward noon, a party consisting
of Paul Luscy, Francois Lavergne, myself and my boy,
aged nine years, left the city in a boat. Paul had been
advised by Dr. Guesnard to take salt water baths, as he
was in declining health. On our way out, we were met

by Captain Taylor, who hailed us and wanted to know where we were from, and whither we were bound. After having informed him that we belonged to New Orleans, and that we had just left Bird Island en route for Bayou Limekiln, he warned us that a band of pirates were believed to be concealed in the neighborhood; enjoined us to keep a sharp lookout, and in the event of our discovering their whereabouts not to fail to keep him advised. On the 11th instant, we went out to fish oysters with Mr. Henry Price. At about 9 o'clock at night we were all resting in our tent, when, hearing the noise of a boat approaching our camp, I left the tent, gun in hand, and cried out : 'Who is there?' Without answering me a single word several men, running toward me, threw themselves upon me. I turned my gun over to them, saying : 'I am not a robber,' believing at the time that they were Custom House officers. At the same time a number of other individuals jumped ashore, armed with guns and bayonets. I rushed under the tent, and, taking up my child in my arms, I cried out : 'I am not a robber ! Here, see my son !' Heedless of my protestations and of this living evidence of my innocence, I, together with my young son, was thrown to the ground and covered with bayonets. In this melee I received a wound in my right arm.

"While imploring for the life of my child I heard the discharge of a gun, and, notwithstanding the bayonets pointed at me, I exclaimed : 'Luscy, brother !' His answer was : 'I am a dead man.' My brother had then fallen into the bayou. I attempted to rise and go to his assistance, but those who were holding me prevented my so doing. They were about twenty-five or thirty in number. They said : 'Catch the man in the water,' speaking of my brother, who had just received a bullet through the abdomen, perforating the spinal column. When taken out of the water, notwithstanding his wounded condition, he was ordered to be pinioned : 'Tie him! Tie him!' I begged them to desist, as he was evidently dying. Then he fell into my arms and said : 'I am lost.' An individual, seemingly a physician, applied a small bandage to his wounds, saying : 'It is useless ; he is dying.' When all was over, these brave and chivalrous men began to busy themselves, some in eating the oysters that we had caught on that day, others in breaking up our small tent and in searching for booty. They only found a pocket-book containing two dollars and six bits, a silver watch and a powderhorn, which they took away. At about 11 o'clock P. M., we were all stowed away in a yawl and taken to the steamer Merchant, in the Mississippi river.

"When this steamer was about to leave, my brother besought them to carry him home and allow him to die in the midst of his family, but this last consolation was brutally denied him, and he was left on shore at the Balize, where he died at 5 o'clock in the evening, on Saturday, the 12th instant.

"This attacking expedition against an unoffending tent and its sleeping occupants was commanded by that brave General, Persifor F. Smith, and Major C. F. Hozey.

"As a proof of the falsity of the statements daily published in the papers of the Second Municipality, I refer to the flattering terms, officially published in the *Picayune* of Tuesday, 15th inst., in which the recorder and the aldermen of that municipality express themselves anent the chivalrous conduct of Messieurs Smith and Hozey, whose sole meritorious act, prompted either through cowardice or intoxication, seems to have been the murder of the only mainstay of a numerous family.

(Signed)   "ELMIRE FRANCOIS LUSCY."

The Luscy family was one of the most honorable and respectable of the lower portion of Faubourg Marigny, and the publication of the above "card" carried much weight with it. While deploring the events that had led to such a tragical ending, and giving the affair the benefit of every mitigating circumstance, the impartial public could not but appreciate the fact that a homicide had been committed in a hasty, unseemly and injudicious manner, and that the affair ought to undergo a thorough judicial investigation. As usual on occasions of public importance, where sectional differences were unnecessarily introduced, the press up and down town took opposite sides, and the controversy, without assuming an acrimonious character, was kept up with spirit. To the "statement" of Luscy, Gen. Persifor F. Smith thought proper to issue a "rejoinder," which had a good effect. Here it is:

" *To the Editor of the Courier:*

" Will you be pleased to insert the following statement of facts, which I would not trouble you with had not Mr. E. F. Luscy, in this morning's *Bee*, published so gross a perversion of them.

"On the night of the 11th instant, with a party of men in boats, searching among the bays leading to Lime Kiln Bayou, I landed at a shell bank, on which was a small tent. I went ashore at the same time with two of the men, and a third followed, the other boats not having yet come up. The two men who landed with me, approaching the tent on the left side, were accosted by one of its occupants, who said: 'Gentlemen, I am no robber, take my gun.' I was then passing by the other (the right) side of the tent. As I came to the front of it, on that side, the two men were receiving the gun he offered, when his brother rushed out of the tent among them, stabbed the two men and turned toward the third. This one drew back and fired at him as the brother was attempting to stab him. The two who were stabbed fell back toward the water, crying out they were stabbed. Upon receiving the shot Paul Luscy turned toward me, who had at this moment fallen over the tent cord, struck me with his knife and then ran into the bayou. As the men who were stabbed fell back, the second boat landed, and the men, hearing that their comrades were wounded, jumped ashore and rushed to the tent, but Major Hozey, who was with them, interfered and prevented any violence, and told Luscy to sit down on the ground, and that he would not permit him to be hurt. His brother was then brought out of the bayou, and was found to be seriously wounded. Every possible attention was paid to him, and he desired to be brought to town. He wished to abandon all his effects, but they were carefully collected and taken on board of the Merchant, and left with him at the Balize. We were not returning to the city by the river, and we could not bring him up. He himself lamented his mistake, and acknowledged that his own violence was the cause of his disaster, but excused himself by saying he had just awakened from sleep and did not know what had happened.

"There were no men but part of the crew of the first boat on the bank until after the whole scuffle was over, and these men had no bayonets. All that Luscy relates of the crowd around him could only have happened after the men were stabbed by his brother, and the others, exasperated at the act, had landed from the boats.

"There was nothing like violence attempted or offered until Paul Luscy rushed out of the tent and stabbed the two boatmen, who were in the very act of receiving the gun which Luscy had offered up of his own accord, and but for that act of violence they would not have been disturbed.

"PERSIFOR F. SMITH.

"June 17, 1841."

After an examination before the Mayor, General Smith and Major Hozey were held to bail in the sum of $5000 each for their appearance before the Criminal Court on a charge of manslaughter. It is needless to say that the grand jury subsequently ignored the bill, and that they were honorably discharged.

Thus ended a dramatic episode, connected with what was supposed to have been the tragic fate of the crew and passengers of the ill-fated ship Charles. What had become of them, and to what destiny they had been doomed still remained a mystery—a mystery which it will be the province of the following pages to clear up.

The judicial investigation that led to the enlargement of the prisoners charged with the killing of poor Luscy, had in no wise tended to allay public excitement or curiosity. The mystery seemed as far from a solution as on the day when the facts were first reported to the authorities. None of the various expeditionary forces, set on foot, had been successful in discovering any, the least, clew to the singular affair, and comments and con- jectures flew about as wildly as ever. Even the French

Consul had advised the war ships of his nation stationed at Vera Cruz and Havana to be on the alert for the mutinied crew or supposed pirates. The "Dunois," being the lightest vessel of the squadron, was accordingly detached Of the various rumors set afloat, the following "canard" will serve as a no uncommon specimen. We copy from a contemporary :

"A gentleman of this city informs us that while endeavoring to hire a boat on the levee Thursday last, the master of the boat, for the hire of which he was in treaty, mentioned that he knew an individual who could furnish a better clew to the late piratical deeds than had been discovered by all the expeditions. On being asked who that person was, he pointed out a Frenchman on board another smack. He added that the Frenchman had been eight days coming up the river, and that a day or two previous to his starting on his return, he had discovered three dead bodies, two of which were floating in a creek on a small island in the vicinity of the Southwest Pass, and a third was half buried in the marsh. On examining these bodies, it was seen that they bore the appearance of having been stabbed with bowie knives, and had evidently not been dead more than a few hours. He further stated that a 'black flag' had been discovered on the island. The fisherman, alarmed, left the spot and made the best of his way homeward.

"This statement our informant was obliged to receive at second hand, as he was unable to speak French to the individual who furnished the information. At our request, the gentleman called yesterday on Recorder Baldwin, and laid before him the above narrative. The Frenchman, who is master of the schooner boat Hornet, was immediately brought before the recorder and substantiated the statements just made. The matter will doubtless undergo further examination.''

Another rumor, absurd and cruel in its character, obtained credence with a certain class, and associated the name of Captain Reybaud with the alleged act of piracy. The charge was repeated in one or two of our local papers, and had no other foundation than the well known character of the Mexican corsair for prowess and acts of daring. It will be remembered that many years previous, the commodore and crew had been prosecuted for piracy in American waters, and this former incident had no doubt led to the belief that the one-armed ''tar'' had resumed his predatory habits. Reybaud had a host of friends in the city, unwilling to allow this stigma to rest upon his honor, and accordingly such men as Armand Pitot, Charles Boudousquié, C. E. Forstall, F. Grima, E. Montégut, G. Lafon, Amédée Ducatel and John L. Lewis protested in the *Courier* against the accusation as groundless and uncharitable, and the more reprehensible as being preferred against an absent man, who at that very time was in Mexico, in the capital of the new Republic of Yucatan, where he was discharging the functions of Secretary of the Navy.

Thus, for days and days, did perplexity succeed perplexity, and all hope of ever probing the mysterious depths of the transaction was fast passing away, when at last, and unexpectedly, on the 25th of June, 1841, tidings reached New Orleans through Charleston papers that '' Captain Gorham, late master of the ship Charles, and his crew had arrived in the port of Charleston as passengers in the schooner Ann, from Attakapas.''

They gave the following account of their adventures : The ship Charles sailed from New Orleans on the 1st of

June, with a cargo of timber and staves, and twenty passengers for Bordeaux.   On the night of the 3d, when about fifty miles from the bar, the ship sprang a leak, and, in spite of incessant labor at the pumps, by 2 o'clock in the morning there was two and one-half feet of water in the hold.   The crew and passengers became terribly alarmed.   A consultation was held with them, and it was determined to return to New Orleans.   The wind at the time was very light, at about north, the Balize bearing north by west.   A new fear arose.   The crew were wearied out with labor at the pumps, and, as the water was gaining on them, they thought the ship would fill and go down before they could reach a port.

The French ship Louis Quatorze was at the time but a short distance off, and the passengers insisted on being put on board of her.   She was bound for Havre.   A boat was immediately dispatched to her from the Charles to ascertain if the captain would receive them.   He consented, and also tendered the use of his boats to aid in embarking them.   This was all happily effected, but gave no sort of relief to the ship Charles, as the water in the hold looked more gloomy and threatening.   After taking a long look at it, the captain and crew came to the unanimous determination to abandon the ship, which they accordingly did on the morning of the 4th, and proceeded on board the Louis Quatorze.   Finding the boats of the Charles insufficient in number to carry them all to the nearest port, Captain Gorham desired the captain of the French ship to haul up, in hopes of meeting some vessel bound for New Orleans or some other port of the Gulf.   This he did for two hours, when, perceiving no sail in sight, he concluded to bear away for Havana.   On the morning of the 10th they fell in with the schooner Ann, from Attakapas for Portsmouth, N. H., on board of which Captain Gorham and crew embarked. But their adventures were not yet ended. The Ann was struck by lightning off Cape Hatteras, and so seriously injured as to render it expedient to turn back to Charleston, where she arrived in a very leaky condition on the 18th.

Some of the passengers signed the following certificate:

"The undersigned passengers, on board the ship Charles, Captain Gorham, declare that on the 3d of June, about 8 o'clock P. M., a leak was discovered, which increased so much in the night that they (the passengers) demanded of the captain to send them on board the ship Louis Quatorze, which was at a little distance. The danger was so imminent that Captain Gorham acceded at once to our demand, and was himself under the necessity of abandoning the ship.

"This is to certify that Captain Gorham did not abandon the ship until he found it impossible to save her, and that we have given him this paper to serve him in case of necessity.

"Given on board the ship Louis Quatorze, in the Gulf of Mexico, the 10th of June, 1841,"

(Signatures.)

The circumstances connected with the abandonment of a ship, unable from the peculiar character of her freight to sink under the heaviest stress of weather, created in Charleston strong suspicions of an attempt at barratry. Captain Gorham, therefore, demanded an investigation, which was held before Judge Gilchrist, and of which the following was the result:

The captain, his two mates and two of the crew were examined, as also a passenger on board the schooner

and some of her crew, and the schooner herself was
searched by the United States marshal.   The Mayor was
present at the examination, and the city attorney, G. B.
Eckhard, assisted the United States district attorney.
Every precaution, it was thought, was taken to obtain
the truth.   Every witness, except the one undergoing
examination for the time, was excluded from the courtroom.   The inquiry occupied about four hours, and resulted in the declaration of the judge that he was satisfied there was no ground for any imputation upon the
captain and crew.   In the course of the proceedings it
appeared that several of the passengers of the Louis
Quatorze had written letters to their friends in the
United States, and entrusted them to Captain Gorham
to be mailed at any port he should first reach.   Three
of these letters were produced and offered to be opened,
if his honor thought the situation and circumstances of
Captain Gorham required their seals to be broken.   This,
however, the judge declined doing.   A bill of exchange,
drawn by Captain Gorham on board the Louis XIV, upon the owners of the Charles, endorsed by the captain of
that ship, was also produced to show how the matter had
been arranged for the conveyance of the passengers.
The bill of exchange stated the object for which it was
drawn, and Captain Gorham declared that the captain of
the Louis Quatorze had entrusted it to him to forward to
her owners, the other two bills of the set having been
left on board.   The circumstances of the bill of exchange and letters were brought out in a manner that
showed that Captain Gorham was not conscious of their
importance, he having closed his account of all the facts
deemed important by him, without adverting to them.
Among other things mentioned by the captain to the
authorities of Charleston was an explanation to the effect

that the blood found in the cabin was the result of a cut in his hand whilst breaking off the neck of a bottle of porter, and the blood on the deck, near the scuttles, was that of the mate, who had wounded himself while making a thole pin for the launch.

Though the mystery attending the fate of the crew and passengers of the ship Charles was satisfactorily cleared up, so far as the charge of mutiny or piracy was involved, nothing could disabuse the public mind of the suspicion that there lurked at the bottom of the affair some evil design, which time would ultimately unearth. Of the private character or antecedents of the " Yankee skipper" nothing was positively known, but no man in his senses could believe that a ship officer, without some sinister purpose in view, would, within sight of the Balize, and with constant opportunities of communicating his condition to some of the towboats frequently cruising about, have adopted the preposterous resolution of abandoning a vessel which, from the nature of her cargo, could not sink, and of leaving her to be discovered under circumstances which naturally inspired the darkest forebodings.   Said a New Orleans contemporary :

"The more we reflect on the conduct of Captain Gorham in abandoning his ship, the more we are astonished and indignant.   If we felt disposed to overlook his desertion of the vessel under circumstances which, as a seafaring man, he should have known, exempted him from danger, we would still be compelled to condemn him for not leaving on board a single line by which the facts of the case might `have been ascertained.   A few words written in his logbook, a letter left on the table in the cabin, would have spared the friends and relatives of the passengers the most cruel anguish, the city au-

thorities a very heavy expense and an innocent individual the loss of life by a deplorable mistake.   For all
this is Captain Gorham responsible.   A fearful weight
of accountability attaches to his infamous conduct.   If
we have a counsel to offer him, it is to avoid Louisiana
in all his future peregrinations.   We know not to what
extremities the execration of our citizens would impel
them, if the guilty author of so mucn mischief were in
their power.''

In the course of time, as the name of Gorham acquired
a world-wide notoriety, information began to reach us
from different sources bearing upon his reputation and
previous conduct.   The slang term '' crooked,'' now a
pure Americanism, fully conveys the opinion in which
he was held by those who knew him best.   The papers
of the country continued to teem with occurrences of his
past life, and from them I cull the following extracts.
The New York *Evening Post* thus describes him :

'' If the captain of the Charles be the same Captain
Gorham, from Bangor, Me., who, a few years since, with
his brother-in-law and some others, desperate characters,
moved into Oswego, in this State, where his store was
fired under such circumstances—*i. e.*, to recover a large
amount of insurance—that public opinion compelled him
to leave the place; who, subsequently, was indicted by a
grand jury of Buffalo on a suspicion of murdering his
own child, by administering to it an excessive amount
of laudanum, and who was cleared by the non-appear-
ance at the trial of his wife, who, it was supposed, he
attempted to kill with a dose of arsenic, to get rid of her
evidence—we say, if this be the same individual, he is
certainly not too good to have been engaged in such an
affair as the New Orleans papers describe.''

The *Journal of Commerce* (New York) furnishes the following contribution to the man's history:

"The name of Captain Wm. Gorham, Jr., if the whole and exclusive ownership of it belongs to one man, is something of a treasure. For Captain Wm. Gorham, Jr., master of the brig Susan Elizabeth, in coming home from Buenos Ayres, in 1839, went ashore, near Bath, Me., to the great damage of the underwriters in this city. The captain on that occasion acted, of course, as agent for 'whoever it might concern,' sold the vessel and cargo, put the money in his pocket, and has not to this day proceeded further in his agency."

That this consummate scoundrel had meditated a breach of trust, an act of barratry, to the prejudice of his employers, there can hardly be entertained an earthly doubt. His plan, after leaving the water-logged ship, was to proceed at once to some port within a short distance from this city, whence it would have been an easy matter to ascertain its movements, follow it to port, and realize the proceeds at an admiralty sale. Hence, when the opportunity of reaching Havana offered itself, he gladly availed himself of it, but his subsequent transfer to, and the stroke of lightning that arrested the course of, the Attakapas craft also blasted and shattered his hopes. For, weeks and weeks were consumed by the crippled vessel in reaching a harbor, and during that time the alarm had been sounded and suspicion aroused in every port. When he reached Charleston the authorities were already cognizant of the singular facts attending the case, and, content with securing his liberty, Gorham was compelled to renounce his criminal project. Such is the theory which the affair naturally presents, and which was subsequently adopted by the press generally.

Piracy in those days was not a matter of such unfrequent occurrence as at this period we may be apt to imagine, though this species of crime, owing to the stern and repressive measures taken by the Federal government, had much abated. Hence the interest taken by our leading citizens and public functionaries in levying forces and issuing armed expeditions. General Persifor F. Smith was by no means an alarmist or a poetical dreamer, but a practical, matter-of-fact and courageous citizen. He knew from experience that the Gulf of Mexico and the Caribbean sea had swarmed in times not very remote with armed vessels of a questionable character, and whether sailing under a black flag or the revolutionary pennant of some neighboring republic, their deeds of blood and rapine had been equally atrocious. No one regretted more than he did the untimely ending of the unfortunate Luscy, for his heart was as kind and as soft as a woman's, though stern and unrelenting to an enemy. Louisianians are proud of him and of his fame, nobly achieved under the frowning battlements of Mexico's fortresses!

CHAPTER XII.

LAFAYETTE SQUARE.

I propose in this chapter to recall old reminiscences anent the square opposite to the City Hall, now the pride and glory of that magnificent faubourg which sprang into existence like a helmeted giant in the arena of Progress, through the genius and persevering industry of such hardy pioneers as Sam J. Peters, J. P. Caldwell, Wm. Freret and other kindred spirits.

As far back as my personal recollections on this subject reach, Lafayette Square in 1836 was a rural patch in the motley quilt of brick and mortar, stone, wood and mud that covered the superficies of the Second Municipality. It was a small but pretty landscape picture, set in a frame composed of various and ill-assorted materials. But, limited in extent as it was, it was almost the only place within the burg which greeted the eye of spring's approach in all its verdure and vitality; of summer's advent in the luxuriance of its foliage; of autumn's days of haze and subdued sunshine, and of winter's cheerless nudity. As was tersely remarked by one of the members of the City Council, it was the only panorama which presented the up-town denizens with a picture of the shiftings of the seasons, showing winter's sojourn to be the shortest, for—

"Here smiling spring its earliest visit pays,
And parting summer's lingering bloom delays."

Considering the mania that prevailed for converting every spot of the "new city" to purposes of business or uses of thrift, perhaps the people should have been thankful that even this small area had been left them to remind them of God's blessed world abroad, and to breathe an atmosphere not wholly noxious or vitiated.

It was the resort of citizens of all ages and of all classes. It was the Parnassus of poets, the Mecca of loafers, the Elysian Fields of juveniles, the Sylvan Shade of lovers, and the Academic Grove of peripatetic philosophers.

In the morning, shortly after the sun had emerged from the horizon, this small plat of ground was made to re-echo the cheery laughter of hundreds of the merry babes who, the owners of round, rosy faces in charge of clean, attentive and affectionate nurses, made the square a scene of juvenile contentment, while others, gamboling under the sycamores, in the tall, rank grass, chased gaudy-winged butterflies or played a thousand of those fantastic pranks from which childhood derives such interest and amusement. At that time, too, it was not an uncommon occurrence to see a few dyspeptic gentlemen and ladies of an uncertain age promenading along the few graveled walks of the resort, some perusing a work on dietetics, others reading James' last novel, or perhaps a work on woman's rights.

From twelve to one the square was all life, hilarity, animation. This was the hour when

"Noisy children just let loose from school"

made it their play-ground, and when with all the hearty joyousness of uncaged birds, or the sportiveness of lambkins, they frisked, leaped, romped and capered till their hour's school recess called them back to study. Here, a group playing leap-frog ; there, a party engaged at battledore. Here, a pair of juvenile gladiators wrestling, and there again, during the Mexican war, a crowd playing at soldiers, divided into two opposite factions, of course ; one led by a bluff, chubby boy, who not inaptly personated General Taylor ; the other, by a sallow, dark-eyed youth, travestying Santa Anna. Happy days of boyhood ! Who, in mature age, is he who, in witnessing the gambols of those guileless youths, does not remember that he, too, was once a boy, when not one of the world's dark clouds had cast their shadows before him?

As a general rule, from noon till evening, the square, comparatively speaking, was deserted. Some poor, fatigued laborer, in the meantime, might be seen taking his siesta under the shadow of one of its trees, or a loafing *habitué*, lying on his back in the dense grass, contemplating the blue firmament, wondering if the regions beyond it were inhabited, and if the people overhead got their liquor on tick. Toward evening, and when the sun had abated much of his noontide vigor, the nurses and their interesting young charges would again make their appearance and move about the square, enlivening the scene with their merry shouts and joyous dancing. The scene was picturesque in the extreme, and hundreds of staid old denizens, reclining on the old, worn-out rustic benches, martyrs of whittling propensities, would view the blithesome capers with unalloyed peals of laughter. But when the shades of night began to fall, when the cerulean heavens became studded with nature's diamonds, when the pale moon shone placidly on things below, and when the light transparent clouds floated above, like the congealed breath of angels, then was the

time that Lafayette Square was the point of attraction.
Then it was that

> " The seats beneath the shade,
>   For talking age and whispering lovers made,"

had their happy and busy occupants.   Then it was that
the poet, as he paced the less frequented walks wooed
the muses and composed " ballads to his mistress' eye-
brows."   Then it was that scheming politicians, crossing over from the old, dingy municipal Hall on the opposite street, met to discuss and determine the plans
of the approaching campaign.   Then it was that poor
creatures, the exhausted state of whose finances made
it inconvenient for them to seek a private lodging, endeavored to seek a cozy spot for the night.   Then it was
that non-paying boarders shaped and moulded into apol-
ogetic forms excuses to their landladies for their involuntary adoption of the credit system.   Then it was that
a couple of sagacious " Ousel Owls "—a mysterious organization much in vogue during the latter part of the
40s—might be seen concerting their schemes for the approaching " buffalo hunt " in the Sierra Madre regions.
Then it was that Cupid, like an expert archer, sat concealed among the branches of almost every tree, fixing
arrows into the bosoms of votaries, who sat on the
benches underneath.   Then it was that many an Anglo-
Saxon Othello upbraided his Desdemona with incon-
stancy, and many a Romeo, under the guise of a brawny
Celtic drayman, poured, in impassioned but unvarnished
accents, the story of his love into the ear of a gentle
Juliet by his side, who had but just escaped from a
neighboring kitchen !

After the firing of the cannon at 9 o'clock, which was
the curfew signal for honest people to repair to their
homes, the crowds would begin perceptibly to thin.

After midnight nothing was heard in the deserted park save the lively chirruping of the katydid or the hoarse, nasal breathing of some poor houseless vagrant, asleep on a bench.   Said the *Delta*, nearly a half century ago :

" If the Scotchman blessed the Duke of Argyle for erecting milestones in his country, we may well call for a benison on him who originated Lafayette Square, and on the Council which tends and beautifies it.   Should that time ever come, so often predicted by a distinguished financier (Samuel J. Peters), when our Council will have a surplus of revenue, we trust that due attention will be paid to Lafayette Square ; that founts of crystal waters will shoot forth their liquid streams from its angles, and that marble statues of art's finest sculpture will ornament its centre.''

This prophecy has never been fully realized.   To Mr. Frank Howard is this park indebted for many improvements that we now behold—the planting of exotic and acclimated trees, and the perforation of an artesian well, whose limpid waters have unfortunately ceased to flow. To the energy of Thomas Agnew—one of the most zealous and honest administrators that the city has ever possessed—are we indebted for the beautiful Schillinger walks which now intersect it.   A few more Howards and a few more Agnews—men of such calibre—would in a few years place New Orleans in the fore rank of the beautiful cities of the Union.   Pluck, energy and intelligence are the only levers to reach this desideratum.

The erection of the statue of Franklin in the centre of the square over twenty years ago is due almost exclusively to the energy of Charles A. Weed, erstwhile proprietor of the New Orleans *Times*, since merged with the *Democrat*, and his enterprising associate, the late

W. H. C. King. This work of art has a peculiar
history, and is the production of Hiram Powers' genius.
When, many years ago, this American sculptor was
struggling at Rome in the pursuit of his vocation,
young, inexperienced and comparatively friendless, but
evincing an aptitude that promised eventual success and
fame, several public-spirited citizens of New Orleans,
with the view of encouraging his youthful efforts and
alleviating his pecuniary embarrassments, came together
and determined to subscribe the sum of $10,000, for a
statue of the immortal sage and philosopher. The order
was, in consequence, given and accepted, and the sum
of $5000 forwarded to the sculptor in part payment. As
years rolled on, Powers, oblivious of his early New
Orleans friends, neglected his contract, and under one
pretence or another—among others, that of the uncertainty of ever obtaining full remuneration—flatly refused,
it is said, to comply with his agreement. It was at this
juncture that Mr. Weed forwarded the amount and
secured the completion of the work.

The physiognomy of the environments of Lafayette
Square is entirely different to-day from what it was at
that period. The City Hall, the Howard mansion, the
Moresque Building, Odd Fellows' Hall, the old Criminal
Court building are all structures of comparatively recent
date. The City Hall was located where now stands
Soule's College, the Recorder's Court and Municipal
Council holding their sessions up stairs. The lower
floor was occupied by the Department of Police, the
captain's office directly fronting St. Charles street,
while the rear was used as a station or temporary prison.
This edifice has undergone outwardly but few modifications.

Such is a brief historical outline of this beautiful little

park, so much admired by strangers.   Under the careful training and commendable attention of Administrator Gauche the place is daily improving, and the gay flower shubs, together with the tropical plants that are to be added, will soon offer us a picture most grateful to the eye.

CHAPTER XIII.

OLD LOUISIANA DAYS.

STORY OF BRAS COUPÉ—THE CUNNING OF A SLAVE—
CABARETS—REMINISCENCES OF THE OLD POLICE—AN
INCIDENT ILLUSTRATING THE CUSTOMS OF THE CHOC-
TAWS—THE FOURTH OF JULY IN THE CAMP STREET
THEATRE—YANKEE DOODLE—ANECDOTE OF THE ELDER
BOOTH—FANNY ELLSLER CHARIVARIED—THE FRENCH
"CRAZE"—LAST DAYS OF ROFFIGNAC.

At a period when the institution of slavery, viewed
under its most humanitarian aspect, had become one of
the pillars of our prosperity and progress, fostered by a
spirit of benevolence and patriarchal affection, a salient
feature of the times was the frequency with which our
African bondsmen would hie themselves into the deep-
est recesses of our forests to escape thraldom for a short
space of time, and enjoy a season of comparative rest.
While yet a boy, I distinctly remember the proximity
of the woods to the sparse habitations that fringed the
outskirts of the town. Marais street was then deemed
the border land lying between *terra firma* and "tremb-
ling prairie," an impenetrable morass, beyond which
none but experienced hunters or fugitives ventured to
enter. In the darkest parts of these thickets and along
the margin of some sluggish bayou or *coulée*, a rude hut

was occasionally to be found, hastily thrown up with willow branches, and securely sheltered from wind and rain by latanier or palmetto leaves, deftly worked into the roof. This was the usual habitation of the runaway negro, until he was driven to seek a new shelter by the professional "slave catcher" with his pack of trained bloodhounds.

Even when not pursued, these outlaws were compelled to emerge at night from their solitary haunts in quest of nourishment. Hence it was that New Orleans, despite the efforts of an inadequate police, became the scene of nocturnal thefts, robberies and assassinations. With the spoils and money thus obtained, a "cabaret" was always ready to supply the hunted-down outcast with powder, shot, whisky and such other articles as were required for his most pressing wants. It was only when, in the course of years, the city had extended its habitable limits beyond Claiborne street that these bold refugees sought new quarters along the borders of Lake Pontchartrain, in the rear of the parishes of St. Bernard and Jefferson.

One of these I well remember, from the terror which he inspired into the stoutest hearts. His reputation for audacity and deeds of ferocity was not inferior to that of "Fra Diavolo," the hero of Italian romance, and, if the truth must be told, no one cared to face this bandit in the woods. The account given of him by Cable is pure fiction. His name was Squier. He was owned by General William De Buys, than whom no kinder or more humane master ever lived. The General, in fact, who was greatly attached to him, had petted and completely spoiled the fellow. Fond of field sports, he had made him his huntsman and usual attendant. He indulged him in every one of those *douceurs* which favorite servants were wont to enjoy ; but these acts of kindness, instead of generating gratitude and love, only resulted, such was the negro's savage nature, in developing a spirit of revolt and insubordination. To escape from an existence of ease and indolence into one of strife and constant danger became a chronic passion, and although frequently caught and punished he would relapse as often into his inveterate habit. On one occasion, when pursued by a patrol of white planters, headed by Mr. Fleitas, of St. Bernard, he bravely stood at bay and defied capture, until he was laid low by a heavy charge of buckshot. From the effect of the wound his arm was amputated, and hence the origin of the surname of *Bras Coupé*, by which he was known thereafter.

For a series of years his escapes, adroit devices to baffle pursuers, and manifold crimes were the subject of entertainment not only in the public prints, but even in the home circle. He seemed to be endowed with the gift of ubiquity. No hound could follow his scent, no officer keep on his trail. If seen in one place, he was soon to be met miles away, laughing at his would-be captors. Even around the domestic hearth, his name of "Bras Coupé" became a familiar word, pronounced in hushed and subdued tones to frighten children. Rewards were offered for his capture, dead or alive, but no one had as yet been found daring enough to confront the fearless brigand.

On April 7, 1837, the following notice appeared in one of the city prints : "The negro, Squier, notorious for the crimes and cruelties he has committed in the neighborhood of the Bayou St. John, has at last atoned for them. Yesterday two men belonging to the guard of the First Municipality were hunting rabbits on the land of Mr. L. Allard (now the Lower City Park), on the other side of the bayou. Impelled by the ardor of the chase, one of them pushed into the swamp somewhat further than his comrade. What was his surprise to be stopped, not by the game he was pursuing, but by a stout fellow taking aim at him with a gun ! The gun was fired at a distance of fifteen paces, and fortunately missed its object. Not entirely a novice in these things, the guardsmen quickly returned the compliment, and with success. Squier, although severely wounded, attempted to escape by running, but was soon overtaken, and died under his blows. We understand that a detachment of the guard will this day be dispatched to find the body.''

This announcement was received with satisfaction by some, with incredulity by others. Cunning and desperate as Bras Coupé was known to be, it was generally believed that he had succeeded with his usual luck in effecting his escape, notwithstanding the severe blows which he had been reported to have received. On the following day an armed posse repaired to the spot, accompanied by the police officers, but despite the most diligent search through the devious paths of the *cyprière*, no trace of the criminal could be detected, although the spot was searched where the conflict was said to have taken place. A trail of blood, soon lost in the slimy waters of the marsh, furnished the only evidence of his presumed fate.

This incident was put down as a police *canard*, and for some time the matter remained shrouded in mystery. Scouting parties, formed at intervals with the view of discovering his retreat, had been sent out, but had invariably returned, disappointed and worn out with fatigue. Week followed week without any additional disclosures, until the public mind, engaged in other subjects, had begun to forget the hero and his exploits, when reliable news of his tragic death unexpectedly reached New Orleans.

It would be amusing to describe in detail the excitement which the event produced. Not only on 'change or at Hewlett's, but in the workshops, markets, and even among families was the subject discussed. A stranger to our city and customs, judging from the general commotion, would have believed that some extraordinary event had just occurred. The daring, the insolence and the utter contempt for law which *Bras Coupé* had ever exhibited were freely commented upon. The wound he had once received at the hands of Mr. Fleitas, and the circumstances connected with his former capture, confinement and escape from the hospital were common subjects of gossip. It was remembered how, when lying prostrate after the surgical operation which had bereft him of a limb, and when reduced by an attack of dysentery to the very verge of death, he had eluded the vigilance of the nurses by flinging himself out of an open window. It was also related how, on another occasion, he had captured a negress who, on effecting her escape from his camp, reported an act of ferocity of which she had been made an unwilling witness. The story concerned the fate of an Irish woman whom he had forcibly carried into the woods, detained for several days, tied to a tree and finally shot to death.

It was on a Monday, July 17, 1837, that one Francisco Garcia, while fishing at the mouth of Little river, on Lake Pontchartrain, met the black desperado. The former had got out of his pirogue to reach for a fish car, which he had temporarily left ashore, when, just as he was about to possess himself of the box, he heard the

explosion of a fulminating cap. Happening, fortunately, to be holding an iron handspike, to which he was
in the habit of fastening his boat, he rushed forward
about seven paces, and came upon a man concealed
behind the trunk of a fallen tree, in the act of resetting
a fresh cap, with his right hand and teeth. Losing no
time, the Spanish fisherman struck him three times with
his ponderous bar, and felled him dead to the ground.

Such was the account given by Garcia, although there
were many persons who, conversant with the character
of the slayer, affirmed that *Bras Coupé's* death was the
result of treachery, as Garcia was his usual purveyor
and friend. The conviction was that Garcia, seduced
by the hope of a large reward, had murdered the man
whom he had promised to protect, and whom he had
found asleep.

Be this as it may, the Spaniard, on accomplishing the
deed, dumped his valuable freight into the boat and
proceeded with it to New Orleans. Reaching Milneburg, the body was thence conveyed to the front of the
Mayor's office, where Denis Prieur, the then chief executive of the city, ordered it to be exposed to public
view on the Place d'Armes, opposite. That thousands
and thousands rushed to that historic square to take a
look at the ghastly remains is a matter of notoriety. No
Mardi Gras procession, no special pageant that I know
of, ever attracted such surging crowds as were witnessed
under that broiling, solstitial sun. Men, women, children ; whites and blacks, freedmen and slaves ; professional men and laborers in their working blouses, all
seemed to have gathered there to satisfy their morbid
curiosity. The body, with its crushed and mangled
head, in a state of rapid decomposition, remained in that
condition from 1 o'clock in the evening until the dark-

ness of approaching night commanded its removal to Potter's Field. The still unhealed and gaping wounds, alleged to have been inflicted by the city guard, who had reported him dead, made the spectacle still more hideous.

It was generally believed at the time that the different municipalities had offered liberal rewards for *Bras Coupé's* capture, dead or alive, and Garcia was much congratulated upon his good luck ; but, when the day for settling came, it was ascertained that only the section below Esplanade street had made any provision for the event, whereupon the sum of $250 was immediately paid the claimant, as promised in the proclamation.

This is a strange story, and it will read more strangely, perhaps, in the eye of the present and growing generation ; but the institution of slavery was one pregnant with constantly recurring changes and new phases. Without entering into any discussion on the abstract right and justice of keeping in bondage a class of people, manifestly designed by the Creator to be "drawers of water and hewers of wood," it is obvious that the form of servitude under which they lived, regarded from the standpoint of practical philanthropy, was a vast improvement on their original condition. It is true that here and there a cruel and barbarous taskmaster was occasionally to be found, but these instances, it must be admitted, formed the exception and not the rule, for every Louisianian positively knows that the planters who thus erred, fell under the ban of social reprobation for that very cause. Whoever attentively reads the old Black Code will observe how stringent were the laws for the protection of the slave. And while I am upon this subject, let me be permitted to say as an historical fact that no master was ever more exacting, despotic, nay, cruel to the negro, than the planter or farmer of African extraction—an anomaly, it is true, but still a fact.

But a truce to digression. I shall now proceed to relate another story. The inner character of slavery times can only be understood by illustrations. Here is a case exemplifying the development of cunning and hypocrisy in the negro race, which the "institution" encouraged.

A certain mulatto, conceiving the design of escaping servitude by concealing himself in one of the numerous packets plying between this port and western cities, hit upon an expedient to provisionally rid himself of his master, whose presence was the only obstacle to his plan. To kill him or do him such bodily injury as might disable him for a time was out of the question, but to put him out of the way by the operation of the law was a master stroke worthy of his Senegambian ingenuity. It happened that New Orleans at that time (1832) was infested by a band of expert counterfeiters, whose skill had baffled the lynx-eyed scrutiny of our bankers and merchant princes, and for the arrest of whom the officers of the United States Bank had offered a large reward. The trail of these criminals had been traced to this city, but the efforts of the police, as usual at that period, had proved wholly ineffective.

One day Denis Prieur, who, ensconced in his magisterial chair, was quietly pondering over the official reports of the "City Guard" anent these shrewd miscreants, was awakened from his reverie by the appearance in his sanctum of a colored man, respectably attired, who whispered to him that he desired to make a private and confidential communication. Being requested to proceed with his statement, the darkey revealed his secret. He said he knew a certain man in the town who had for some time been holding private interviews with these counterfeiters, and that many things led him to believe that the man was a " suspect," who, if arrested, could impart valuable information. The Mayor was non-plussed. He knew the party denounced to be a just and upright citizen, but as his profession was that of a printer in the publishing office of the *Bee*, engaged occasionally in lithography and engraving, he deemed it prudent to dispatch a court officer. Meanwhile, the informant, contrary to his expectations, was forcibly detained for the purpose of a confrontation, which, taking place a few moments afterward, revealed the strategem so cunningly devised. The master stood aghast at the impudence of his slave, and Prieur, while enjoying a hearty laugh over the ludicrous termination of the affair, sentenced the abashed culprit to be publicly whipped and pilloried. In his trousers pockets were found forged letters of manumission.

I have had occasion in these reminiscences to advert sometimes to the existence of " cabarets." These public houses of entertainment were a great eyesore and a serious source of danger to the peace and good order of society. They abounded in the vicinity of markets and of such other places where negroes were wont to congregate. The cabaret was a species of grocery, dram shop, gambling house and " fence " or depot for stolen goods, all combined. A contemporary, speaking of this common nuisance, described them as follows :

" The whole batch of cabarets in our city merits one sweeping anathema. These groggeries are fruitful nurseries of vice and crime. Felony holds there its headquarters, and roguery of every kind finds a safe retreat within these obscure recesses. We have good reason to believe that one-half of the cases of robbery, murder and arson which occur in New Orleans are hatched within these dens of iniquity. If they deserve censure from no other cause, the fact of vending liquor to slaves, of encouraging gambling among the lower classes, of conniving at pilfering and other delinquencies, should be sufficient to subject them to a searching scrutiny and to condign punishment whenever detection follows."

These social pests were mostly controlled by foreigners of a low class, chiefly Catalans, whose predilection for negro concubines was scandalous. Several accumulated large fortunes and became prominent citizens.

Of the police force in "Old Louisiana Days," the preceding pages have given a sufficient account. A more worthless and contemptible body of men never assumed the functions of office in any other city. The following examples, taken at random, will better illustrate:

On the 11th of July, 1831, two men, members of the City Guard, named Miro and Clure, were sentenced by the judge of the Criminal Court to two years' hard labor, with ball and chain, on the public streets, for having, under the authority of a search warrant, stolen from the proprietor of a cabaret the sum of $200, which they took from the drawer. Having been sent back to their prison quarters (then situated at the corner of St. Peter and Chartres) to serve their term, they contrived to break through the roof and descend to the street in the rear. They were in full view of the guardhouse, where no one seems to have observed them. Just as they were about to effect their successful escape, they happened to attract the attention of some laborers who were at work on St. Anthony Square, just back of the Cathedral. One of them had a dagger in his hand, and threatened to kill whomever should attempt to stop him; but the workmen, undismayed at the sight of the knife, knocked him down with brickbats, and bore him off a prisoner. These worthies had to serve their time.

Another incident, which happened at a later date, and which related to a projected attack upon the City Treasurer's safe is worthy of mention. The names of the officers implicated were Rockwell and Greenough. It appears that the crime had been for a long time meditated and discussed between the parties privy to it; but it also happened that during the interval every particular connected with the scheme had been communicated to Captain Harper. Anxious to catch them in the act, he patiently awaited the development of their plans. On the 29th of May, 1841, he received private information from one of his spies that the attempt would be made on that night. He accordingly secured the cooperation of Lieutenant Winters, and together they repaired to Lafayette Square, where they lay *perdu* in the tall grass. The municipal building occupied the site on which Soulé's College now stands.

After the night had partly set in, their vigilance was rewarded. Greenough and Rockwell, accompanied by another confederate, whose name is not given, appeared upon the scene, seemingly in close consultation. Creeping cautiously toward them, the captain overheard their conversation. It was then settled among themselves that Greenough and the confederate were to pick the lock, or, I should rather say, unlock it, (for they had provided themselves with a false key) and with an axe, which they had brought with them, were to batter down the fragile depositary. But one obstacle was in their way—the night watchman, at the door of the building. This man happened to be a Dutchman, faithful to his trust. He was a thick-headed and honest fellow, inclined, however, to be exceedingly credulous. To Rockwell was assigned the difficult task of putting to sleep the vigilance of this modern Cerberus, this model watch-dog of the Treasury. Rockwell went to him unhesitatingly, and engaged him in conversation. He knew Rockwell as an officer of the force, and this circumstance alone dispelled all suspicion from his mind. Rockwell told him that some rowdies were disturbing the peace at the corner of Poydras and St. Charles, and he went to see about it, but hurried back to his post before the conspirators could effect their purpose. Then other devices were resorted to in order to entrap the janitor, but the latter was immovable, At last, incredible as it may seem, Rockwell persuaded the soft-pated Teuton that there was a most extraordinary horse, of surpassing size and beauty, on exhibition on Camp street, and offered to show it to him. Unsuspicious of any trickery, and fond probably of curiosities, he accepted the proposition, but, as the reader may imagine, this phenomenal quadruped, this winged Pegasus, had taken his aerial flight. Disappointed, they retraced their steps, and, as they were crossing the square, Rockwell induced his companion to look around for sleeping vagrants and suspects. He agreed to this, and the first people they espied in the square were Captains Harper and Winters, lying flat upon the grass. "Here is a loafer," exclaimed the Dutchman, as he poked Captain Harper's ribs with his wand of office, as a hint to get up and move toward the guardhouse. But as this course would have brought the watchman close to the City Hall, where the burglars were operating, Rockwell interposed, "Never mind their sleeping, leave them alone." So saying, he stooped over the prostrate form, and recognized his own captain, who instantly sprang to his feet and seized the criminal. On hearing the noise occasioned by the arrest, Greenough and his accomplice incontinently fled, but were subsequently lodged in jail.

These and others, which I might relate, are extreme cases, it is true, but if an estimate is to be formed from the withering terms in which the press were in the habit of denouncing the police in general, specially during the terms of office of Nicholas Girod, Roffignac and Prieur, my criticisms will not be found unduly severe.

One of the characteristic elements of which the motley population of New Orleans was composed in ancient times was the Indians of the tribe of "Chactas" (Choctaws). When Louisiana was originally settled by the French, the colonists found in the territory included in the grant bestowed on Law, and subsequently on Crozat, a nation of these warlike savages, sufficiently powerful to bring into the field a force of nearly 20,000 braves. They lived along the lake coast, including Biloxi, as far as the country of the Alibamons. Under the influences of civilization—that is to say, of whisky, powder and tinseled jewelry—these people were induced to be friendly to the white settlers, and their allegiance often proved efficacious and opportune in the wars waged against the Natchez and Chickasaws.

In the course of time their nation, decimated by constant warfare, disease and debauchery, dwindled away to such infinitesimal proportions that their influence entirely ceased.   Push-ma-ta-ha, the last of their chiefs, faithful in his friendship to the American government, left a brilliant and honorable record.

The history of this race and of the savages who inhabited Florida is an interesting study.   Without omitting to note the profound researches of l'Abbé Rouquette, the subject, I may say, has been treated with a master hand by the late Dr. Charles Deléry in a compendious work, which I had the privilege to read some time ago with great relish and profit, unfortunately in manuscript form.   It is to be hoped that the production of this once prolific and versatile Creole author will see the light of day ere long.

Fragments of this erratic race still exist.   I have seen some on the prairies of St. Landry and along the banks of the Têche, in the vicinity of Charenton; a few are yet gathered in some portions of Avoyelles, but their principal encampment seems to have been established across the lake, in the neighborhood of Covington. They used to flock to New Orleans at times in considerable numbers, their usual places of resort in the daytime being the Place d'Armes and lower markets, where they were wont to peddle their wares.   In the nighttime they usually pitched their camp along the Bayou St. John.   The police never arrested them for misdemeanors or crimes, but turned the offenders over to the chief of their tribe for punishment, the exemption, it was claimed, being based upon treaty stipulations or immemorial usage.   The following occurrence is a fact in point :

In the year 1832, the master of a schooner lying in the Old Basin, who was about to set sail for the Tchefuncta river, applied in the night-time to Captain Dutillet, of the City Guard, for assistance against a band of Indians who had taken possession of his craft and wanted to be conveyed to St. Tammany. Inquiries revealed the fact that the party consisted of a young fellow, who had recently been adjudged guilty of homicide, and that the others were the ancients and relatives of the deceased, whose duty it was to carry out the decree of death. According to their laws, the execution was to take place in the presence of the assembled tribe to which the culprit belonged. Another law, bearing on the subject, was that should the criminal escape or conceal himself, his next of kin was, as a matter of course, to undergo his punishment. Compromises were permissible, and ransom paid to the friends of the slain was recognized by their code.

The skipper, as was to be expected, demurred under the circumstances to the forcible seizure of his vessel for any such purpose. Aided by his lieutenant, Bonseigneur, Dutillet repaired to the Basin and effected the arrest or rather the release of the captive. He was taken to the guardhouse, where he told his story. He was cool and undemonstrative, and seemed to take in the situation as an ordinary occurrence. With the phlegm befitting an Indian he related to the bystanders in broken French that, having been attacked by three worthless young bucks of his nation, he had shot one to death and put the other two to flight. "Me kill Indian, me die." His name was Eh-hé-lum-abé; his countenance was kind and expressive. Much sympathy was manifested for his fate, but, aware of the fatal consequences that might result to his father, brother or son, he deprecated every attempt offered to save his life. He begged to be taken back to the schooner, where his squaw and children had been left.

Moved by compassion, Dutillet proceeded to the

vessel in quest of the Choctaw chiefs. After several long parleys they agreed to admit the Indian to ransom in the sum of $100. Thereupon a subscription list was circulated among our people, the money collected and the prisoner released.

From these grave subjects let me turn for a moment to the theatricals and amusements of the period.

An incident which _occurred in the Camp street theatre may be worth recording. It is certainly characteristic of the times.

It was a Fourth of July night, a holiday then celebrated with greater *éclat* and outward manifestations of patriotism than at the present day, that this temple of Thespis was filled to repletion with a crowd, the majority of whom were backwoodsmen from the Western country. Great preparations had been set on foot by the manager to make the performance an acceptable and *recherché* affair, particularly to our musical *dilettanti*.

The leader of the orchestra was an old Frenchman, whom I remember well. He was afflicted with almost complete deafness, occasioned by the explosion of a caisson at the battle of New Orleans, and how he managed to direct his artists with such ability has ever been to me an unfathomable mystery. For several weeks he had had his musicians rehearsing the overture of the opera of " La Dame Blanche "—a novelty then—and when, after many wearisome efforts to attain perfection, he saw the acme of his ambition about to be crowned with success, visions of entranced audiences, tumults of applause and *salvos* of *encore* filled his imagination with rapture. At last, the long desired occasion, fraught with such pleasing anticipations, finally arrived.

As I have already said, the house was jammed. It

was a hilarious, promiscuous and uproarious audience.
They had come to have fun, and fun they were determined to have.

Seated in front of the footlights, with waving *baton* in
hand, the bent form of old man Desforges was to be seen,
giving the three consecrated raps. The magnificent
symphony began. Never had the music of Boieldieu
been interpreted with such effects of pathos and sweet-
ness, when, all of a sudden, a call for "Yankee Doodle"
was heard from the galleries. Heedless of the interruption, the orchestra proceeded with the music, when the
cry of "Yankee Doodle" was taken up again, and began to resound from dome to pit. The deafening noise
reached old Desforges' ears like the murmur of a gentle
breeze, wafting upon its wings faint echoes of applause.
Mistaking the cause of the uproar, the musical leader
was delighted. He had attained, as he imagined, the
goal of his ambition, and, throwing his whole soul into
a supreme effort, was about to give additional language
and expression to his charmed violin, when crashes following crashes gave notice that the work of demolition
of benches and chairs had commenced, amid angry
shouts of "Yankee Doodle."

At this stage of pandemonium the curtain was pushed
aside, and Mr. Caldwell made his appearance. Turning to Mr. Desforges he shouted to him to stop. "The
people don't want that," he said, "they want Yankee
Doodle."

The old man realized the situation. He stood up in
a stupor, and only had time to gasp out, "Yankee
Dude!" Then, stung to the quick by the affront put
on him by the populace, he shrieked out in quick, pip-
ing tones: "You want Yankee Dude? Well, you no

have Yankee Dude! Because why? Because not necessair.''

At this outburst of rage and pluck, the audience broke out into plaudits and shouts of laughter, and the overture *was* finished without further interruption. They had had more fun than they had bargained for.

This anecdote reminds me of another, the scene of which occurred in the same theatre, about the year 1836, and of which the elder Booth figured as the hero. This eminent tragedian, father of the gifted actor whose late death has bereft the American stage of one of its proudest ornaments was, it may be remembered, addicted at times to spells of inebriety, which brought on prolonged attacks of mental failure. He had many friends and acquaintances in New Orleans who admired his erratic genius and loved his sympathetic nature. When in one of these convivial moods, he would indulge to such an excess as to completely lose all recollection of his professional engagements or appointments. I have had frequent occasion to notice in the files of old papers severe and pungent criticisms upon his repeated failures to appear in his advertised characters, necessitating the substitution of one play for another. Whenever he was announced in the part of Richard III, his favorite character, the attendance was so large as to exclude even standing room.

It was on the occasion of one of these debauches that the following occurrence, not posted on the bills, took the whole audience by surprise. He was playing to Caldwell's Richmond, when, during the battle scene, Booth, conceiving the duel to be a reality, fought long and desperately, and attempted to slay his antagonist. Caldwell realized his danger at once and skilfully parried all his thrusts, but, finding himself hotly pressed, whispered to Booth, as a stage cue: "Die, Mr. Booth, it is time for you to fall." Straightening his apparently misshapen form, and waving his gleaming sword on high, he exclaimed with sonorous voice: "As long as Richard wields this blade, he'll never die." The public understood the situation, and the curtain was rung down amid peals of laughter.

From music and actors, I shall now turn to a theme interesting to the disciples of Terpsichore. The singular adventure which befell Fanny Ellsler in New Orleans merits some attention.

In the afternoon of May 11, 1841, a report was industriously circulated that the celebrated *danseuse* intended to regale a party of "choice spirits" at the ordinary of the St. Charles Hotel with a magnificent banquet, after the close of her engagement at the theatre. With this proposed entertainment the general public had nothing to do, although, as it was then said, it would have been in better taste had not pains been taken to spread the news. Later in the afternoon, a second report was started that such of her worshippers as had not been included in the list of invited guests had determined upon giving her a grand serenade, while the feast was going on. Very little attention was paid to either of these rumors until the preparations for the ovation had begun, and, singular as it may appear, the entrance into the barroom of the St. Charles Exchange (the most frequented place in the city) was selected as the rendezvous for perfecting the necessary programme for the out-door part of the entertainment. This naturally attracted the attention of every passer-by, each of whom was given to understand that a public demonstration, similar to those that had been made in other cities.

was to be inaugurated as a token of the adoration of the people of New Orleans for the divine " Sylph.".

But a number of persons, who recollected the disgraceful scenes enacted in Baltimore, some time before, when a score of toadies, converting themselves into asses, had drawn her carriage through the streets, objected to the city of New Orleans vying in such folly with any other town. They, therefore, determined to break up the projected scheme, and to organize a counter serenade. The idea was a foolish one, perhaps, but nevertheless they supplied themselves with every instrument known as constituting the paraphernalia of a charivari band. No sooner had Ellsler's admirers begun their musical *fête* than the opposition opened their concert of discordant sounds. They continued the performance, until the serenading party were compelled to stop. At this point, just when the contending parties were about coming to blows, a wag rang an alarm of fire, and the engines rushed to the spot, with their bells ringing, and put an end to the conflict. This unexpected reinforcement made the anti-Ellsler people masters of the field. Shouting and screaming, combined with the tooting of horns, the beating of drums, the blare of tin trumpets, enlivened the scene and drew thousands of spectators thereto from every quarter. The fire laddies, suspected by the serenaders of complicity in the plot, were assailed by the latter, but were in turn supported by the rioters. The scrimmage that ensued then assumed enormous proportions, and was only quelled by the engines being put to work and pouring streams of river water upon the combatants. With the exception of a few battered hats and bloody noses, no great injuries were sustained in this serio-comic battle. From one of the upper windows of the

once famous caravansary, Fanny Ellsler, it is said, surveyed with tearful eyes the discomfiture of her crowd of
admirers, and left the city on the following day, fully
impressed with the conviction that, whatever their
faults in other respects, our people would never tolerate
abject fawning or servile adoration.

The French Revolution of 1830—*les trois jours de
Juillet*—and the consequent accession of Louis Philippe
to the throne, as "king of the French," threw our
friends of Gallic nativity into such a state of excitement
and frenzy that the feeling was properly denominated
the "French craze." Upon the receipt of the glad
tidings cannon were fired, bonfires lit at every street
corner down town, and mass meetings held, in which
furious bombast predominated over common sense. On
public as well as on private buildings the tri-color
floated beside our national emblem. Nothing was to be
heard except of the grand revolution that was to accom-
plish great wonders for France, and draw her into a
closer alliance with republican America. The City
Council became infected with the prevailing fever, and
adopted a series of resolutions appropriate to the occasion. Not even did our State Legislature, supposed to
be a more conservative body, escape the contagion, for
that august embodiment of concentrated wisdom went
to the lengths of adopting an "address to the people of
France," congratulating them upon the restoration of
their liberties, and appointing W. C. C. Claiborne, one
of its members, as a messenger in charge of the precious
document. Not to be behindhand in these manifestations of general rejoicing, our importers and merchants
subscribed to a fund for a "dinner to be given to the
captain of the first ship under the tri-color flag that

should reach this port.'' This part of the programme was not realized until the ensuing year, under the circumstances which I am now about to narrate.

It was on the 7th of April, 1831, nearly nine months since the overthrow of the Bourbons, that the French ship Zelia, from Bordeaux, moored at her wharf opposite the Cathedral. She was the first French vessel which had made her appearance at our port since the glorious achievement which, to use the jargon of the period, had ''restored to France her liberty and independence.'' Agreeably to a resolution adopted by a number of citizens, the battalion of artillery fired a salute of 101 guns in honor of the new flag. Nor was the banquet forgotten. It went off, of course, with the *éclat* usual on such occasions and with an appropriate accompaniment of toasts and speeches. The '' Parisienne '' was sung in the midst of clashing goblets, and the succulent viands were literally devoured in commemoration of the event.

On the day that the ship was about to leave port, on her homeward voyage, a large delegation of Frenchmen, headed by Messieurs Auguste Douce and Pierre Nogués, escorted Mr. Claiborne to the vessel. On crossing the gangway leading to the deck, the plank being extremely narrow, Mr. Nogués, who was carrying a magnificent silk flag, tumbled over into the river; but the water being shallow and the flag bearer very tall, the pretty and costly emblem, a donation of our fair creoles, escaped injury, save that caused by a slight immersion in the turbid Mississippi. Mr. Claiborne took charge of the precious gift, as well as of the more precious parchment-engrossed ''Address,'' and proceeded on his mission.

Speaking of the political errand of the last named gentleman, the *Courier*, a leading French paper, not inaptly said :

"This measure, besides being rather tardy, is believed to be without a parallel in the local legislation of the Republic. The people in their elementary capacity have already given expression to their enthusiasm, and have not instructed their representatives to act in their behalf. It is, moreover, an usurpation of the rights of the Federal Government, which alone controls our Federal relations."

The last public act of Mayor Roffignac, in his character of chief executive of New Orleans, will prove a fitting close to this chapter. The following letter and valedictory throw strong rays of light upon the policy of his administration. They were both written and delivered on the eve of his departure from his native country, and repel the idea that our people were non-progressive in early days. To him, as I have already said in a former sketch of his life and services, is due the impetus first given to the wheels of government. His letter to the City Council was couched in the following terms:

"NEW ORLEANS, April 12, 1828.
"*To the President and Members of the City Council:*

"GENTLEMEN—If it were in my power to portray human feeling, I would attempt to express to you the lively sense of gratitude awakened in my breast by the flattering terms in which it has pleased the Honorable City Council to manifest its satisfaction with my efforts, during the last eight years, to merit the confidence reposed in me by my fellow-citizens. I would not, however, be doing justice either to the people who have, during that period, honored me with an almost unani-

mous vote, or to you, gentlemen, whose wise counsels
have so frequently guided my measures, were I not to
acknowledge how much assistance and support, in the
exercise of my functions, I have found in the general
approval of my constituents, and in the firmness of the
magistrates who compose the Municipal Council.

"In the government of a city, just as in that of a
State, no useful forces can exist except such as are derived from public opinion, and this opinion never manifests itself spontaneously, except when the measures
proposed are profitable to the mass of the citizens.
Keenly alive to the importance of this commercial city,
now advancing in the front rank of the metropolitan
centres of this Union, I have been anxious to introduce
all the improvements which the progress of the age has
placed at our disposal. I have been of opinion that a
slow advance was not in keeping with the spirit of the
age, nor with the wants and interests of an active and
enterprising generation. I have thought, in other words,
that this great mart of so many wealthy States should
be in a position to offer to industry and commerce
everything needed to facilitate and hasten their operations. I have not shrunk, in order to bring about these
useful results, from borrowing capital, as I am convinced that the financial resources of an opulent city
like ours, with its yearly increasing revenues, will suffice to liquidate its liabilities through a funding system,
both gradual and little onerous.

" Success, gentlemen, has crowned our hopes, thanks
to your co-operation. New Orleans, at this day, offers
guarantees of prosperity that assure her future.

" The expressions of regret which you have so kindly
uttered are, believe me, reciprocated on my part.
United to you by common duties; in full accord as to

our intentions, although differing at times from the means proposed, I have found, in your indulgence and in the favor of my fellow-citizens, a full reward for my services. I am happy to carry away, in my temporary separation from this city, where my sweetest affections and my fondest memories will ever cluster, the assurances of your friendship and of the esteem of my fellow-citizens. I pray you to accept the expression of the sentiments of respect and attachment which will ever bind me to you and to our people.''

This noble letter, at the time when he was about to lay aside the cares of office to take a needed rest, was read by the whole community with sincere sympathy, as his resignation was felt to be a public loss. He had devoted eight years of his life to the service of the city and thirty years to that of the State, in trying and difficult positions, from which he had always emerged as pure as refined gold. He was a model official in every respect.

On the eve of his departure, he proceeded to the Council Chamber, where preparations had been made for his reception. The recorder, as usual, presided. On his appearance, the members rose to their feet, and offered him the seat of honor. This he declined, and modestly taking a position in the aisle, near the right-hand row of chairs, he delivered the following remarks:

''Gentlemen—At the time when the relations which have so long bound us together are about to be severed, I have deemed it my duty to repair to this hall to enjoy once more the pleasure of meeting those members of the City Council who have lent me their powerful assistance in my difficult duties of mayor, and to thank you again in person for the address which the Council has condescended to transmit to me. Its contents affix the stamp of honor on my official career.

"There are situations in life when the emotions which one experiences become an obstacle to the expression of thought.   Such, gentlemen, is the position in which I find myself at this moment.

"Eight years ago, this day, and at about the same hour, I appeared for the first time within these precincts to take the oath to support the law and do all in my power for the interests and well-being of my constituents.   This oath, I declare to you, has been religiously observed, and I have seconded by every means at my disposal your patriotic views in the furtherance of the growth and prosperity of this interesting capital.

" I can not conceal from myself the fact that, in the course of my career, I have committed many mistakes ; but they were involuntary and excusable, my intentions being pure.

"To-morrow I shall resume once more the character of a private citizen, and, in doing so, will feel great satisfaction if the manner in which I have acquitted myself of my duties has earned for me the title of a good citizen.   This last quality is eminently due to the gentleman elected to succeed me, and whom public esteem has elevated to the position.   I sincerely hope that he will escape the opposition of enemies, which a faithful discharge of public duty is likely to create.   If this good luck has not been my lot, I have at least the consolation of knowing that I harbor malice against none.

" I trust, gentlemen, that you will be pleased to act for me as intermediaries with my constituency, and that you will repeat to them what I have just declared within this hall, that if I have been so unfortunate as to commit errors, they were not the result of design.

"I am about to revisit the home of my birth. There, as elsewhere, I shall ever carry in my heart the recollection of lovely Louisiana, my country by adoption; and be assured that I shall neglect no means to shorten the absence which will separate me from her. I beg you, gentlemen, to accept the assurance of the feelings of sincere gratitude which your repeated acts of kindness have filled my heart."

The last expressed wishes of Roffignac were never realized. He died a tragic death in his *chateau* in France, a few years afterward, just as he was preparing to return to the city he had loved and served so well.

CHAPTER XIV.

OLD LOUISIANA DAYS.

NEW ORLEANS IN 1788—ITS DESTRUCTION BY FIRE—
NEW ORLEANS THREATENED WITH A GENERAL MASSA-
CRE—SAVED BY A SLAVE—GRANDJEAN THE CONSPIRA-
TOR—THE LEGION—ITS HISTORY—A SHAM BATTLE—
THE FAUBOURG ST. MARY—ITS ORIGIN AND PROGRESS
—SAMUEL J. PETERS—BERNARD MARIGNY—DOUBLE
DEALING—THE OLD GRAVIER CANAL—ORLEANS NAVI-
GATION COMPANY—ORGANIZATION OF THE POLICE—THE
STORY OF THE GIQUEL-BROOKS AFFAIR—INTREPIDITY
OF JUDGE JOACHIM BERMUDEZ—HEROISM OF HIS WIFE
—THE "WASHINGTON GUARDS," THE NUCLEUS OF THE
WASHINGTON ARTILLERY.

To one who loves to delve into the dust-begrimed, worm-eaten and somewhat musty records of generations long gone by, the student frequently stumbles upon unexpected revelations and surprises. No history furnishes a wider field for romance, thrilling episodes and dramatic incidents than that of our State. These have never been thoroughly and deftly written, since they require the pen of a Macauley, a Thiers or a Motley to bring them forth from their chiaro-oscuro recesses into the bright sunlight of the realistic.

What more beautiful and Van Dyke-like portraiture of character can a historical writer select than that furnished, for instance, by our public personages during the first decade of the present century, including the period of excitement and terror created by the Aaron Burr "fiasco." Here we would see Claiborne, halting, procrastinating and ever needing the rod of Wilkinson to urge him on. There the General, whom Jackson, suspicious of treachery, had advised the Governor to watch —imperious, bombastic, but plucky to the core. Further on Daniel Clark, the libertine and shrewd moneymaker, always bent on mischief and discord, suspecting everybody and suspected by all. Then we would be made acquainted with Livingston, Davezac, McDonogh, Hall, Derbigny, Lislet, Bellechasse, Macarty, Sauvé, Destréhan, and a host of others, without omitting Pére Antoine as a central figure, not as they are dryly delineated in the annals which we possess, but as they lived, moved, spoke and thought.

The warfare for supremacy, so long waged between the two antagonistic races—Saxon against Gaul—their gradual intermixture and final harmonious blending, despite the prejudices engendered by religion, diversity of customs and early training ; their rivalry in the fields of politics, literature and commercial progress ; these also would constitute an instructive and yet an entertaining and amusing theme, where the imagination, without any disregard to truth, might be allowed to wing its flight amid scenes of almost Acadian picturesqueness. Is not this an unexplored mine, inviting and remunerative to a diligent prospector?

I am led to these remarks by the information that a work of this character is now progressing, and is in the hands of one whose pre-eminence in the walks of science and of humanities fits him so well for the task. A renowned ecclesiastic, whose whole life has been devoted to the training of the youth of the country, and whose leisure hours are dedicated to the wooing of knowledge and polite literature; his undertaking should be looked upon as an auspicious omen in the history of letters.

The great fire that occurred in New Orleans, of which the following is the official account written by Gov. Miro to His Majesty, the King of Spain, is far more graphic and pathetic than that given out by any of our local writers, as a comparison of their merits will readily show. I need, therefore, no apology for having rescued it from oblivion in its long sleep among our old archives, and for publishing it *in extenso*. The translation is a literal one :

"On the evening of the 21st of March, 1788, at 1:30 o'clock, a fire broke out in the private residence of Don Vicente José Nunez, paymaster of the army. (This building was situated at the lower corner of Chartres and Toulouse streets, on the woods side.) *Eight hundred and fifty-six buildings* were reduced to ashes, including all the business houses and principal mansions of the city. A wind from the south, then blowing with fury, thwarted every effort to arrest its progress. The parochial church and presbytery (*casa de los curas*) were involved in the common disaster, together with the greater part of its archives. The Municipal building (*casa capitular*), the barracks and the armory, as well as the arms deposited therein, except 150 muskets, met the same fate. The public jail was also destroyed, and hardly had we time to save the lives of the unfortunate prisoners.

"We succeeded in saving the Custom House, the

tobacco warehouses, the Governor's and Intendent's buildings, the general supply store of provisions and blankets for the Indians, our park of artillery, the Royal Hospital, the Ursulines Convent, the barracks set apart for the dragoons and resident regiment, and several private edifices fronting the river.

"As soon as we perceived that the progress of the fire was being hastened by unceasing gusts of wind, and that the whole city was evidently in danger of destruction, our principal aim was directed toward the removal of our supply depot (*almacen de viveres*), as this was our sole dependence for future subsistence. We had previously taken out of the artillery quarters every implement necessary to cut off the fire. We carried off from the treasury and deposited on the river banks all of your Majesty's treasures, in currency and silver, over which a guard was kept, attended by that care against risk consequent on the confusion and disorder which necessarily occur at such a time. The papers belonging to the Auditor's (*contaduria*) and Secretary's departments were transferred to places of safety, and, when subsequently returned to their respective custodians, none were found missing. With the exception of some slight injury to the armory and a small quantity of war materials left in the park; of the mislaying of some articles in the storehouse at the time when we took out some artillery implements (not an unexpected contingency); of the loss of a small quantity of flour that had been worked into biscuits for delivery at Natchez, and of a little damage to the building that had been purchased for experiments in the manufacture of snuff, the loss of your Majesty has been trifling.

"Hemmed in on every side by the raging flames,

and mindful of the obligation we were under of extinguishing the conflagration and cutting off its further
communications, we could not close our eyes to the dire
necessity staring us in the face—a dearth of provisions
for the morrow. On the spur of the moment, we took
every measure suggested by humanity and our sense of
duty to prevent the pangs of hunger from being added
to the sufferings of the helpless victims of this terrible
calamity, and, with this object in view, I ordered that
the stock of biscuits that had been rescued from the devouring element should be distributed among the needy
applicants, inasmuch as most of the bakeries had been
swept from existence.

"If the imagination could describe what our senses
enable us to feel from sight and touch, reason itself
would recoil in horror, and it is no easy matter to say
whether the sight of an entire city in flames was more
horrible to behold than the suffering and pitiable condition in which every one was involved. Mothers, in
search of a sanctuary or refuge for their little ones, and
abandoning their earthly goods to the greed of the relentless enemy, would retire to out-of-the-way places
rather than be witnesses of their utter ruin. Fathers
and husbands were busy in saving whatever objects the
rapidly spreading flames would permit them to bear off,
while the general bewilderment was such as to prevent
them from finding even for these a place of security.
The obscurity of the night coming on threw its mantle
for awhile over the saddening spectacle; but more horrible still was the sight, when day began to dawn, of
entire families pouring forth into the public highways,
yielding to their lamentations and despair, who, but a
few hours before, had been basking in the enjoyment of
more than the ordinary comforts of life. The tears, the

heart-breaking sobs and the pallid faces of these wretched people mirrored the dire fatality that had overcome a city, now in ruins, transformed within the space of five hours into an arid and fearful desert. Such was the sad ending of a work of death, the result of seventy years of industry. I herewith enclose to your Majesty a plan exhibiting the actual condition of the city.

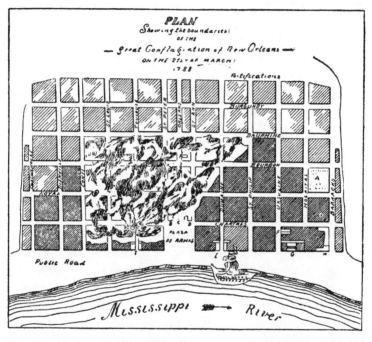

A. Cemetery.	D. Capuchins' Quarters.	G. Royal Hospital.
B. Prison.	E. King's Stores.	H. Barracks.
C. Church.	F. Ursulines' Convent.	I. Government Buildings

Note.—All the buildings fronting the river were saved. The settled parts of the town are indicated by the black squares; the others were open town lots

"To alleviate in part their immediate wants, camping tents were distributed to those who applied for them, and we agreed to distribute daily one ration of rice, on your Majesty's account, to every one, without distinction, who solicited the same. The number of these persons amounts to 700, who will continue to be provided for during the continuance of their extreme necessities. Many have taken temporary lodgings with families that were so fortunate as to escape unscathed, and to such an extent have the compassionate feelings of the latter shone forth that on the following day there was not a single human being without shelter.

"One of my first measures was the sending of three ships to Philadelphia, directed to the care of our resident minister, besides the issuing of several permits, to enable us, within the shortest possible delay, to receive a supply of provisions, nails, medicines and other articles of first necessity, at reasonable prices, for which purpose we drew from your royal coffers at this point the sum of $24,000 on account, for the payment of 3000 barrels of flour, which I have already ordered.

"The people not embraced in this general misfortune have in general voluntarily offered to subscribe to a fund for the rebuilding of the edifices most needed. The ecclesiastical corps, represented by their vicar, has suppressed for the time being the collection of all parochial tithes. Colonel Maxent has exhibited on this occasion evidences of the most considerate charity, having afforded a home and maintenance to a very large number of families, who had sought a place of refuge at his residence. He sold me the stock of rice and tobacco that he had on hand at the market prices ruling before the fire, and even offered to go up to the post of Pointe Coupée (*el puesto de Punta Cortada*), for the purpose of getting the signatures of those who might be willing to subscribe for the relief of the needy.

"The loss occasioned by the destruction of the buildings has been estimated at $1,080,000, exclusive of merchandise and personal effects; and as this fact can not now be ascertained with any degree of certainty, unless through the declarations of parties interested, we have issued an edict prescribing that, within a delay of eight days, every victim shall furnish me with a detailed statement of his loss. This order has not been complied with as yet, for the reason that many families have retired to a distance of eight and ten leagues from this capital, and have not been apprised of it in time. Hence, I must suspend until next mail a statement of our total loss, which, we suppose, will exceed $3,000,000.

"The mind of every one to-day is chiefly absorbed in the expectation of that relief which the benevolent disposition of your Majesty gives them cause to hope for. Opinions are divided into two classes; one is 'that of the landed proprietors, the other that of the merchants. The first want free trade in this province, and ask that foreign crafts, whatever their nationality, may be allowed ingress into our port. The second, aware that the point had already been mooted in the Provincial Council (*Ayuntamiento*) of this city by one of the members (*regidores*) with the approval of his colleagues, have presented us with a memorial, the object of which is to induce us to influence your Majesty against the suggestion, and in this demand they, too, go to extremes. They solicit me to crave your permission to allow the inhabitants in general of these provinces to bring cargoes here from any European port without any distinction whatever. There is no doubt in my mind that either of these concessions would rapidly develop the prosperity of the colony, and build up in a short time this now desolate capital; but, as the first project is wholly opposed to our policy of not allowing in the Gulf of Mexico of any ship not bearing our flag, under the pretext of only coming to the river; and, furthermore, as regards the second, inasmuch as the interests of the monarchy may require that preference should be given to some foreign nation, France for instance—a friend allied to us by such strong ties—I merely confine myself to recommend the prorogation of commerce granted by the royal letters patent (*cedula*) of January 22, 1782, with the privilege that during the space of three years the people here may avail themselves of foreign crafts, with the same exemption from duties as is conceded by Art. 5 of said royal letters patent.''

The loss by this terribly destructive fire, as officially ascertained and made known to the Spanish Cabinet afterward, was declared to amount to the sum of $2,-595,561.

The foregoing letter loses much of its idiomatic force and beauty through the free translation which the genius of the Spanish language compels one to adopt, although some passages therein must forcibly remind the scholar of some of the imaginary scenes depicted by Defoe in his ''Plague of London.'' Governor Miro was not only a thorough diplomat, but a polished classic.

While conning, some time ago, over the pages of our ancient municipal records, my eyes chanced to stray upon certain passages of a message forwarded to the aldermen of the city, by Mayor John Watkins, on September 28, 1805. As their contents are not referred to by Mr. Gayarré in his work on Louisiana, I think it will be both interesting and instructive to reproduce them in their entirety:

''GENTLEMEN OF THE COUNCIL—Agreeably to my promise, some time ago, permit me to enter into the particulars of some of the circumstances relative to the conspiracy which had for its object to call to arms the negro slaves in our midst to burn down our city, and to slaughter its inhabitants. A mulatto, named Célestin, was the first man to give warning of the existence of this abominable project.

" It seems that a white man, a fresh importation from St. Domingo (where he has doubtless served an apprenticeship to the crimes which have precipitated that unfortunate island into an abyss of destruction), had been for some time employed as a workman in the shop of Mr. Duverné, a respectable citizen of the faubourg St. Mary, at whose place Célestin also had been engaged to work. One day the wretch, whose name is Grandjean, confided to the latter a plan relative to a general insurrection of the slaves, the success of which was to be secured at the cost of the lives and fortunes of the whites. Célestin, guided by natural sentiments of humanity, like a faithful slave, and without loss of time, imparted the information, with all its details to Mr. Duverné, who, in turn and conjointly with Célestin, apprised me of it, accompanied for that purpose by Colonel Dorcière. Measures were immediately taken to not only disconcert the plot and arrest the author, but to secure also sufficient proof to convict him of the atrocious crime which he was meditating against the peace of the Territory. With this object in view, we advised several free colored people, both intelligent and of excellent character, to get themselves introduced to Grandjean as persons well disposed to second him in his undertaking, and who were, under this cloak, to draw from him all the particulars of his conspiracy, in order to qualify themselves to testify eventually before the courts. The plan proved a success, for Grandjean opened himself fully to them, and explained his plans, which were to be car-

ried out in the following manner: He said that, being
the principal agent, he was to be known only to ten
persons, who were to be the apparent leaders.   These
ten chiefs were to communicate the secret to ten others,
and so an *ad infinitum*.   Couriers were to be sent to
the blacks at Natchez and to those of adjoining points.
Commandeurs or negro drivers particularly were to be
won over, and on a given day, at an appointed hour, the
decisive blow was to be struck.   The insurgents were to
make themselves masters of the different streets of the
city, take forcible possession of the soldiers' barracks
and of the different public stores, surprise the State
House and other government buildings, massacre every
one who offered resistance, and finally set the city on
fire, if it could not be reduced to subjection otherwise.

   " These particulars once known, it became necessary to
take steps to inform the whites of the situation, without
creating unnecessary alarm.   In consequence, Colonels
Bellechasse and Dorcière, Mr. Duverné and myself,
went at an hour agreed upon with a detachment of *gen-
darmerie* and surrounded the house.   Colonel Bellechasse,
who had fortunately screened himself completely for the
purpose, was able to hear from the lips of Grandjean
himself the substance of the horrible things that I have
been relating.   We then made an irruption into the
apartment—Grandjean was taken and led to the jail,
where he is now detained while waiting for his trial and
the just punishment which he deserves.

   " With regard to the reward to be awarded to Célestin,
there is no doubt that application to that effect should be
made to the Territorial government; but, while awaiting
its decision, and in the uncertainty of its final action, if
the recollection of his important services has not faded
away through lapse of time, it must behoove you, it seems

to me, gentlemen, to break the fetters which now bind this faithful servant, and to invest him with that dignity of freedom which he refused to accept at the price of your blood.

"With regard to the colored people who have so nobly contributed toward the discovery of the plot, they will find an adequate reward in some honorable testimonial of your esteem and acknowledgment of their claim on public gratitude."

Acting upon these suggestions, the City Council appointed two of its members, Messrs. Pédesclaux and Arnaud, to confer with Mr. Robelot, Célestin's master, in reference to his manumission. In consideration of the sum of $2000, agreed upon by experts and paid by the corporation, Célestin became a free man, and an object of envy and admiration to blacks and whites alike.

Nor were the colored men forgotten, who had so firmly stood by the citizens of New Orleans. Not only were eulogistic resolutions adopted by the Board of Councilmen, but more substantial favors and tokens of consideration were bestowed upon them. This class of our population, it must be said to their credit, notwithstanding the anomalous condition which they occupied, invariably proved themselves honest, industrious and conservative citizens. In periods of public calamity they were always to be seen in the front ranks cheerfully performing every service assigned to them. During epidemics, the females braved every danger and were considered by our physicians as the most competent and attentive nurses in the world. The acts of heroism displayed by the free men of color at the battle of New Orleans, under the command of Savary, D'Aquin and Lacoste, extorted the admiration of Jackson and fill a

glorious page of Louisiana history.   These lines are but
a small tribute to their worthy past.

But what of Grandjean? As he had committed no
overt act to incite the slaves to insurrection he escaped
the death penalty, but was convicted of the lesser offence, and sentenced to serve a life sentence in the chain
gang employed upon our public streets.   Exposed at the
pillory and whipping post with the convict's red bonnet
and parti-colored trowsers and jacket, and dragging a
fifty-pound ball attached to his ankles, he was for many
years to be seen, toiling and panting with other criminals. in cleaning gutters and grading our highways with
batture sand.

The most thoroughly equipped and disciplined body
of citizen soldiery that Louisiana ever possessed in *ante-
bellum* times was, without doubt, the organization popularly known as the "Legion."   Its origin dates from
the period of our territorial government.   At that time,
several companies, composed of Creoles and of Frenchmen who had seen active service in Europe, were
formed and consolidated.   Governor Claiborne, in his
correspondence with the President, when Louisiana
was threatened with invasion by Burr's adherents, mentions them as bodies that could be depended upon in
case of an emergency.   They constituted the nucleus,
around which gathered in subsequent years other organizations of a similar character, so that, when in 1814
the British invaded our soil, a body of troops, known as
the Battalion of Orleans Volunteers, stepped into the field
fully armed and equipped for action.   They proved
themselves trained veterans, and their prowess and effi-
ciency are now a part of our country's history.

In the progress of time, this small corps increased in

strength and stability with such rapidity that it became necessary to incorporate it into a Legion, which was successively commanded by generals of repute, such as Cuvellier, DeBuys, Lewis and Augustin. Such is the outline of its formation. Nearly every nationality was represented in this organization. The Germans had their Yaegers, the Spaniards their Cazadores, the French their Voltigeurs, Cuirassiers and Lanciers, the Americans their Washington Guards and Louisiana Grays, the Creoles their Grenadiers, their Sappers and Miners, the Irish their Emmett Guards, each appareled in gaudy and appropriate uniforms. There was even a mounted corps of Mamelukes. The Orleans Battalion of Artillery, set on foot by such veteran officers as Dominique You, Major Gally and Gen. Benj. Buisson, and composed of the *élite* of our Creole young bloods, was perfect in every detail and always ready for immediate service.

By a special act of the Legislature, the Legion was required to assist the Mayor in *all cases of tumult, when the police found themselves unable to preserve the public peace*, and in April, 1830, the city voted it a yearly allowance of $2000 in compensation for the service.

It was about that time that the Louisiana Legion turned out for the first time in a body to go through the evolutions of a *petite guerre*, or sham battle, in Marigny's field, jointly with the uniformed bodies of the First Brigade, which had been invited for the occasion. About 120 men of the Fourth Regiment of United States Regulars, stationed in the city under Major Twiggs, appeared and formed a reserve corps in the rear of three columns of attack, headed by Lieutenant Colonel Cuvellier and directed against a point which was defended by a corps of infantry and two field pieces, under the command of Major Daunoy. The onset being successful, a pontoon bridge was thrown by the latter over Marigny's canal. A retreat was ordered. This operation enabled him to take a new position on the opposite bank, and to resist with advantage a body of troops much stronger than his own, supported by two field pieces and two troops of cavalry under Captains Vignié and Ed. Ducros.

The mimic conflict was admirably planned and conducted, and after the firing had ceased, a copious breakfast *champêtre*, offered to the general staff, the United States troops and the uniformed companies of the brigade, terminated a military feast, which was marred by no accident and attended throughout by the most hearty good nature and cordiality. In addition to two cavalry companies from the parish of Jefferson, there were two companies from St. Bernard, the Louisiana Guards, the Lafayette Riflemen and the Cadets, who, with the United States troops and the Legion, formed a total of nearly 2500 men, of all arms, when they returned to the city.

When the war with Mexico first broke out, and volunteers were being called upon to proceed at once to the assistance of our beleaguered men on the Rio Grande, the Legion answered the call within twenty-four hours. It readily furnished the contingent required, which was among the first to reach the scene of operations.

The object of the Legion was to encourage military ardor and discipline. Every holiday or State occasion was taken advantage of to display this spirit. Thus on the feast of St. Barbe, the patroness of Artillerists, the Orleans Battalion were wont to turn out in splendid array, with a bouquet of flowers inserted in their *mousquetons*, and proceeded to the Cathedral to hear mass and take up a subscription for our orphans' asylums. This yearly practice was religiously observed every 8th of December. Their flags and banners were usually blessed by the bishop during these public ceremonies. Every Sunday witnessed some marked display or procession, either a drill on the Place d'Armes or an excursion to some rural retreat.

The days of the Legion are now things of the past, but they yet linger in the recollections of old inhabitants like faded and regretted glories.

Much space has been devoted in these preceding pages to accounts of the foundation and gradual development of the "city" proper (*le carré de la Ville*), though frequent references have been made to its suburbs. I now propose to give a faint outline of the rise and progress of the faubourg St. Mary, now composing the First District of New Orleans.

To two citizens of alien birth and parentage, James H. Caldwell and Samuel J. Peters, are mainly due the creation and commercial prosperity of this now famous centre of our metropolis. The first was the soul of enterprise, the latter the embodiment of financial skill and daring. One was the designer, the other the architect. While leading and wealthy Creoles, such as Marigny, Vignié, Montégut, Millaudon, DeBuys, DeFeriet, and a host of others were listlessly dreaming of the possibilities in store for their native city, the Anglo-Saxons, under the guidance of audacious speculators and far-seeing prospectors, were at work with tireless energy in laying out the ground.

It is related, and the story rests upon authenticated tradition, that these two gentlemen had originally made choice of the lower faubourg as the future theatre of

their financial operations. The harbor of that part of
the city offered advantages which no other point presented, not only on account of its great depth of water
and the security of its levees, but of the cheap construction of wharves. To attract the shipping to that
locality by means of warehouses and cotton presses; to
erect on Elysian Fields, opposite the terminus of the
Pontchartrain railroad, a first-class hotel; to construct in
that vicinity a larger theatre, and to locate there their
gas and waterworks plants—these were the first schemes,
precursors of still greater, projected by these prescient
and public-spirited men. With this object in view,
Bernard Marigny was approached by the parties, and,
after considerable haggling, consented to yield, at a
fabulous price, a large space of territory, constituting
nearly the whole of his ancestral plantation. When
every necessary document had been drawn up, all the
parties in interest met at the notary's office to ratify the
agreement and conclude the sale, except Mrs. Marigny,
who, it was surmised, had purposely absented herself at
her husband's suggestion. As her dotal and parapher-
nal rights were involved in this matter of transfer, her
refusal to ratify the contract broke up the project. Mr.
Peters, it is said, was so enraged at this act, which he
bluntly denounced as double-dealing, that, turning to
the Saxon-hating Creole, he cried out: '' I shall live,
by God, to see the day when rank grass shall choke up
the streets of your old faubourg,'' a prophecy that has
unfortunately been verified to the letter!

The reader must not suppose from this incident that
the Creole population blindly indulged in the senseless
prejudices of their once popular tribune or approved his
opposition tactics. On the contrary, they upbraided
him for his course in bitter terms, both in conversation

and in print, and this fact drew upon him in after years
that strong opposition which checked his political aspi-
ration, and lost him the governorship. It was evident
to them that he was no safe adviser or leader. But, as
a matter of fact, this evidence of a narrow-sighted policy
only served to widen the breach between the antagonistic races, and to add fuel to the continuance of those
unfortunate broils and encounters, then so frequent and
fatal.

Canal street was not by any means, as some people
suppose, the dividing line of the contending factions,
inasmuch as many of the most enterprising American
merchants and business men of the period, including
Mr. Peters himself, had their principal establishments
in the French quarter. Chartres street, the great thoroughfare of the day, was dotted as far down as Toulouse, with magnificent and attractive stores, among
which the jewelry bazaar of Messrs. Hyde & Goodrich
will long be remembered by old-timers. The firm of
Peters & Millard, doing then an extensive grocery business, was located on Old Levee street, not far from
Bienville, while such merchants and bankers as Saul,
Montgomery, Zacharie, etc., were all domiciled down
town.

The refusal of Mr. Bernard Marigny to participate in
the advantages offered by the financial magnates not
only sealed the doom of his own immediate section and
brought about the eventual decline of the "*carré de la
ville*," but was the event from which dates the surprising transformation of that once gigantic quagmire,
known to-day as the First District, into a new and wonderful city, the centre of progress, wealth and refinement, with its attractive public buildings, immense
warehouses and stores and palatial residences for its

merchant princes.   The New Canal, the Waterworks,
the St. Charles and Verandah hotels, the Gas Works,
the St. Charles theatre, the introduction of square stone
pavements, were not a few, although among the first, of
the improvements inaugurated by those men of iron,
and notwithstanding the financial crash of 1836-37,
which, for the nonce, paralyzed every industry, the
work of progress and go-aheaditiveness steadily went on.

In order to attract further trade to that fast growing
portion of the city, the subject of improving and widen-
ing the old Gravier canal, now the New Basin, to its
opening at the Lake, became a vital question.   The
Marigny canal on Elysian Fields street, and the Carondelet afforded ample water-ways, it is true, for commercial communications with the Lake and Gulf ports, but
the inhabitants up town complained that they derived
no immediate advantage therefrom, and were completely
shut out from the traffic by pretended monopolistic
privileges and legislative grants.   This was in 1830.

The act of the legislative council of the Territory of
Orleans, passed in 1805, incorporating the Navigation
Company for the purpose of improving the internal navigation of the Territory, had failed to produce the beneficial effects expected from its provisions.   Although
twenty-five years had elapsed since the incorporation of
that company, its operations had been limited to the
keeping of the Bayou St. John in an imperfectly navigable state, and to the opening of the canal and basin,
previously constructed by the Baron Carondelet.   Pre-
tending to an exclusive right to improve the navigation
of the Island of Orleans, the object of this company appeared not to have been to make improvements, but to
distribute enormous dividends among themselves.   It was
nearly ten years since this company had purchased the

Canal Gravier, for an insignificant sum, and although excessive dividends had been constantly declared since that time, no proposition seemed to have been offered for the opening of that canal. By an act of Congress, passed on the 16th day of April, 1816, a large square of ground was donated to the Navigation Company, for the purpose, it was presumed, of enabling it to make further improvements. This tract of land was divided into lots and sold, but the proceeds were not applied to the facilities of navigation, but distributed, it was reported, among the stockholders. Little, however, as had been done by the company in the way of meliora-tion, much had been done in the way of exacting tolls. These were so large as to keep down the commerce of the lakes, to depress the industry and retard the growth of all that part of the State which lay to the eastward of Lake Pontchartrain, and to cause loud and just com-plaints from the people of the adjacent States and Ter-ritories.

Descanting upon this subject, a paper said :

" The most sanguine calculations would insufficiently appreciate the advantages to arise from the making of a safe, easy and cheap communication between the city and the Lake. To the city this advantage would be found in the greatly increasing quantity and cheapness of all building materials and in the cost of the articles of first necessity ; in the additional commerce which will be drawn from the neighboring States, and in af-fording ample protection against inundation from the breaking of the levee at any point above the line of the canal. The advantages of that part of the Gulf which sends its produce to market through the Lake are too obvious to be mentioned, and the whole State must nec-essarily derive benefit from the increasing population and wealth of any part. With this view a railroad company has been incorporated. Whether the application for an incorporation for the purpose of constructing a railroad instead of a canal proceeds from an idea of the superiority of the former for the conveyance of passengers and merchandise, or was founded on a misty notion with respect to the rights of the Orleans Navigation Company, is a matter of conjecture. Much has been written and various opinions entertained in relation to the superior advantages offered by the different modes of transportation. Greater expedition must be conceded to railroads, and those will probably be preferred for the conveyance of persons. But for the transportation of bricks, lime, shells, sand, lumber, firewood, etc., it is believed that a straight canal from the Lake shore to some convenient spot in the upper part of the city of New Orleans, by which these articles could be landed there, from the same vessel in which they have been first laden, is preferable. The opinion which seems at this time generally prevalent is rather more favorable even to the canal and bayou of the navigation company for the transportation of these articles than to the railroad. Still, it is believed that the stockholders in the railroad company will be fully remunerated without extending their exclusive privileges beyond the limits of their charter. They have the exclusive right of constructing railroads to the city ; but we ask for the privilege of making a canal, the same to revert to the State at the expiration of twenty-five years.''

The foregoing remarks, trite and commonplace as they may appear to us at the present time, were the expression of that far-sighted policy which brought about the reclamation of thousands of acres of swamp lands. The struggle for the construction of this important water way

was long and painful, and, when won, contributed beyond measure in settling and thickly populating with
hardy and industrious citizens all that territory which
extended from Baronne street to the uninhabitable
morass beyond. The Third Ward, as it stands to-day,
is the product of that noble work accomplished by persevering and spirited citizens, whose race seems now extinct. The manual labor and engineering work, it may
be observed here, were intrusted to *Simon Cameron*, of
Pennsylvania, a notorious hater of the South, who subsequently became a United States Senator. In those days
he was a contractor of national reputation, and as he was
very careful in concealing his negrophilistic propensities, the contract was readily awarded him. Hundreds,
not to say thousands, of laborers and mechanics were
employed from abroad to inaugurate the work, but, when
the yellow fever set in, a dreadful pestilence broke out
among the unacclimated strangers, and hecatombs of de-
caying carcasses were to be daily found along the banks
of the stream now lining our erstwhile renowned "Shell
Road." For a time obstacle after obstacle seemed to
seriously impede the successful performance of the contract, but, with the vim and energy characteristic of the
Saxon and Celtic races, every obstacle was finally overcome and a new route opened to Lakes Maurepas, Pontchartrain and the Gulf of Mexico. The Milneburg railroad, a triumph for the Marigny followers, be it said *en
passant*, destroyed all further hopes of carrying on the
railway scheme.

As no community can thrive, prosper and expand
without adequate protection to person and property, an
important resolution relative to a new organization of
the city guard was adopted by the Council. Under its

operation the members of that body were required to be acquainted with both the languages then in vogue, to-wit: the English and French, to establish satisfactorily their moral character, and to prove a residence of not less than one year in the city.

For years past, the insufficiency, the laziness, the insolence and the tyranny of the city guard had been constant themes of complaint. In the performance of their duties they were either culpably remiss or daringly despotic. On the one hand, acts of open villainy were perpetrated within the limits of the municipality, and almost before the eyes of the guard, without the least impediment being afforded to their successful accomplishment. On the other, indiscreet but unoffending citizens were not infrequently aggrieved and outraged by those stupid and impudent hirelings. In short, the police system was as loose in discipline, injurious in its operations, and contemptible in its character as any that ever disgraced an enlightened city. It was not difficult to trace those abuses to their source. The old city guard was composed principally of foreigners, the lees and refuse of the town, of individuals picked up in the lowest haunts of vice, and admitted as members of that department of government without the slightest moral qualification and without inquiry into their fitness for the station they assumed. Generally acquainted with but one of the two languages most in vogue, and several, in some instances, ignorant of both; utterly regardless of the responsible character of the duties which devolved upon them, and totally unfit by habits, manners and birth for their new occupations, they constituted in general a most worthless and infamous pack of fools and knaves, without the slightest value in regard to the performance of their functions, and yet formidable to the citizens, on account of their acts of unprovoked and lawless oppression. It was evident that little could be expected from such a motley assortment of French, Spanish, German and Swiss adventurers, nine-tenths of whom had been but a short time in the country.

Notwithstanding every attempt to remodel the force on a stable and efficient footing, such was the prejudice entertained by honest citizens against an organization that was looked upon by the whole community with unqualified opprobrium, that many years elapsed before, by slow gradations, the corps was improved with competent officers. To be a policeman was a badge of degradation, and it was not before Recorder Baldwin's first advent to office that the body was noticeably bettered. Winters, up town ; Youennes, in the Second District now, and Eugene Mazerat, in the Third, gave tone and character to the organizations under their control, and when Mayor Crossman assumed the reins of government he was enabled through their instrumentality to reconstruct a force respectable in numbers and reputation, which subsequently became the nucleus around which has gathered the present police.

It cannot be expected that within the compass of a few pages the subject which I have so imperfectly broached should be fully developed. The history of the First District is one of wonderful achievements and surprises. Pluck, genius and sagacity are the groundwork upon which its commercial importance and *élan* were founded.

A tragical event, connected with the defence of a magistrate's habitation and home, attracted, in 1836, general attention and became the subject of universal interest. The story is worth relating.

This deplorable catastrophe was the outgrowth of a judicial decision in a case in which much sectional and racial feeling had been displayed. It was termed the Giquel-Brooks affair. It seems that in a *rencontre* that took place on Royal street, the latter had been shot to death under circumstances denoting malice and premeditation. Serious troubles had previously existed between the parties. A trip to Mexico, undertaken by Brooks, had put a temporary stop to their quarrel, but, on his return, after an interval of several months, he resolved to definitely settle the matter. An interview was, therefore, agreed upon, during which Mr. Giquel indulged in very provoking language. It only served to widen the breach. Irritated by this conduct, the deceased withdrew, and immediately sent a friend with a demand for satisfaction. The reply was a request for fifteen minutes' time for deliberation, which was granted, but, instead of awaiting the return of the messenger and delivering his promised answer, the challenged party forthwith repaired to the office of the Recorder of the Second Municipality and preferred a charge against Brooks.

Thus stood matters, when the adversaries again met in Royal street, near St. Peter. An affray resulted, and the unfortunate Brooks, shot through the heart, lay stretched upon the pavement. Giquel was conveyed to the Mayor's office and admitted to bail on an appearance bond.

This unfortunate occurrence threw the whole city into a state of great commotion, for the deceased was generally liked and esteemed. He was buried the same evening, and his funeral *cortége* was followed to the grave by a large concourse of friends and citizen soldiers.

At the close of the judicial proceedings before the

committing magistrate, the privilege of bail was revoked ; whereupon, he was committed to prison on the charge of murder.

Public opinion was pretty equally divided as to the propriety of the course of Judge Préval in withholding from him the benefit of, what some deemed, a constitutional right ; the people up town, who had taken sides, as usual, against the Creole, warmly espousing the former's ruling. Among the military organizations—a crack one, by the way—which, from its character and high-toned membership, exercised a great influence in the upper section of the city, was the "Washington Guards," of which Brooks for some time had been an active and highly esteemed member. They had attended his funeral in a body, and had vowed over his grave that justice should be meted out at any and every cost. The friends of Giquel, on the other hand, were not less active or persevering. They engaged eminent counsel, and resolved to exhaust every legal remedy before giving up the struggle. It was evident that the antagonistic parties were terribly in earnest, and reasonable men began to apprehend mischief.

Thus stood matters, when, on September 2, 1836, a writ of *habeas corpus* was applied for before Joachim Bermudez, judge of the parish court, and father of our lamented late Chief Justice. Upon the bench, he was the ideal of the upright magistrate. Cold, austere, and yet scrupulously attentive, he kept under perfect control the impulses of a naturally passionate and impressionable temperament ; heedless of friend or foe, and unswervingly obedient to the call of duty and honor. Out of court, he was one of the most amiable, entertaining and amusing *raconteurs* I ever knew. Brave to a fault, he had been engaged in his earlier years in several affairs of honor, and was known to be as expert with the pistol as he was familiar with his Civil Code. He was proud of his noble Spanish lineage, of his race and of its traditions.

Such was the man before whose tribunal angry faces soon grouped themselves. The atmosphere of the court room was filled with threatening rumors and dire menaces, and, as the judge calmly surveyed the turbulent element before him, he inwardly smiled at the idea that any populace should ever conceive the idea of frightening him from the performance of his judicial functions.

After the traditional *oyez*, *oyez*, *oyez* of the sheriff had been commanded, the attorneys, after offering evidence, commenced the argument, which was prolonged not only during that day, but continued to the following. No man in that room was a more attentive listener than the judge, who, note-book in hand, jotted down every authority cited and each salient point. Upon his strong and impressive face, in his jet-black eyes, set under shaggy eye-brows, not a trace of emotion, not a clue to the inward workings of his intellect could be traced. When the case was finally submitted, leisurely taking up the papers, he calmly informed the lawyers that he wished to deliberately read the evidence before announcing his opinion, which, he added, was nearly made up. Two hours afterward, amid the muttered curses of the baffled enemies of Giquel, the latter was released from confinement on a fifteen thousand dollars' bond.

To a casual observer it was evident that trouble was brewing, and that the life of the intrepid judge was in great peril. Friends crowded around him to afford him protection, but these he quietly dismissed, simply remarking that the only danger he apprehended was a skulking assassin's bullet. Face to face he feared no man.

On the evening of the 5th of September, 1836, while quietly enjoying a smoke at home by the side of his devoted wife, a violent ringing of the door bell apprised them of the presence of visitors. These consisted of three friends, one of whom was Toutant Beauregard, a young dentist, who had come in haste to inform him that a party of desperate men were banding together to lynch the judge, and offering their services for his protection. Bermudez said nothing, but there was something grim and terrible in his smile at this attempt to overawe the independence of the judiciary. Absenting himself for a few moments, he returned with his household weapons. Delivering a beautifully chased double-barreled shotgun to Beauregard, he simply remarked : "It is loaded." Then placing his broad-sword against the mantel-piece corner, he quietly resumed his seat by a side table, on which were resting two formidable cavalry pistols, and added: "Now let them come." Of the five persons composing the group in the parlor of that silent mansion on Bayou Road, between Rampart and Burgundy, none appeared so cool and unconcerned as the intended victim. As the hours sped on every neck was craned to catch the least suspicious sound. The night was hushed in death-like stillness, and, save the hurried pace of some belated wayfarer, nothing seemed to denote the proximity of danger. All of a sudden a crash was heard at the door, which flew wide open from the violence of an unseen pressure. As quick as thought, Beauregard rushed to the spot with gun in hand, but a heavy stroke from a cutlass bore the weapon down, which was harmlessly discharged. An enraged crowd then poured into the sitting-room, but were dumfounded at the sight of Mrs. Bermudez, who, grasping her husband's sabre, had placed herself between the latter and his assailants, and by frequent and well directed blows was compelling them to retreat in shame.

Meanwhile the judge was not idle, as a corpse on the carpet and the escaping form of a mortally wounded aggressor fully attested. His brace of pistols had done their deadly work. Beauregard and his two companions followed in pursuit, and must have done some service, as several were wounded in this disgraceful affray. A dead body was discovered later on in Esplanade street.

One of the victims was a member of the "Washington Guards." Fearing that if a military parade attended the funeral some disturbance might again disturb the public peace, Captain Hozey, who was a man of nerve and sound judgment, ordered the soldier companions of the deceased to turn out in citizens' clothes. He was a thorough disciplinarian, and, after the obsequies were over, so confident was he of the fidelity of his men to the cause of law and order, that he proffered their services to the Mayor as a guard to the judge's residence. But the proposition was gratefully declined, as public opinion had too strongly set in against any renewed disorders. Peace and calm reflection had reassumed their mastery.

Such are the sad details of an affair which, forming part of the history of our judiciary, has been long a subject of comment among the older members of the bar. Judge Bermudez seldom spoke of the subject, and only when questioned by intimate friends. I believe no one regretted the occurrence more than he did, for he was kind, chivalrous and humane, never exhibiting anger except under strong provocation.

CHAPTER XV.

OLD LOUISIANA DAYS.

A UNIQUE SCENE IN COURT — ZACHARY TAYLOR AND
WM. O. BUTLER — KENTUCKY TROOPS ASKING FOR THEIR
DISCHARGE — JEAN GRAVIER — HIS EARLY HISTORY AND
MISERABLE DEATH — A SAD RECORD OF INGRATITUDE —
HISTORY OF THE BATTURE CASE — THE CLAY MONUMENT
— THE LAYING OF THE CORNER STONE — MASONIC CERE-
MONIES — PUBLIC ADDRESSES, ETC. — THE INQUISITION
IN LOUISIANA — PRINCES IN EXILE — LOUIS PHILIPPE IN
NEW ORLEANS — THE MARIGNYS IN PARIS — AN EDITOR
MOBBED — HIS PRINTING OFFICE GUTTED — THE TROOPS
CALLED OUT.

The Fifth District Court of New Orleans was, on Friday, July 7, 1848, the scene of a singular occurrence.
On that occasion there appeared as litigants before Judge
A. M. Buchanan no less personages than the Whig candidate for the Presidency of the United States and the
Democratic nominee for the Vice Presidency. I allude
to Major Generals Zachary Taylor and William O. Butler.
The judge looked unusually dignified and impressed,
and appeared to be struck by the peculiar coincidence.
These two distinguished postulants for the highest offices
in the gift of the people, heroes on many glorious battle
fields, were dressed in the simple garb of citizens, and

acted as though they recognized their amenability to the tribunals of the country. *Cedant arma togæ.* It was a grateful and practical illustration of our republican institutions. A large concourse of spectators were in attendance, among whom were officers of the army and members of the bar, attracted by the novel character of the proceedings. Such a thing as the candidates of the two great political parties being brought " into court " had never happened within the memory of the oldest clerk or sheriff, and they never expected to look upon the like again.

The cause of the appearance of these illustrious officers before our judiciary originated in this wise : Some of the volunteers who had recently arrived from Mexico, tired of the dull routine of camp duty and the strictness of military service, had determined to obtain their discharge by an application to the courts. Accordingly a petition was prepared and presented to Judge Buchanan, which set forth, in substance, that George W. Eames, Wm. P. Payne, Thomas M. Davis, etc., of the Fourth Regiment of Kentucky Volunteers, had enlisted and been mustered into the service of the United States " for the term of the war with Mexico ; " that on the 2d of June, 1848, at the city of Mexico, General Butler, then commander in chief of the army, published general orders to the brigade in which petitioners were serving, that the war was ended ; that petitioners marched to Vera Cruz, and were thence transported to New Orleans, where they arrived on the 5th of July ; and, after demand and refusal of their discharge, they, in pursuance of their rights and privileges as citizens of the United States, which they enjoyed in common with every other citizen under the Constitution and laws of the United States, entered the city of New Orleans without asking the permission or consent of Col. John S. Williams (colonel of their regiment) Gen. Wm. O. Butler or Gen. Z. Taylor; in consequence of this act they had been arrested and placed in the custody of Sergeant Proctor, and are now in his custody and defrauded of their rights; that, by the terms of their enlistment and contract, on the 4th of October, 1847, they had bound themselves to serve the United States faithfully for and during the *term of the then* existing war with Mexico, but for a no longer period; that the war with Mexico had expired; that they had been duly notified of this fact by a general order issued and published at Ayutla, in the Republic of Mexico, on the 2d of June, 1848, by Major General Butler; that this was the only way known to the laws of the United States by which, as soldiers, they could be officially notified of the expiration of their term of service.

They therefore respectfully asked that a writ of *habeas corpus* might issue in their behalf, directed to John S. Williams, colonel of the Fourth Regiment Kentucky Volunteers; Major General Wm. O. Butler, Major General Zachary Taylor and Brevet Brigadier General Geo. M. Brooks, by whose joint orders and authority they had been deprived of their liberty and kept in custody; and that they might receive their full and final release, and further their final discharge from the service of the United States as soldiers thereof.

The answer or more technically speaking, the "return" of General Taylor to the writ, set forth in substance that the said complainants were soldiers of the United States, by voluntary enlistment, and as such belonged exclusively to the command of General Butler, who was now in court and ready to answer for their supposed illegal capture and detention. He further said that he had not at the time of the issuing of the said writ, nor had he at any time since, in any way disturbed or restrained the personal liberty of the said complainants, and prayed to be hence discharged. General Brooks' answer was similar, and disclaimed any interference with their personal freedom.

The answer of General Butler was a square and unreserved denial of the right of the volunteers to the relief applied for.

The case of the complainants had been entrusted to S. S. Prentiss, the most fervid, eloquent and brilliant orator of the South. His effort was masterly.

The points involved were two-fold—1. Could the war be said to have terminated before official proclamation of a treaty of peace? 2. At what place were the troops to be disbanded? At the place of their enlistment or at the first point of American territory reached?

Judge Buchanan decided the case against the applicants. After an exhaustive review of the salient objections offered, he thus concluded his opinion:

" In the meantime, and pending the unavoidable delays attending the mustering out of the service and paying off of the different corps enlisted for the war, it appears to me absolutely indispensable that the military organization should be preserved. Without the salutary restraints of military discipline, an army degenerates into a mob, and the worst of mobs, the terror of any community which may be unfortunate enough to be in contact with it. The military organization seems to me no less indispensable in the interest of the soldier himself during the necessary delays which must elapse between the landing of the Fourth Kentucky Regiment, for example, at New Orleans, and its discharge at Louisville. For, how can the muster rolls be verified at

Louisville, unless the men are kept together in New Orleans, and on the passage up the rivers Mississippi and Ohio?

"In conclusion, I may be permitted to say that I do not see any good reason for the anticipation of evil expressed by the eloquent counsel of the petitioners, should the orders of the War Department be allowed to take effect in relation to the volunteers. The eulogium which that gentleman has passed upon the care and attention bestowed by the distinguished Commander in Chief of the army in Mexico upon the comfort and wants of his troops is no less just than exalted. The troops have certainly been forwarded thus far on their way home with unexampled dispatch, and we are fully warranted in believing that the concluding stages of their return route will be equally expeditious. Should I grant the prayer of these petitioners, I might find myself obliged to add to my already somewhat onerous duties those of mustering officer and paymaster of the forces. I doubt whether our gallant soldiers would benefit by my assumption of these novel judicial duties. But, without any jest (which is, perhaps, misplaced upon this really important occasion), my interference in the premises, it appears to me, would be liable to the grave charge of unconstitutionality, by trenching upon the special department of the executive authority of the nation."

These proceedings, so novel in their character, and so far-reaching in their effects, had become a *quasi* national question, and had assumed to some extent the character of an important factor in the presidential campaign, then pending. Prentiss, as it is well known, was a strong, if not an original supporter of the gallant hero of Palo Alto and Buena Vista, and the capture of the

Kentucky vote and adjoining States was a matter of deep concern to the Whigs. Viewed in that light, the case was semi-political.

A peculiar feature of this application for a writ of *habeas corpus* was its striking analogy to the question involved in the defence of General Jackson before Judge Dominick A. Hall, when charged with flagrant contempt. The reader will remember that on that occasion, the French citizens, who had enlisted to defend Louisiana from invasion, claimed their discharge on the ground that the enemy had retired from our territory, and that a treaty of peace had been concluded between the belligerent powers. General Jackson refused their request, basing his action upon the fact that if such was the fact, the same had never been officially promulgated or made known to him by his government. Then it was that Louallier, a Frenchman by birth, but a patriotic member of our State Legislature, energetically protested against this view of the case, in an able but rather intemperate article published in the Louisiana *Courier*. Thereupon Jackson caused him to be arrested. A writ of *habeas corpus* was issued in his behalf in Judge Hall's court. Old Hickory, to use his characteristic expression, "jugged the judge," and sent him out of his lines. Thus it will be perceived, one of the main incidental points of the question, as to the effect of the treaty, rested upon its "promulgation."

The decision of the court was acquiesced in cheerfully and promptly by all parties in interest, and warmly commended by the Federal authorities in Washington. Though harshly dealt with as they thought the Kentuckians remained within their barracks, attentive to their duties and obedient to the orders of their superiors, thus giving the highest evidence of their patriotism and respect for the laws of their country.

In a dingy cabin, situated in the most retired spot of the obscurest portion of the faubourg St. Mary, passed away from life on the 1st day of October, 1834, at the age of ninety-five years, Jean Gravier, a native of Bergerac, department of Dordogne, France. He had been a resident of New Orleans for nearly half a century, and was known by everybody for the heavy monetary transactions in which he had been engaged, and the vast land speculations into which he had plunged. He had been the possessor of untold thousands, accumulated by dint of thrift, sagacity and scrupulous honesty—a wealth subsequently scattered to the winds by envious, artful and dishonorable schemers. After having been the lord and master of that vast extent of territory, which once formed the faubourg St. Mary, besides its valuable *banlieu*, as it was then termed, he died in a condition of abject indigence, occasioned by vexatious law suits instituted by former beneficiaries of his unbounded charity and munificence, and only left muniments and evidences of title to very large estates.

Louisianians may well afford to throw a few flowers, I will not say upon his tomb, for he had none, but over the memory of one of our most remarkable city founders. Though reviled and derided by people whose low instincts precluded them forming a just appreciation of his character—he was in the Christian meaning of the term the type of a good Samaritan. With his emaciated body was also interred the recollection of his many good deeds. During the last period of his earthly career he had been the object of attack from designing ingrates, who sought by every means known to the law to dispossess him of his long-acquired acres, and to precipitate him in his decrepid and imbecile state into a condition of hopeless embarrassment. Those who enjoyed his friendship and confidence invariably avowed that notwithstanding these cruel persecutions, he never recriminated or injured any one, but bore his misfortunes with fortitude and resignation. In fact, at the very time when perfidious advisers were urging him on to his ruin, he never brought suit against any of his debtors, although it was a well-known fact that many among them were in a condition to easily liquidate their liabilities, and by so doing have relieved him of his pressing necessities.

Though reduced to penury and abandonment by the wretches whom he had enriched, it can not be denied that in every situation in life, his doors were ever open to the needy and the unfortunate. A fact not generally known is that he was a physician by profession. Combining a thorough knowledge of chemistry with a long medical experience, he had devoted a large portion of his life to the successful treatment of the sick, not for the sake of lucre and speculation, but solely in the interest of suffering humanity. Notwithstanding the weight of advancing age, he would hie himself on foot wherever called, and unlike certain members of the faculty that we all wot of, never looked around the poor man's bedroom to ascertain the value of his furniture. In the cholera and yellow fever epidemics that preceded his death, and scourged New Orleans with such a merciless hand, his efforts night and day were unceasing, and to his superior knowledge in the science of healing is probably due, during that eventful period, the preservation of the writer's maternal grandmother's life.

What adds humiliation to the catastrophe which deprived the community of this virtuous citizen, was the state of complete want into which he had fallen, being destitute of the most ordinary necessaries of life. Not one among the hundreds whom he had frequently succored through the sad vicissitudes of life, ever came to his deserted habitation, or offered him the least comfort or relief. Hungry, helpless and unhelped, they allowed him to die like a dog—I know of no expression more applicable to his fate—without even the last rites of religion. And yet among these were some who owned properties derived from his benevolence ; others, who had purchased from him entire squares of ground for a mere pittance, though of great value, paid in cotton seed, old clothes, and other rubbish ; others, incarnate Shylocks, who had foreclosed their mortgages on large plantations, at the very period when his financial straits rendered it materially impossible for him to redeem his engagements. They fell upon him like birds of prey upon the dying soldier on the battle-field, and never ceased their tormenting attacks upon his quivering frame until life itself had become extinct.

But I am mistaken when I say no one visited him in his dying moments. Several lawyers with litigating claimants at their heels attended his agony, and obtruded their noxious presence upon the privacy and sanctity of his last hours on earth, without bestowing a single thought upon his comfort, spiritual or physical. They had come to witness his demise, as a matter of judicial form, and to affix the seal of the law to his papers and effects. What cared they for his body or its proper inhumation ? Is it needless to say that they never gave a thought to his funeral—one worthy of a man who had played such an important part in the city's history—except to convey the information of his death

to the town sexton. Fearing to be called upon to con-
tribute a few dollars, they notified none of his friends,
so that Jean Gravier, who had been thrice a millionaire,
was buried in a pauper's grave. His corpse, covered
with the vermin-eaten rags that had enveloped his
body during his long, lingering sickness, was thrust
into a rude cypress coffin, thrown upon a dray, taken
out without any attendants to the old Catholic cemetery, and there literally dumped into a slimy hole,
which had been dug with difficulty through the decay-
ing and crumbling fragments of those who had preceded
him in that last dismal abode. Not even a cross or
wooden tablet was erected to mark his final resting
place, where friend or wayfarer might have stopped to
ponder over the strange fortunes of a man who had
exceeded by a quarter of a century the span of life
allotted to frail mortality—a life spent in alternate seasons of opulence and squalid poverty. Forcibly does
his fate recall to mind the lines of the poet :

> " Optima quoque dies miseris mortalibus,
>   Prima fugit; subeunt morbi, tristisque senectus,
>   Et labor, et duro rapit inclementia mortis!"

Connected with the growth and incipient development
of the city of New Orleans, the life of Jean Gravier is
replete with historic interest. His long and celebrated
litigation, begun in 1806, and involving the right of
ownership in and to the " batture " in front of the city,
above Canal street, constitutes in our jurisprudence an
era as marked and distinct as that which subsequently
characterized the " Gaines Case "—a case which, in the
opinion of ancient denizens, yet living and cognizant of
facts of universal notoriety, dispossessed thousands of
their rightful properties and of their honest earnings.

Not so with the batture case **referred to,** which now forms part of the domain of our **State history,** and the particulars of which are described in an entertaining manner by Mr. Gayarré in his treatise on the "American Domination" of Louisiana. This immense and valuable tract, acquired in part by Edward Livingston, as transferee of Gravier and in consideration of professional services rendered, was "a piece of land of comparatively recent formation." "It had been occupied," says that author, "as a common by the city for many years previous, and the title which the city had to it was, in the opinion of the inhabitants, unquestionable. It had happened, however, that Livingston had prosecuted with success his claim, and in pursuance of a decree of the Superior Court of the Territory, the plaintiff had been put in possession by the sheriff. A few days afterward Livingston employed a number of negroes to commence the digging of a canal which he projected to make in a part of the land decreed to him by the court, but the citizens assembled in considerable force and drove him off. On the day following, Livingston went again to the land in question with a view of exercising his rights of ownership, but was again opposed by the citizens."

The history to the title to this most valuable piece of property is little known, though connected with an event fraught with interest to the Catholic church. It had been originally owned by the Jesuits and purchased in parcels. The first acquisition was made in 1726 from Bienville, Governor of the province; the second from the same party in 1728, and the residue in 1743, from a Mr. LeBreton.

In the year 1763, the order of the Jesuits having been abolished by a Papal bull, all their estates were forfeited to the crown. Although the province had been already ceded by France to Spain, yet as the treaty had been kept a profound secret and was not put into execution until six years thereafter, the edict of confiscation was enforced for the benefit of the former nation only, and under it the property was seized and disposed of. The portion of this land, adjudged to the city, was purchased by persons from whom it passed to Bertrand Gravier, Jean's brother, who cultivated it as a plantation.

The various phases which the contention over this possession of our river front assumed are fully described in our several histories, to which the reader must refer for details and particulars. Suffice it to say, that Gravier's claim to the ownership of the land was finally confirmed. It was worth millions of dollars. Engaged meanwhile in interminable law suits, the natural offshoot of this protracted litigation, he found himself compelled, as we have already seen, to dispose by piecemeal, and for trifling values, large sections in that growing part of our city.

Some time ago, while looking over a lot of old musty records, my eyes chanced to fall upon a partial list of property advertised at his succession sale. I say partial, for the estate to be disposed of then comprised only that portion extending from Dryades street back to Bolivar. This was several years after his death. What disposition was made of the residue of his property I am unable to say, but the records of the old "Probate Court" are still attainable, I believe. One thing however is undoubted, that at the time of his demise, he was possessed of a fortune sufficiently large to have warranted the outlay necessary to have furnished his prostrate frame with proper nourishment, and his vermin-covered body with a decent Christian burial! Gravier street is now the only reminder left of his name and good deeds.

A remarkable event in the history of New Orleans was the laying and dedication of the corner stone to the monument of Henry Clay, at the intersection of Canal and Royal streets. Under the auspices of the "Clay Monumental Association," of which I happened to be an humble member, this tribute to the memory of a great and good American was raised in commemoration of heroic deeds achieved in the councils of the nation, on behalf of American industry, nationality and honor.

It is needless to say who Henry Clay was. No one came nearer in touch with the people than he. He was not only a typical Southerner, with all his vices and foibles, but a statesmen above the prejudices of section, caste or sectionalism. His eloquence was magnetic. His popularity was immense. Under the spell of his silvery voice, thousands were attracted under his banner, and unswervingly stood by him. In Louisiana, where he was a frequent visitor, and in which state his daughter had been married to a member of the Duralde family, he was looked upon as one to the "manner born." His frequent sojourns with his intimate friend, Judge Alexander Porter, of St. Mary, are well remembered by the old time inhabitants of Franklin, and have furnished material for very pleasant reminiscences.

Saturday, April 12, 1856, the anniversary of the illustrious orator's birth, was the day selected for the commemorative manifestation. It was a great occasion of gala in New Orleans. At dawn loud peals of artillery awoke the slumbering city and announced the approach of the auspicious event. Manual work and trade were practically suspended, and the town seemed to have turned out *en masse* to enjoy the delightful spring time and do honor to the event. Early in the morning our streets began to be thronged with people, and military companies with music and banners, as well as civic societies, were to be seen moving from every direction. The galleries on Canal street, especially those in the vicinity of Royal street, were crowded with beautiful and gayly attired ladies. Difficult would be the task of describing at length the brilliant pageant which was to be seen along every avenue leading to the spot about to be consecrated to the memory of the illustrious orator and sage. In the procession our uniformed companies, firemen, benevolent societies and trades unions had been assigned appropriate positions. At 1 o'clock P. M., when the ceremonies were about to proceed, the large platform erected for the accommodation of the " Clay Association " and invited guests was surrounded by a compact mass of upturned faces.

The laying of the corner stone was entrusted to the Masonic fraternity of which Henry Clay had been an active and illustrious member.

The ceremonies began by the officers of the Grand Lodge, clad in their appropriate regalia, reading the Manual Prayer, after which, in a cavity of the stone, the following memoranda were placed :

1. Life of Henry Clay, by George D. Prentice.

2. Life and Times of Henry Clay, by Calvin Cotton.

3. Private correspondence of Henry Clay.

4. The names of the President of the United States and his Cabinet, of the Governor of Louisiana and State officers, of the Mayor of the city of New Orleans and city officers, the officers of the customs, and the officers of the Clay Monumental Association; also copies of the daily papers of New Orleans, April 12, 1856, a copy of

the Civil Code of Louisiana, and one of the several coins of the United States.

5. A brass plate bearing the incription :

" This corner stone of a monument erected to the memory of Henry Clay was laid on the 12th day of April, A. D. 1856, A. L. 5856, by the M. W. G. Lodge of Free and Accepted Masons of the State of Louisiana ; W. M. Perkins, Grand Master ; H. H. Dorson, D. G. M. ; S. O. Scruggs, J. G. W.; L. Texada, S. G. W.; S. C. Mitchell, G. T.; Samuel G. Risk, Grand Secretary.''

At the conclusion of this ceremonial a portion of the militia, tired with marching and exposure to the sun, filed off toward their armories. The spectacle presented as they moved away in the distance, with music and flaunting banners was grand. Then came the singing of a French ode, composed by that gifted Creole poet, Dominique Rouquette, set to music by Prévost, the leader of the French Opera, in which the entire troupe of artists, accompanied by their orchestra, participated. Listened to with enthusiastic applause, it was one of the great surprises of the occasion.

Judge Theodore McCaleb then delivered the oration. As might have been expected, the distinguished orator handled his fruitful theme in a masterly manner. He began by reviewing the present grandeur, prosperity and power of the American Republic, and the influence which the wise counsels of Clay and our other great statesmen of the last fifty years had exercised in bringing about this glorious consummation ; continued by an allusion to the power of the sculptor's art in ancient and modern times to perpetuate grand and heroic deeds, and to inspire the youth of the country with ambitious thoughts ; compared the lives and achievements of Clay and Jackson ; reviewed the evidences of the love for the

Union which still throbbed in the hearts of the American people, and concluded by an eloquent appeal, in the course of which he denounced the proposition, which was being actively discussed, of forming a great " Southern party " to resist the aggressions of the North.

The discourse of Judge McCaleb was succeeded by an address from that accomplished daughter of Alabama, Mme. Octavia Walton Le Vert, which was read in a very effective style by the popular young orator, Charles D. Dreux ; after which the festival concluded with the reading, by the author, M. F. Bigney, Esq., of an interesting ode. I regret that space prevents me from publishing it in its entirety. It began as follows :

> " Lonely the mill boy wends his weary way,
>   Too soon inured to toil. A mother's wants—
> A widowed mother's—claim his young regard,
> And labor is a pleasure. Sometimes thoughts
> Prophetic of the future, start his soul,
>   And give ambition wings. Golden and grand,
> The hills of Fame, in the dim distance, rise
> All spangled o'er with triumphs, and he feels
> That he can mount with an earnest tread,
> And wreath a fadeless chaplet for his brow;
>   Nature is his instructor—trees and flowers;
> The sparkling gems in Night's cerulean dome;
> The springtime warblers, and th' insensate clod,
> All teach him wondrous love. Bright as the sheen
> Of an archangel's wing, his thoughts take form
> In rudimental beauty, but his tongue,
>   As yet unskilled in verbal witcheries,
> All vainly strives to give them fitting speech."

It concluded as follows :

> " Gone is the peerless commoner, self-made,
>   Whose acts were all a triumph; who, to gain
> The proudest honors in a nation's gift,
> Would ne'er forsake the right; and now, his praise
> Falls from all lips in heart-felt gratitude.

Fitting it is his cenotaph to rear
In view of the glad waters of that tide
Whose commerce speaks his constant eulogy;
This is the corner stone; and here to-day
Assembled thousands see it fairly laid.
Above, to bear his fame to latest time
In monumental marble, shall arise
The faint translation of a grateful thought
Which swells in every breast for Henry Clay."

A detachment of the Mobile military, consisting of the Mobile Cadets, infantry and rifles, under the commands of Captains Sands, Chamberlain and Bissell, which had arrived in the morning, assisted in celebrating the day. Quarters were provided for them at the St. Louis Hotel by the " Continentals," and a number of invited guests, including Governor Wickliffe, ex-Governor Hébert, Mayor Lewis, and other representative gentlemen, sat down to a sumptuous banquet at that noted hostelry. Numerous toasts were drank and speeches made, and "the feast of reason and the flow of soul" was kept up for several hours, when the greater part of the company repaired to the St. Charles Theatre, by invitation of Manager Ben. DeBar.

Thus ended the ceremonies of the laying of the corner stone of a monument, which for nearly four decades has been a proud landmark in the history of New Orleans. It is to be regretted that so much has been said about the removal of the statue. It is not long ago that the *fiat* went forth. Whether the mandate will be obeyed or not, is, at the time I am writing these lines, a matter of conjecture. Monopolies usually carry the day over patriotic attachments. Iconoclasts are not lacking in this generation. The " almighty dollar " seems to have invaded the sanctuaries consecrated by the affections of our fathers, and to have expelled therefrom those holy memories which sanctify, as it were, the glorious past. Around the base of that bronze "a counterfeit presentment" of a pure and great American patriot, cluster events not easily forgotten, not the least important of which was the congregation of that noble band who, in 1874, under the inspiration of a Marr, and the fervid appeals of an Ellis and an Ogden, summoned an oppressed community to arms, and taught tyrants how frail was their tenure upon the fealty and respect of the people.

It was in later years, a very short time before the internecine war between the States, that the bronze statue of Henry Clay, molded and executed by Hart, a native Kentuckian, was placed upon its pedestal.

If it be a grateful duty on the part of a historian to rescue from oblivion the meritorious deeds of men, who have contributed to the cause of humanity and civilization, far more noble is the task which conscience imposes upon him to turn aside the shafts leveled by the hand of calumny. A long suffering victim from this system of persecution was Pére Antoine, the weak and charitable monk who, for more than fifty years, officiated in our midst. What makes his case more deserving of sympathy is the fact that the thrusts directed against his good name and religious character should have been aimed at him in the very house of his friends, and by persons high in authority in the church itself. The charges that have been preferred against his ministry are numerous and are even now recorded in the archives of the propaganda at Rome. Of this fact no doubt exists. Hence, the wide divergence in opinion which now exists, not only among the laity of Louisiana, but on the part of the Catholic clergy at large, as to the verity of the accusations laid to his charge. Among these is that of his attempt to introduce the Inquisition in the colony, which so alarmed the fears and conscience of the Spanish governor as to induce that functionary to exile the fanatical priest beyond the jurisdiction of the territory. In this matter there is an intermixture of truth with fiction, which gives a far more sombre coloring to this episode than the facts will justify, and this I propose clearly to demonstrate to the most obtuse and prejudiced reader. Let a plain, unvarnished statement of the facts unfold the tale. It is a historical fact that wherever Spain exercised dominion, whether in Mexico, Peru, Cuba, or her North American possessions, the peculiar institutions of the mother country were engrafted upon it and became a part and parcel of her colonial system of government, subject only to such limitations and modifications as might be imposed by the King. State and church, of which the Santa Hermandad formed a not inconsiderable part, being blended together by almost indissoluble ties, the Inquisition by the mere transfer of the territory from France to Spain, became *ipso facto* incorporated into its political machinery. Thus we find that in 1769, immediately after the unfortunate execution of the Louisiana patriots and the unfurling of the Spanish flag upon the Plaza de Armas, Governor O'Reilly, in assuming charge of the new acquisition of his royal master, issued his *Bando de Gobierno*, or rules, for the government of the people, in which edict, among other equally important matters, I find the following article : "The principal object of the institution of the tribunal of the Santa Hermandad being to repress disorder and to prevent the robberies and assassinations committed in unfrequented places by vagabonds and delinquents who conceal themselves

in the woods, from which they sally and attack travelers and the neighboring inhabitants, the Alcalde
Mayor Provincial shall assemble a sufficient number
of members or brothers of the Santa Hermandad (Inquisition) to clear his jurisdiction of the perpetrators
of such evil deeds, by pursuing them with spirit, seiz-
ing or putting them to death.'' This was on the 25th
of November, 1769. Now, when we bear in mind that
Pére Antoine landed in New Orleans in the year 1779,
ten years after the event above recorded ; that he was
instituted curate of the Parochial Church of St. Louis
on the 25th of November, 1785, and was sent back to
Spain by Governor Miro in the beginning of 1789 for
an alleged attempt to introduce the Inquisition here,
the charge naturally falls to the ground. As instituted,
defined and limited by General O'Reilly's supreme
edict, we clearly see that the formidable society whose
erstwhile excesses in Europe and America had sown so
many seeds of discord even in the bosom of the church
itself, had been shorn of all its former powers and entrusted solely with duties preservative of peace, order
and government. This fact should always be borne in
mind if we desire to arrive at the exact truth and to
analyze fairly and conscientiously the motives of the act
which led to his expulsion from the colony. O'Reilly's
Bando de Gobierno was never repealed, and such being
the case, was as obligatory upon the Governor as it
was upon the humblest layman. Another fact which
it may be well here to notice is that in Spain the duties
of the Holy Office were relegated to the Capuchin
monks, of which order Pére Antoine was a member.
Hence, it can not be a source of much surprise that he
should have been commissioned by the superior of the
fraternity in the mother country, to whom he owed re-

spect and obedience, with the duty of putting into operation the existing law. This letter he received on the 5th of December, 1788. It caused him much anxiety and trouble. The duties imposed upon him by his beloved parish church were onerous and demanded all his care and time. In this perturbed condition of mind he kept his appointment secret, and it was only in the beginning of the following year that he concluded to apprise Gov. Miro of the fact by laying before him his commission as the head of the Holy Inquisition in Louisiana and the instructions which he had received from Spain.

From all the facts which I can glean from contemporaneous data, the attitude of Pére Antoine toward the chief of the civil authority of the colony was humble, respectful and by no means intolerant. He informed that functionary that he had been urged in a letter received by him from the "competent authorities" to discharge his new duties with the greatest fidelity and zeal, and in conformity with the *royal will*. To give effect to the mission entrusted to his fidelity he requested the Governor to furnish him with a *posse*, as required by the rules laid down by O'Reilly. To this course Miro was averse. As the secular arm was necessary to enforce the law, a simple, manly refusal on his part would have sufficed to strike the proceeding with nullity. But he followed a different course. He received the friar with apparent cordiality, promised to grant him his request, at the very time that in his mind he was planning the ruin of his unsuspecting countryman. In this whole transaction the conduct of Miro was insincere, unjust, arbitrary and unworthy of the reputation of one of Louisiana's most enlightened governors. When Pére Antoine went back to his parish, his mind was apparently relieved, unsuspicious of any lurking danger. But within twenty-four hours after the interview, a platoon of soldiers filed into his bed-room and forcibly carried him to a ship about to sail for Cadiz. This was done in accordance with orders issued from headquarters. Thus, like a common male-factor or convicted felon, was the priest transported beyond the seas.

Miro, in a special report bearing date June 3, 1789, thus speaks of the affair : '' When I read the communi-cation of that Capuchin, I shuddered. His Majesty has ordered me to foster the increase of population in this province * * * The mere mention of the Inquisition uttered in New Orleans would be sufficient not only to check immigration, which is successfully progressing, but would also be capable of driving away those who have recently come, and, I even fear that in spite of my having sent out of the country Father Sedella, the most frightful consequences may ensue from the mere sus-picion of the cause of his dismissal.''

Such is, I believe, a correct version of the humiliating difficulty in which the good and, perhaps, misguided old man became involved. As to the Inquisition itself, al-though constituting a part of the governmental ma-chinery of State, its existence in our State was merely nominal. I do not think that O'Reilly's ordinance was ever enforced. If so, it must have been under another designation, and under a different system.

As the general reader is aware, New Orleans was visited, in 1798, during the administration of the Mar-quis de Casa Calvo, by the exiled Orleans princes, one of whom, traveling under the name of Philippe de Co-mine, subsequently became known as Louis-Philippe, King of the French.

During his sojourn among us, which was of several months' duration, he was a familiar figure in our streets, and in his association with our people was unpretending and democratic. His early training had served him in good stead, not to speak of the rough edges which a wandering life had tossed him against. He had taken up his residence with Philip Marigny, father of Bernard and grandfather of Mandeville, whose late demise has been so deeply regretted, and enjoyed the hospitalities of the neighboring gentry, who strove to make him and his brothers as happy and comfortable as possible. He was also for some time the guest of Julien Poydras, whom he accompanied to his home in Pointe Coupee, with the view of studying the inner history of plantation life and African slavery. Whatever may have been his conclusions in relation thereto I have had no means of determining, but, if one may be permitted to judge from his subsequent actions, there is reason to believe that the rigidity and sternness with which through his fleet, armed cruisers, he enforced the suppression of the traffic in human flesh off the coast of Africa in after years, were in some measure prompted by his early reminiscences and experience in Louisiana.

His associates and "cicerones" in his rambles around the city and suburbs were the D'Aunoys, the DeClouets, Col. Bellechasse, and, last, though not least, the gritty Irishman named Daniel Clark, who was then occupying the important post of American consul. These gentlemen, together with the Spanish Governor of the province, introduced him as well as his brothers into polite society, where he was charmed by the graces and the captivating manners of our Creole beauties.

When they left New Orleans for Havana, such was the affection entertained by our people toward those unassuming and grateful scions of royalty that several of their most intimate acquaintances escorted them on board of their ship as far as the Balize, where they parted with unaffected regret. A belief long prevailed here that Mandeville Marigny was Louis Philippe's godson. Such was not the fact, and no one would laugh more heartily over the story than Mandeville himself. The fact is, that on the occasion referred to the Colonel was not yet born, and his father a boy not yet out of his teens. The following are the facts from which the mistake originated : Many years ago, I can not remember how long, old Bernard, once a four-fold millionaire, having wasted his patrimony in wine, women and cards, bethought himself of repairing to France and of reminding the reigning king of certain obligations, some pecuniary as well, which he had incurred toward the Marigny family. Louis Philippe received him with open arms at the Tuileries, lodged him royally, allowed him a seat at the family dinner table, and otherwise treated him with the greatest con-descension. But that was all. Louis Philippe, in his old age, had become as miserly and penurious as Ber-nard had been shiftless and prodigal in his younger years. At the mere mention of a pecuniary payment or the suggestion of an annuity, the avaricious king pricked his ears and opened wide his eyes in utter astonishment. The fortune hunter had brought along with him one of his sons, Mandeville, and through him peace between the two courteous disputants was brought about. He was to enter the French army, and, through the patronage of his royal protector, it was thought he would soon ascend every rung of the military ladder. This proposal met the acceptance of the parties in interest and the youth was at once sent to the College of St. Cyr, which he left, a few years later, a full fledged lieutenant in a crack cavalry corps. But the young Creole soon tired of the service. Accustomed from early youth to a life of activity, adventure and rough exercise, he soon became fatigued with the dull routine of a city garrison in times of peace, and longed for the broad savannas, the tangled forests, the impenetrable marshes, the mighty rivers of his Louisiana home. Had France been at war with some foreign power at that time, the case might have been different, perhaps. Besides, there were ominous signs in the political sky. The international difficulty over the French spoliation bill was exciting a very acrimonious debate in the French House of Deputies, and the trend of public opinion was becoming insultingly hostile to the United States. American tourists in Paris were placed in a very awkward position at times from uncomplimentary remarks uttered in *cafés*, restaurants, theaters and even *salons;* and duels resulting therefrom were not uncommon. In this condition of affairs, after attending his cousin, Bosque, who, though a cripple, had the good fortune to vanquish on the field of honor one of the traducers of his country's good name, Mandeville shook the dust of Paris from off his feet, and returned home without delay.

It was on a beautiful Sunday morning, on the 30th of August, 1835, that a multitude of excited mechanics gathered on the grass-covered grounds of the Place d'Armes. Their object, as far as could be learned, was to protest against the further employment of slave labor in workshops or factories of any kind. The first speech delivered at that meeting having had a tendency, by reason of its revolutionary sentiments, to provoke a general disturbance of the peace, Mr. John Culbertson, then filling the duties of mayor *ad interim*, ordered the police to at once arrest the speaker and disperse the unruly assemblage. The order was executed to the very letter. But other large crowds having in the meantime gathered in various quarters of the city, particularly in the faubourg St. Mary, where the standard of revolt had been openly planted, several companies were detached from the Louisiana Legion for service, and succeeded after some resistance in quelling the disturbance. Three or four of the ringleaders were taken into custody on the charge of inciting riots. A judicial inquiry having been determined upon and held, the conduct of the acting mayor was fully approved. During four days the city was kept in a state of ferment and excitement, and violence was only repressed by the efforts of the police and the firm attitude of our citizen soldiery.

It was not long, however, before the smouldering embers of discontent and anger burst forth anew with greater intensity among those who had battled on behalf of law and order. It was an outbreak of general indignation, and had been occasioned by an ill-timed and inconsiderate squib which had appeared in the editorial columns of the *Advertiser*, a widely circulated sheet, against the members of the Legion. These were taunted with their foreign birth and were plainly told that if a war were ever declared against France, they would prove recreant and traitors. Such was not the truth, for the greater part of our Creole chivalry and manhood had honorable representatives in that organization. The real *gravamen* of their offending consisted in the fact that they had taken arms on the side of the government against an unruly mob.

The soldiery were, of course, incensed at this direct insult, while the feelings of their friends were no less inflamed. Groups congregated around street corners to discuss the situation, and the angry effects of wounded honor were not long in manifesting themselves. They therefore repaired to the office of the obnoxious paper, in Chartres street, to arrest the parties connected with the outrage. They there found Mr. J. C. Prendergast, one of the proprietors, whom they compelled to lead them to the residence of Dr. Vernon, the responsible editor, but finding that the libeler had effected his escape, they conducted Prendergast to the police station, where he was seized by the crowd and threatened with death. Such most surely would have been his fate had not the active intervention of the Mayor, the Attorney General, the judge of the criminal court and of many members of the Legion itself, rescued him from his peril.

Prendergast was thus saved from the fury of an angry populace, while on their way to the public square, with a halter round his neck. He was put into the jail for safekeeping. Vernon had escaped. On the first intimation of a popular outbreak, the thoroughly affrighted editor had taken to flight, and, reaching Lake Pontchartrain, hastened to Mobile, from which propitious haven he never emerged until the storm had spent its fury. Pending these events, surging crowds had gathered in thousands around the now doomed newspaper office and had proceeded to wreak their vengeance. The building was partially gutted, the presses overturned and large quantities of type hurled through the windows into the street. Whatever fell under the

hands of the almost ungovernable multitude was dam-
aged, if not wholly destroyed. Again were the city
and State authorities called upon to interpose their
power and influence, but their efforts proved partially
successful. The arrival of the U. S. troops, under
Col. Twiggs, which had been hastily summoned from
their garrison at Bay St. Louis, finally restored peace
and relieved the community of the moral and physical
strain to which it had for several days been subjected.

The sequel is easily told. Prendergast, having made
a suitable explanation and apology, was restored to
public favor. Dr. Vernon, the author of the senseless
pasquinade, returned from his place of confinement.
The negroes were put to work, as they had done before,
without further molestation, and "peace reigned in
Warsaw" once more.

I knew Prendergast well in later years. He was a
genial, warm-hearted Irishman, brave as a lion and
gentle as a child In politics he was an enthusiast.
Locofoco-ism was his *bête noire*, and, unlike the majority of his countrymen, was ever ready to defend, extol
and propagate the tenets of Whiggery. When he left
the *sanctum* of the *Advertiser* he cast his fortunes
with the *Tropic*, one of the sprightliest, most tren-
chant and aggressive papers that ever appeared in New
Orleans. The chief editor was the celebrated Col.
McArdle, of Mississippi, who wielded a caustic and
powerful pen. All of its editors were fighting men who
recognized the "Code" as the supreme arbiter of personal differences. Prendergast remained some time with
them, and, being a practical printer, was of great
assistance to the concern. Tiring, a few years after, of
the financially unproductive connection, he determined
to launch out on his own account in the Third District,

and established the *Orleanian*, in the Marigny buildings, on the levee. This paper he conducted with signal ability during the rest of his life, which closed some short time after the war. During and after the famine of 1845-46 in Ireland, when the exodus from that unfortunate island first began, and thousands sought a home in our city, Prendergast was indefatigable in his efforts to alleviate the distress and relieve the necessities of such of his countrymen as needed immediate assistance. He caused temporary quarters to be established in the row of three-story buildings in which his printing office was situated for the reception of the emigrants, where committees, appointed for the purpose, acted the part of good Samaritans and obtained for them employment at once. His paper was, of course, the medium through which this important work was accomplished. The *Orleanian* was the official journal of the Third Municipality until the consolidation of the city in 1852, and had the contract for all the public printing in that rather impoverished section. For years he manfully fought the battle of adversity, and when death overtook him in his journey through life, it carried off a poor, but fearless and honest man.

CHAPTER XVI.

OLD LOUISIANA DAYS.

COLORED MECHANICS — THE SLAVE TRADE — NEGRO DANCES — THE GAME OF RAQUETTES — THE ST. DOMINGO REFUGEES — LE CAFE DES REFUGIES — L'HOTEL DE LA MARINE — THE LAFITTES — WERE THEY PIRATES? — THE STORY PLAINLY TOLD — ANCIENT BUILDINGS — PÈRE ANTOINE'S BAKER — THE OLD PONTALBA BUILDINGS — THE GOVERNOR'S RESIDENCE — THE COLONIAL STATE HOUSE — L'HOTEL TREMOULET — LE VEAU QUI TETE — THE VOYAGEURS — TRAVELING ON THE MISSISSIPPI — KEEL BOATS — A WORD ABOUT TIGNONS — THE OLD FORTIFICATIONS — THE ORLEANS COLLEGE — THE FRENCH BARRACKS — REMINISCENCES OF THE BATTLE OF NEW ORLEANS.

During the two or three decades that followed the transfer of Louisiana to the United States, the tide of immigration was slow and uncertain. Several causes had contributed to this result, one of which was the stagnation of business occasioned by our war with England. A scarcity of white manual labor having ensued, it became necessary to substitute slaves and free colored people in all mechanical pursuits. Thus it was that in our factories and blacksmith shops bosses or foremen would be whites, while the operatives were either blacks or mulattoes. And so with other trades, such as brick-layers or masons, carpenters, painters, tinsmiths, butchers, bakers, tailors, etc. In fact, had not the progress of the country, from the condition of unrest under which it had been laboring, developed itself into the proportions which it has since assumed, there can not be the least doubt but that all the lower mechanical arts would have been monopolized in the course of time by the African race. But the reverse fortunately took place, by reason of the influx of white immigrants, so that even the branches of industry, which had by common consent surrendered to the colored population as too menial for the white race, were wrested from them by the encroachments of foreign labor.

It was at this phase of our municipal history that the problem began to manifest its latent difficulties, and that the excessive amount of European labor in our glutted market brought about that reduction of wages that has to-day pauperized the honest *American mechanic.* This evil weighed heavily on the community at the time, and so continued for years, until, just immediately before the breaking out of hostilities, the owners of slaves raised to a trade were compelled to dispose of them to sugar and cotton planters, in regions where rivalry with the white industrial class was not so disadvantageous. But even there all mechanical professions were soon filled by immigrants, who, being stimulated by the spur of necessity, consented to work at scab rates and carried off the palm of industry.

On board of the pilot boats of the Balize were a number of black and colored boatmen, than whom no smarter sailors or rowers could be found. Their songs, while deftly feathering their oars, were an indispensable accompaniment to their fatiguing labors. The blacks were generally composed of newly landed Africans, as the slave trade was still secretly being carried on. It is a well established fact that such philanthropists and negrophilists, as John McDonogh eventually proved to be, were by no means behind the times in dealing with human flesh, as fast as it was imported to our shores from the coast of Africa, as can be shown by referring to their business advertisements in the *Moniteur* of 1806. Even at a much later period, these kidnaped victims were openly smuggled into the Mississippi waters, either by the way of Barataria, Lafourche or other bayous. A chronicler of that period says :

" We can attest that upon a plantation belonging to the United States authorities we saw a number of newly arrived negroes from the coast of Guinea, who had been carried into the Mississippi in 1816, as captured prizes, by United States armed vessels, and who were afterward disposed of by public sale, under the Marshal's hammer, to the highest bidder, in accordance with the prevailing law for the disposal of captured slaves."

Subsequently, Congress altered this policy, and captured Africans were transferred to Liberia. When speaking to one another they would make use of no other tongue than their own Congo *calabash*, of which, of course, a stranger could not understand a word ; but, being very quick of ear, they soon learned the Creole idiom, then spoken by everybody. They could never master the pure French, which was mostly in vogue among the Franco-American population.

There were among these Africans, both among the males as well as the females, several magnificent specimens, who were justly considered as models of physical development. They were generally reverenced among their countrymen as kings or princes. They claimed to have been the offspring of sovereigns in their African wilds, and to have thence been ruthlessly abducted by traders, who had brought them over the sea. Whether descendants from princes or not, it is to be acknowledged that certain fellows pointed out in the Congo dances were distinguished by something of a royal bearing. They were of robust frame, broad shouldered and muscular. When attired in scant costume for the *bamboula* their almost herculean conformation was noticeable. Two of these that I saw were blacksmiths, and were called by all the African womanhood *candios*, which means kings.

These illustrious ebony-hued personages were looked upon as the great dancers of the circle, the leading spirits in the mazes of the Congo Saturnalia. They inaugurated the universal hubbub by a signal given to the *tam-tam* beaters. Selecting their female mates, they would place themselves in the midst of a ring of yelling, yelping and stamping crowds, who looked upon their saltatory feats with every manifestation of delight. The public exhibition was continued until, fairly exhausted, they would sink to the ground. Judging them by these performances, one would have said if in their country those only were elected kings who could jump the highest and dance the longest, their kingship was no sinecure. He would have been astounded also by their supernatural extravagances, their unnatural contortions, and by the band of weird-looking Bacchantes, each of whom seemed to vie with the others in ridiculous capers. Their music, as the reader is already aware, consisted in beating long drums, called *tam-tams*, made of empty barrels with a sheep-skin cover, in the rattling of the jaw-bones of horses or mules, and the tooting of wooden horns shaped like those of a cow. To these a tambourine was sometimes added, but the article was evidently a modern innovation.

What made these dances so odd and peculiar was the vibratory motions of the by-standers, who in different styles contributed to the lascivious effect of the scene, while the principal characters were going through the figures. The performances were usually greeted by the vociferous acclamations and clapping of hands of all the assistants, and toward the close there followed such a whirling of the whole mass that one might have imagined a group of serpents interlacing one another, and casting a charm upon the throng of dancers and spectators.

While speaking of Congo amusements, I must not omit to mention the game of *raquettes*, as it was played among us in our city's early days. Let the reader transport himself in imagination to one of those wide, level meadows that were to be seen extending from the Bayou road to Elysian Fields. In these wild and unobstructed pastures the two parties, into which the company of players had first divided themselves, would select a piece of ground and measure out the distance between their respective quarters or stations, usually half a mile. At the extremities of this line two poles were erected, and the intervening space was covered by a paper frame, which had to be pierced by a ball before a victory could be claimed. This game had originated with the Indians, particularly with the Choctaws. The contending clans were known as the *Bayous* and the *La Villes*. The latter were the players of the city proper ; the former represented the Bayou St. John settlements. The contestants were picked out by the opposite leaders, and the number of members equalized as nearly as possible.

The ball was about two inches in diameter, and the

spoon-shaped *raquettes* were proportioned to the size of the missile. Their handles were about eighteen to twenty inches long. The ball could only be thrown with the *raquettes*, as the use of the hand was strictly prohibited. Wrestling and throwing one another down constituted part of the exercises. Frequently it would happen that just as a player was about to strike the goal, he would be unexpectedly hurled to the ground by a more alert antagonist. All fighting, beating or boxing was expressly forbidden. After the first throw in the air, which was called the *bamboula*, the whole crowd would eagerly watch the descent of the ball and rush for it. The game was then fairly started. From that moment the projectile was to be seen speeding through space from one end of the field to the other ; groups would become interlocked in their efforts to reach it, and many in consequence would suffer from severe falls.

It would sometimes happen that in this general scramble, when contestants were unable to extricate themselves from one another, a new *bamboula* would be demanded by both sides. Then the ball was again tossed in the air, and to the player it was the most exciting part of the pastime.

These games were played on regular days. They always began in the afternoon, when the sun was on its decline, say from 4 to 7 P. M. in the summer season. The running, wrestling and dexterity of the players were not only very exciting spectacles, but the eager crowd of spectators and acquaintances, running into the thousands, that usually gathered on the "raquette green," made such occasions a source of social entertainment. The vicinity of the grounds was covered with improvised places of refreshment, small booths for all sorts of cakes, fruits, sweet beer, ice cream, etc. Indeed, there could

not be a more pleasant evening spent than in attending
these erstwhile popular games and amusements. There
were also contests played between whites and Indians,
the latter belonging to the party of the *Bayous*. The
colored people were very much devoted to this entertainment, in which many of them excelled. Among
these every old-timer will remember "Lapin," so
named from his nimbleness of foot. When the contest
was over, they would go home singing doggerel rhymes
of their own composition, in mockery of the losing
party. As the prize usually consisted of a pretty silk
flag, of fanciful design, the trophy was borne along at
the head of a procession, as it slowly wended its way
toward the city. The whites took a great interest in
these field sports, encouraged them with their cheers,
and always evinced the kindest feeling toward them.

During the year 1809 many immigrants, numbering
eight thousand, white as well as black, made their way
into Louisiana, then known as the Territory of Orleans.
This incident, which so much contributed to the ex-
pansion and improvement of the city of New Orleans,
demands some explanation, as it forms an interesting
feature in the annals of our metropolis.

It will be remembered that, after the general treaty of
peace concluded at Amiens, France, under the guidance
of the First Consul, had sent a large military force to
the island of St. Domingo for the purpose of subduing
the revolted colony to the authority of the mother
country. Of the failure of this expedition the historical
reader is cognizant, which was owing to the ravages of
yellow fever among the unacclimated troops. Upon the
retirement of the latter, the country lapsed into the
power of the Africans, who, under Christophe, waged

a war of extermination, not only against the Caucasian race, but against the mulattoes and griffs as well. The struggle continued for a considerable time, when, overpowered by superior numbers, the Europeans and the colored people were forced into exile.

They sought and found a refuge in the island of Cuba, on the south side, toward the coast of Hayti. The point they selected was Santiago de Cuba. Being received with open arms, not only by the Spanish authorities, but by the inhabitants of the country, they set about repairing their fallen fortunes and establishing farms and plantations, with the aid of the few faithful slaves who had adhered to them in their adversity. Matters prospered with them for a time, but, just as they were beginning to reap the fruits of their industry and thrift, a thunderbolt fell at their feet. This was the announcement of the invasion of Spain by Napoleon, the imprisonment of King Ferdinand at Bayonne and the rupture of friendly relations between the two countries. Under such circumstances, these French subjects were ordered either to leave the island or abjure their nationality. They preferred the former, and for a second time prepared to emigrate. Packed in narrow spaces, in leaky and unseaworthy ships, these victims of adverse destiny were shipped to New Orleans, with barely the necessaries of life allowed them.

The importation into the territory of slaves from abroad without special permission from our government was an act forbidden under heavy pains and penalties by Congress, and as many of these expelled colonists were attended by a large retinue of their bondsmen, it became a matter of anxious consideration to determine whether they should be allowed to land or not. Included in the prohibition was a large number of colored freedmen, who afterward became useful and honored citizens, as was testified by the valor they displayed during the battle of New Orleans, under the leadership of their compatriots, D'Aquin and Savary. Governor Claiborne severed the Gordian knot by informing them that they would be permitted to come on shore conditionally. He ordered their release, therefore, from the quarantine station and submitted the whole matter to the Federal Executive.

Viewing the question as a *casus necessitatis*, the President confirmed the course of his pro-consul in Louisiana, and his action was afterward approved by the two branches of Congress. The accession of this large number of immigrants caused a considerable stir, as the reader may imagine, in the ranks of our little community, whose population within the narrow bounds of the city proper, in 1810, did not exceed eight thousand souls. These contributed in the course of time, with the means they had brought with them, in forwarding several improvements, not the least of which was the erection of an elegant theatre on St. Philip street.

Another was the establishment of a coffee house, called the *Café des Refugiés*, in the neighborhood of the old market, between Maine and St. Philip. This place became during a number of years the recognized headquarters of the *Colons de St. Domingue*, as they were called, and here it was that the famous liquor, *le petit Gouave*, was also concocted, whose invigorating qualities some of our people may yet remember.

Adjoining it was the *Hôtel de la Marine*, the boarding house and rendezvous of all the adventurous spirits of those times. It was in that building that dozens of Sicilians were butchered in 1857, on the occasion of the Know-nothing riots on Orleans street, when Norbert

Trepagnier was almost cut to pieces by Italian Demo-crats. In the course of a few years the establishment was enlarged, and in 1815 Mr. F. Turpin became its proprietor, and advertised it as follows :

" NAVY HOTEL.

" Coffeehouse, Public Baths, Table d'Hote and Board ing House."

It seems that the worthy manager not only catered to the inner comforts of his patrons, but also contributed *babulum* to the amusements of the general public, as may be seen from this characteristic notice :

" ROPE DANCING.
" On the Tight and Slack Rope.

" Mr. Medrano has the honor of informing the inhabit-ants of New Orleans and its vicinity that, on Sunday evening next, 6th instant, he will give another exhibi-bition of rope dancing at the Navy Hotel.

" He will execute the same feat as on last Sunday, of standing on his head, with his legs crossed, on a pole thirty feet high ; but instead of having one circle of fireworks at his feet, he will have three, one on his feet and one on each hand.

" He will dance on the tight rope divers steps, and execute many extraordinary feats too tedious to men-tion. He will appear on the rope in man's clothes ; an empty bag will be given him, into which he will enter, when it will be tied above his head ; he will then be seen to come out in the character of an old woman of eighty, and in that dress dance to the tune of Yankee Doodle.

" On the slack rope, with fireworks to each arm, he will represent a windmill, and turn with such velocity as to render it impossible to distinguish his form—with a number of feats equally surprising, that can not fail to please the public.''

These exhibitions were given in the immense court-yard, which can still be seen at this late date, together with the old sleeping apartments above the galleries.

In this quaint hostelry was frequently to be seen on an evening the familiar figure of the dashing General Humbert, who had become an intimate of '' mine host,'' Turpin. Here it was that in his declining years he was in the habit of conversing anent those times of the French Republic, in the affairs of which he had taken a con-spicuous part, or of relating amusing incidents of the fight at Chalmette, or of expatiating upon the brilliant prospects of his friends, Morelos and Hidalgo, to achieve the independence of Mexico. The men, who had fought under Lafitte, and Dominique You and Beluche, would crowd around him and crane their necks with delight as they listened to his stories of war and deeds of daring. The bronze faced veteran, with rubicund nose, was as vigorous as ever, and as addicted to his cup. His mind was filled with military schemes and expeditions. He was intent at that period on undertaking some grand military enterprise in favor or South American inde-pendence, the struggle of the colonies with the mother country having reached its climax.

And now that I have mentioned the names of Lafitte and his desperate crew, I shall say a few words con-cerning their real character and pursuits ; that is to say, before they were pardoned by President Madison, inas-much as their subsequent career reveals another story. There has been such a glamor of romance blended with fiction thrown around them that the whole truth should as well be told.

We must first bear in mind that the bulk of the mercantile class of New Orleans at the time these men engaged in their operations consisted of people of French extraction, either of European birth or natives of the French West India islands. Hence, during the long wars that were waged between France and Great Britain, those who comprised that portion of the population of Louisiana viewed the enemies of their race with feelings of undisguised hostility, and although the American government was not actually at war with the English nation before the year 1812, still so deeply seated was the irritation caused by her haughty and arrogant bearing on the ocean that our authorities winked, as it were, at every naval enterprise undertaken by French merchants or ship owners against British commerce or navigation in the West Indies or in Mexican waters. In this state of affairs and actuated by such feelings, sundry naval expeditions from the coast of Louisiana, and more particularly from the harbor of Barataria were fitted out, some of the most influential and respectable French commercial firms being interested in these naval armaments. The vessels sailed under the authority of French letters of marque, as cruisers.

When, in the course of time, the English had captured all the French West India islands, Guadeloupe, Martinique, etc., these privateers were deprived thereby of friendly harbors and markets for disposing of their captured prizes.

In consequence of this new condition of things, the corsairs, Lafitte among them, bethought themselves of obtaining letters of marque from the government of Cartagena, and of establishing intercourse with the merchants of New Orleans through the Barataria Canal. Now, it was impossible for the United States Govern-

ment openly to encourage the introduction of goods
and merchandise into the territory, coming, as they
did, from an illicit source, inasmuch as, not having yet
broken off all friendly relations with Great Britain, they
could not sanction any contravention to our neutrality
laws. The privateers were willing and anxious to pay
the customs import duties for the goods thus thrown
upon the New Orleans market, but they were precluded
from so doing by these considerations and the instructions emanating from Washington.

Hence, a system of smuggling merchandise into
the Barataria market grew up, and the practice was
kept up so openly and undisguisedly that the very contractors of the United States army, engaged in the purchase of clothing for men and officers, were in the habit
of repairing to the mouth of the Barataria Canal, and
of there receiving cloth for transportation in carts and
other vehicles to the city proper. In this manner the
Federal officials connived at the introduction of contraband goods. When, in later years, an expedition was
undertaken against the privateers of Barataria, and
Pierre Lafitte was made a prisoner, no proceedings
were instituted against any of them on the charge of
piracy. They were merely indicted for violating the
revenue laws.

It is not my purpose here to enter into details as to
the salient features of the lives of the Lafittes and of
those who were attached to their fortunes. Martin, De
Bouchel and Gayarré, in their respective works, have
fully accomplished this duty, that is, so far as our own
local history is concerned. The question : Were they
pirates? is one that is frequently asked and unsatisfac-
torily answered. From my researches, and they extend
to contemporaneous publications, executive documents,

official reports from local authorities, Federal navy reg-
isters, and other authentic sources, I have been forced
to the conclusion that they became pirates and outlaws
as soon as they left the jurisdiction of the United States
and took up their abode in the province of Texas. The
proof is incontrovertible.

After their establishment had been broken up by
Commodore Patterson, notwithstanding their heroic services at the battle of New Orleans, they were looked
upon with distrust by the American authorities in general, and by Beverly Chew in particular, who was
then the collector of this port. Barataria, closely
watched, had ceased to afford them shelter and im-
munity. They began, therefore, to cast about for new
scenes of operations, and, having purchased through
their financial agents, Sauvinet and Laporte, the eight
vessels which had been captured from them and sold as
prizes, they embarked for Port au Prince, vowing
vengeance against the inhospitable Americans. There
can be no doubt that from that moment they had resolved upon a course of piracy. Dominique You, one
of their leaders, was himself a Creole of St. Domingo,
and expected to be received by the government officials
of that island with open arms. But such anticipations
proved futile. Their reputation had preceded them,
and this fact, coupled with various suspicious captures,
attributed to them, caused the Haytiens to close their
ports. They were only allowed to revictual their ships,
but no other indulgence could be obtained. Thus frus-
trated, they determined to repair to Galveston and occupy
that sandy waste. The place had just been abandoned by
Aury, who, together with Gen. Long, were the leaders
in the movement of Texas independence. Forty of them
met together on board of a Mexican rebel ship, and,

having gone through some nondescript naturalization ceremony, in a document which they all signed, they proclaimed a provisional government and appointed themselves its officers. They at once unfurled the black flag, the red flag, the Mexican flag, the Cartagena flag, and every other flag which ingenuity could devise. It was not long before their crimes were heralded throughout the world, and provoked a special proclamation from the President. Armed cruisers were sent in pursuit of the wretches—the Lynx, the Porpoise and the Enterprise, being the fleetest, were in constant service. Their depredations were carried on not only in the Gulf and Caribbean sea, but extended over the Atlantic coast as far as Charleston and Savannah. Their favorite place of operations was around the island of Cuba, whose numerous inlets served them as favorite lurking places. Not even was the coast of Louisiana spared, as the numerous forays in the bays of Calcasieu amply evidence. It was on the occasion of one of those expeditions that Lafitte was compelled, by order of the commander of the Enterprise, to hang a fellow, Brown, in Galveston, from the yard-arm of one of his schooners, and to deliver the rest of his fellow-pirates for trial in New Orleans. During the whole period embraced within the years 1817-21, Lafitte was directing these depredations, under his lieutenants, Dominique, Beluche and Gambie, surnamed *Nez Coupé*, the most brutal and cowardly assassin of the band. A man by the name of Desfarges, together with eighteen other confederates, was caught red-handed off the mouth of the Balize, by a United States cruiser, and brought to New Orleans to be judged. Upon hearing this, Lafitte hurried to the city, engaged counsel, John R. Grymes, for his defence, and was not idle in working up a sen-

timent among the rabble in favor of the imprisoned parties. A howling mob of scoundrels in our midst rallied
around the rickety prison, adjoining the arsenal, and
threatened to tear it down. Several companies of the
Legion were called out by the Governor, and kept guard
over the building during several weeks. Balked in this
attempt, they threatened to set the whole city on fire,
and, notwithstanding the vigilance of extra patrols,
actually succeeded in applying the torch to the State
armory and in destroying several buildings in the
vicinity of the jail. Meanwhile, the pirates were
brought to the United States District Court to be tried,
and, notwithstanding the persistent efforts of their able
lawyers, were adjudged guilty and sentenced to be hung.
On hearing this result, Lafitte, armed with letters of
recommendation from some of the most influential merchants and politicians, lost no time in taking passage
for Washington, to see the President. Being amply
provided with means, he cut a conspicuous feature in
the capital for some time, and with the assistance of Livingston and Davezac, who held high positions at court,
succeeded in obtaining an audience. What means he
used to attain his end is impossible to explain at this
late day, but the fact is that he was enabled to secure
the liberation of all, with the exception of Desfarges,
who, being their captain, it was thought should be
made an example. As to the latter, the decision of the
President was carried out, and he was hanged at the
foot of St. Anne street, from the yard-arm of one of our
cruisers.

A particular circumstance connected with the leniency
exhibited toward these ruffians was the fact that, several
weeks after their liberation, many of them were again arrested on the high seas, for deeds of a like piratical

character. Of course, the press was incensed against
the chief executive, as we read in the papers of the
period.

Lafitte's prestige was gone. On his return to Galveston, of which he pretended to be the Governor under
the authority of the Mexican Congress, he was quietly
given to understand by the captain of the United States
armed schooner Enterprise, that he would have to
decamp, if he wished to avoid a bombardment. This
he finally consented to do, after having vainly attempted to seduce the officer from his line of duty by a
profuse hospitality. The establishment was broken up,
some eight hundred in number. The common property
was divided into shares, and the crew disbanded.
This was in 1821. Some followed Lafitte into the
waters of Yucatan ; others, like Beluche, who rose to
the rank of Commodore in the Bolivian navy, went with
him to Cartagena ; others, like Gambie, doomed to assassination at the hands of his own men, returned to
Barataria, expecting something to turn up, while the
balance, resolved to lead new lives with Dominique
You in New Orleans, went back to their old homes, and
finally died in our midst, converted into useful citizens.

One of the most ancient buildings of New Orleans was
the bakery of Cadet, at the corner of St. Peter and
Royal, who was succeeded by Joseph Vincent, and is at
present occupied by Manessier as a confectionery store.
It was then a one-story structure, with a Spanish tile
roof. Cadet used to be Pére Antoine's purveyor of
bread for the poor, and the last receipted account—which
was found among the latter's effects after his death—ag-
gregated a little over thirteen hundred dollars. This
single item furnishes. more than any panegyric which

my pen can bestow, a sample of the extent and measure of the holy man's benevolence. Not very many years ago, the outlandish appearance of the upper part of the rear building would attract the eye of the stranger. It was a remnant of the abandoned old bakery, and with its quaint old chimney was used as a sort of mill for grinding coarse flour to a finer grade.

In the year 1794 another fire broke out in the city, which, though not quite as disastrous as that which preceded it six years before, was a source of great affliction and misery to the humble classes. According to the statements of eye-witnesses, we know that several thousands were left homeless and became dependents upon public charity. That year signalized several important events in our history, among which may be mentioned the completion of our Cathedral Church, the inauguration of our sugar industry and, lastly, the construction of the Carondelet Canal. The names of Boré, Baron Carondelet and Almonester are the names of that period. To the latter especially is the honor of public liberality attached. On each side of the "Place d'Armes" were rows of stores and dwelling houses. They were constructed during the short period of O'Reilly's administration. They were in the style known as *briquetés entre poteaux*, *i. e.*, partly of bricks, between posts. The roofs were covered with tiles, baked or burned in kilns of domestic manufacture, before the introduction of flat tiles from Nantes and Havre. They were, indeed, relics of the earliest improvements of the Louisiana colony. I may say incidentally that the character of some of our roofs is an unerring indication of their age or of the *régime* under which they were constructed.

The most ancient or primitive were covered with cypress
shingles.   Again, in order of time, followed the hollow
red brick tile, after which again, for a long number of
years, the French flat tile came into vogue.   It is only
within a comparatively short space that slate coverings
have been generally adopted.   One of the most ancient
brick buildings in that quarter of the town stands at
the corner of St. Peter and Chartres, opposite the old
City Hall, or former Cabildo.   It is erroneously supposed
that this quaint structure, so decidedly Moorish in its
design and style of architecture, was formerly the residence of our Spanish Governors, and that it was within
its walls the festival was given by O'Reilly, during which
the unfortunate Lafreniére and his co-conspirators were
arrested, to be from thence transferred to their gloomy
dungeons.   The palace, which these dignitaries then
inhabited, fronted the river, and was situated on Levee
street, between Toulouse and St. Louis.   The Governor's
official residence was at the corner of Toulouse, further
down the street, and had been constructed during the
French domination.   It is more than probable that
the house about which I am now writing was used for
the accomodation of the officers connected with the
Cabildo.   Early in the present century it was a place of
public entertainment for travelers, as was also the
"Trémoulet House," opposite the river landing, at the
corner of Old Levee and St. Peter, afterward Baron
Pontalba's residence.   This old moresque edifice, at the
time that General Jackson reached the city in 1814, to
take charge of its defence, was a restaurant and lodging
house combined, and its proprietor received none but
people of condition and quality.   He was a jolly old
Frenchman, and a Vatel in the culinary line.   Its name
was unique : *Le veau qui tête*, the "Sucking Calf."

One who used to patronize this establishment in his younger days once told me that its customers were the cream of our *bourgeoisie*. There was a continual ebb and flow of guests in the upper *salons*, where visitors were wont to take their meals upon small, neatly covered tables, attended by polite waiters. These rooms were appropriated for dinners *à la carte* exclusively. There was, besides, a *table d'hôte*, where repasts were served at fixed hours. To a stranger no fitter place could be found, if he was desirous of initiating himself into New Orleans French society, into that part of it, at least, which constituted the moving, active, mercantile portion, as busy as bees, traveling up and down the river coast from what were called its posts. These were settlements, such as the post of Opelousas or the post of Natchitoches, which were current expressions, handed down from the times of the colonial *régime*, to denote the various trading and military points along the margin of the Mississippi.

In those days, it was not the North American adventurers that were the pioneers in the commercial establishments then extending throughout our State. Trading was the special branch of French immigrants. These were indefatigable in organizing mercantile agencies over the rural sections of lower Louisiana, even in the nooks and recesses of inland bayous, and of far away stretching piney wood ridges. In later years, when the appliances of steam had opened new avenues to more active operations in the inland water courses and tributary streams of our great river, North American merchants and traders began to establish branches throughout the country. The natives of the soil were not inclined to follow commercial pursuits. Agriculture was their sole occupation. In this respect, the son followed the example of his father, and of his ancestors. The earth furnished him with comfort, wealth and even luxury. Hence foreigners, *les nouveaux deballés*, as they were called, enjoyed an undisputed monopoly. Navigation and trade with the parishes and posts of the interior were carried on mostly in what were then known as coasting boats. But when more distant regions were to be reached, as, for instance, the posts of Natchitoches, or of Opelousas, or of Ouachita, barges, which had been constructed on the upper Mississippi, the Wabash, the Ohio or Illinois rivers, and brought to the city with their Canadian crews, were the conveyances most usually employed. These flat-bottomed boats, very long and narrow, were splendidly adapted to traveling in sinuous, crooked bayous, such as those that constituted the Red river branches, and the numerous and intricate water courses which lead, in the season of high floods, from the Mississippi to the Atchafalaya, Opelousas and Attakapas settlements. These barges or long keel boats were partly covered with raw ox hides, wound or bent in the form of a tunnel over a wooden framework, so as to protect the freight or cargo from sun and rain, and to shelter passengers and crews while taking their meals or indulging in rest. This mode of locomotion was romantic, and not devoid of a certain charm. It was the primitive conveyance in which the ascent or descent of the river was accomplished from New Orleans as high as Pittsburg. These voyages would consume generally forty or fifty days, when undertaken with the current, and at the stages of low water the danger from snags, stumps and sawyers was frequently imminent. Before the use of steam power, the crossing of the Mississippi from point to point

against the current was the most difficult part of navigation, and this was done by means of a large square
rigged sail.   When a point had to be doubled, the crew
were put on shore, and a long *cordelle*, or rope, was
slung around the breast of every man, who was made to
pull the craft, like a beast of burden, while a couple of
hands on board the vessel, armed with long poles,
would keep it at a convenient distance from the shore,
and aid its course by occasional pushes or pulls.   In the
evening the crew, being completely worn out, as the
reader may conjecture, the boat was made fast to the
river bank, and a hot supper would be prepared ashore,
where the men would stretch themselves out on the cool
ground or furze, by the side of a blazing fire, whose
smoke would drive away the usual swarms of buzzing
mosquitoes.   Such were, in part, the hardships of our
early navigation, *endured by the brawny Canadian voyageurs.*

From this subject let me now digress to another.
When the Spanish Governor, Estevan Miro, in 1786,
took command of the province of Louisiana, he published, in accordance with the practice pursued by his
predecessors, a sort of manifesto or message, called *un
Bando de buen Gobierno*, in other words, rules for the
people.   In this document various observances were
enjoined.   Among others, it was declared that people
would be punished with the greatest severity who were
found living outside of the lawful relations of the matri-
monial state, and that persons of color, particularly
women, would be vigorously prosecuted should they
not abandon their lax and idle mode of living.   Nay,
this Governor, whose administration proved him to have
been a mild and tolerant official, went so far in his edict

as to forbid this class of females to wear any jewels or
ornaments of value, or to adorn their hair with feathers ;
se coiffer de plumes.　In lieu thereof, he ordered the use
of a handkerchief or bandana.　The custom of wearing
this sort of headgear was almost universal among the
industrial classes in olden times.　It was called the
tignon.

After the arrival of Carondelet as Governor of Louisiana, and during that part of his administration which
covered the period from 1792 to 1796, the city of New
Orleans was strongly entrenched within a line of fortifications, and enclosed with ramparts, deep ditches and
picket revetments.　These protections had been thrown
up against the possible incursions of hostile Indians
and servile insurrections in adjoining parishes.　There
were no issues from the little town except through
three main gates—the Tchoupitoulas, the Bayou Road
and the *chemin public*, the latter skirting the river front
from the actual location of the United States Mint, downward.　At or near each one of these gates sentries were
stationed night and day, keeping ward and vigil over
the safety of the people.　After the American government took possession of the country, these works were
allowed to crumble into decay, and I find in my
researches into the city's archives that, as early as in
1805 and 1806, under the administrations of Mayors
James Pitot, and John Watkins, the revetments were
being used in the filling up of the trenches, which had
become dangerous to public health.　As late as 1816
there were left few traces of their existence, with the
exception of a little coquettish looking fort, called " St.
Charles," at the foot of Esplanade street.　It was dismantled some time in the year 1821, and the ground

ceded temporarily to the corporation. As to the old
bastions once standing at the four corners of the old
carré, they were completely razed to the ground. The
gate leading to the Bayou Road overlooked a drawbridge
which spanned a wide and deep ditch at that point. In
my boyhood days the place was still called *la porte du
bayou*. Under the masterly and energetic hand of
James Pitot, our first elected Mayor, the spirit of enterprise developed itself to a surprising degree in the first
decade of the present century. Among other beneficial
results was the encouragement given to immigration,
whose tide began to flow in with unabated rapidity.

In 1812 was erected, immediately on the outskirts of
the city proper, the building known as the "Orleans
College," out of which nursery of education sprang into
the world a number of Louisianians that have been
justly esteemed for their intellectual attainments. This
institution faced St. Claude street, which had been
recently laid down upon the plan of the contemplated
extension of the city as a thoroughfare behind Rampart
street. The object of the authorities in opening this
new street was to group around it a certain number of
residences, or, in other words, the colonization of a new
faubourg. But the project proved futile, and for a
number of years the college continued in its isolated
position ; for, being surrounded by an almost unfathomable morass, the people were loath to locate their
domiciles in this noisome neighborhood. How many
car loads of "cotton seed" it took to fill up this dismal
swamp, it would be difficult to say. In the course of
time, as *terra firma* was steadily advancing, improvements were pushed beyond the structure. It then
became necessary to demolish a part of the college
building in order to open Ursulines street through St.

Claude.   For this reason one may see the two extremities or wings of that ancient building (the college),
each resting on the edges of the two streets above mentioned.

On leaving the city proper from Fort St. Charles,
at the foot of Esplanade street, and following the
main road along the Mississippi river, with a view
of visiting the battle fields of 1814-15, one would meet
two lines of defence before reaching the spot.   The first
line ran along to the woods on the ground occupied by
the late Touro's unfinished almshouse.   There a sort of
tête de pont had been thrown up to protect the public
road.   A ditch or canal, of considerable depth and
extent, with a low earthen breastwork on its front, was
still to be seen in 1816.   The second defensive line, about
one mile distant from the former, had been constructed
in the immediate neighborhood of the spot where the
United States Barracks stand to-day.   There was a line
of breastworks connected with bastions, one of which
formed also a *tête de pont*, to cover the public road.
That locality, for long years thereafter, was converted
into an open-air public garden, on the river front,
enclosed with a beautiful orange hedge, and from which
one could enjoy delightful breezes as well as a magnificent view of the stream as far as the eye could
reach.   All along this route, the main road for pedestrians was on the summit of the levee.   It was dotted
with a continuous row of fine country houses.   The
slope of the lands from the bank of the river toward the
swamps was very gradual ; and immediately behind the
cultivated fields, mostly covered with stalks of Indian
corn, were the open pasture grounds in which numerous herds of neat cattle, sheep and goats were seen
browsing.

From this second fortified or rallying point and proceeding two miles lower, the visitor would reach the battle scene and the famous entrenchments, which, in 1815, the British on the 8th of January unsuccessfully attempted to storm. Here in 1816 part of the works was already dismantled. That portion which had formed the bastion or small fortalice by the edge of the river was barely recognizable. The breastworks of the line, the *fossés*, the banquette, the glacis, were still in a good state of preservation. Only a few months had elapsed since the chivalry of England had there met with such signal defeat, and already the hand of man had been engaged in converting those appliances of misery, war and desolation into fields of peace, plenty and prosperity. *And yet a few years* later they were all swept away.

The old Barracks constructed by the French were completed in the year 1758. These buildings, fronting the river from the rear of the Ursulines Convent to Barracks street, were in a good state of preservation when taken possession of by the American government. Their record is historical. Here had been stationed in regular succession the French regiments of the line, until in 1763 Louisiana was ceded to the Spanish monarchy. Then came their occupation in 1769 by the troops of the cruel O'Reilly and his successors; then their transfer in 1800 to Laussat, the Prefect, and three years thereafter their delivery to Commissioner Wilkinson. The Barracks proper formed a single building, nearly a square and a half in length, two stories high, built of brick, plastered with a coating of lime, and having on its front as well as in its rear a wide gallery supported by a row of strong, square pillars, also constructed with the same material, *i. e.*, bricks

plastered with cement made of mussel shell lime.   A
remnant of these most ancient military quarters, at the
intersection of Chartres and Barracks streets, is still
one of the salient features of the neighborhood, having
first been converted into a private dwelling house, the
erstwhile family residence of the Charbonnet family,
afterward the domicile of a Catholic seminary, and
lately the scene of a terrible Sicilian *vendetta*.   With
the exception of this building, the Barracks were entirely demolished to make room for modern stores and
houses.   Between the high walls of masonry enclosing
the area of the structures and the levee or river bank
there was an open *plaza*, or parade ground upon which
the garrison troops were wont to drill whenever the
usual review and inspection within the enclosure were
omitted.   This open space constitutes now the site of
the two squares of buildings traversed by Gallatin
street, the most noted cesspool of immorality, assassination and crime ever known in New Orleans in ante-
bellum times.   It was upon that spot and not in the
Place d'Armes, as is popularly believed and authorita-
tively asserted by several writers, that Lafrenière and
his associates in martyrdom were publicly shot to death
by Spanish soldiers, in the presence of the cruel and
bloody O'Reilly.   It was, also, within the walls of
those gloomy barracks that the judicial farce, called a
trial, was enacted, and the warrant for their execution
probably sealed and signed by the tyrant.

CHAPTER XVII.

OLD LOUISIANA DAYS.

THE INDIGO CULTURE — REMINISCENCES OF FAUBOURG
ST. MARY — JEAN GRAVIER — THE DISMAL SWAMP — LE
QUARTIER DES DAMNES — THE MACARTY CREVASSE —
THE SHELL ROAD — MICHOUD'S HUNTING GROUND —
SKETCH OF EARLY SETTLEMENTS — THE BAYOU ST. JOHN
— LA TERRE AUX LEPREUX — THE LEVEE FRONT — FAU-
BOURG LIVAUDAIS, NOW THE FOURTH DISTRICT — REMI-
NISCENCES OF DANIEL CLARK — ALEXANDER MILNE'S
OLD CASTLE.

During the administrations of Governors Galvez and
Carondelet, the tract of land which became thereafter
known as the *Faubourg Ste. Marie* consisted of a large
plantation owned by Jean Gravier, who acquired his
title from the government sales that took place after the
expulsion of the Jesuit fathers from the colony. The
latter had purchased the same by notarial act, in Paris,
from Bienville himself, and it is evident that the confiscation of their property was an act of arbitrary spoliation.
This immense estate, extending on its front from Canal
to Delord streets, had been for a number of years devoted
to the culture of the sugar cane and of indigo. This last
branch of industry was then being extensively carried on
along the lower coast of the Mississippi delta, in the

Red river parishes, and upon the boundless prairies of southwest Louisiana, where this tropical plant may still be seen growing in wild luxuriance. Its frequent destruction by swarms of locusts and parasitic insects was the main cause why this former *staple product* of our State was made to yield to the supremacy of sugar, which, besides being a surer crop, was also far more remunerative. But one of the reasons which greatly contributed to this result, eight years before the cession of the territory, was the extremely unwholesome condition of the process for its fabrication and the consequent prevalence of disease among the slaves at certain seasons of the year. The great mortality which ensued was attributed to the peculiar exhalations that poisoned the atmosphere during the whole period of fermentation. This was a great drawback, as may naturally be supposed, and constituted an important factor in the consideration of profits. The quality of the Louisiana indigo was rated in the commercial marts of the world as next to that of Guatemala, which was estimated as superior to that of India.

In the rear of the Faubourg St. Mary, in close proximity to the site of the once well known Freret cotton presses, on Poydras street, lived, in 1816, the only surviving brother of the elder Gravier, one of the original purchasers of the plantation, which, a little before the year 1803, was laid out, as per plans, into a suburb. Called by his neighbors "Doctor" Gravier, because he attended the sick without remuneration, and effected cures by means of simples and Indian herbs, this singular old man led a hermit's life, forsaken by the world, in an old shanty surrounded by weeping willows, amid the ghastly scenery of a Louisiana swamp. To the casual observer he always looked like one absorbed in the solution of some moral problem, or in the sorrows of a bitter disappointment.

No ordinary courage was required to venture alone within the precincts of that forbidding and desolate spot. Encircled, as it then was, by low cemeteries, along the edges of the fathomless morass, the dismal willows could be heard uttering plaintive sounds with every gust of wind, as it rushed through closely interlocked cypress thickets. There were still to be seen fragments of old indigo vats and other vestiges of that industry. No wonder, then, that this remote part of the town was invested with the glamour of romance. With many it was associated with scenes of foul deeds and midnight murders. Some would assert that hunters had stumbled by accident upon overturned trees, within whose cavities human skeletons had been discovered. Others pretended that fire-flies or *ignes fatui* were to be seen in the warm summer nights flitting or hovering over the graves of departed spirits, while others, still more timorous and superstitious, shuddered with affright at the portentous hootings of owls in the small hours of the morning.

Now, all these gloomy forebodings of ignorant people had their origin, of course, in the very nature of the locality. Bats and other night birds were to be expected in such surroundings. As to *feux follets*, they were indigenous to swamps inaccessible to the tread of man, and impregnated with a petroleum-like substance oozing out of decayed stumps. The marsh was alive with slimy, dangerous and shining reptiles of every species. The croaking of bull-frogs, from the avuncular *wararron* to the diminutive and adolescent *grenouille* was incessant, and, to complete the description of this

scene of misery and martyrdom, the swarming and buzzing of insects and the shrill cries of sea gulls, joining
in a demon's chorus, made a residence in such a waste
a matter of utter impossibility.

From the foregoing statement the reader will easily
infer how it was that this portion of the outskirts
of the Faubourg St. Mary was looked upon by the community as unhallowed ground—a Golgotha, where the
carcasses of men and animals had been heaped together,
as in a charnel house. For a long time it was studiously
shunned for residential purposes by many decent families;
but, in the course of years, the stories of buried treasures by pirates, of midnight assemblies of desperadoes
and other legends of a similar character were forgotten
or scouted at, and, at the present day, few of the old
survivors of that period would remember them, were not
their memories occasionally jogged. Although the old
willow trees have disappeared from our sight, still is
their recollection preserved by the name of the street
which intersects their former location. The Workhouse
and the several cotton presses established at the crossing
of Claiborne and Poydras streets stand now in the very
midst of the quarter once known as *le quartier des
damnés*. I must not omit to mention, in connection
with this subject, that a canal, named after Poydras,
ran through this tract of land—a cesspool of pestilen-
tial effluvia and a menace to the salubrity of the corporation.

It was in the spring of the year 1816 that a crevasse
occurred at the upper end of Macarty's plantation (now
the town of Carrollton or rather the Seventh Municipal
District of New Orleans) which inundated the rear
portions of the plantations which extended from that

point to the city. The waters, surcharged with the calcareous and slimy particles peculiar to the Mississippi river, were spread over the whole space covered by our swamps and reached as far as the corner of Canal and Bourbon. In the city proper it appeared all along Dauphine street, where it apparently found its level. By this casualty all the low and depressed parts of our city environs were marked by a line which appeared upon the walls and fences, after the subsidence of the overflow and the retiring of the element into the lake and adjacent bayous. This incident provided a valuable and accurate topographical survey. Everywhere was this water mark distinctly visible. Thus the fact was ascertained that the greatest depression was to be found all along Canal street, which has since required an incredible amount of "filling" to bring up to a level with the other parts of the town. The Bayou Road, on the contrary, in the neighborhood of Claiborne avenue, as well as several other isolated tracts, were ascertained to be the most elevated, having escaped the almost universal submersion.

The beautiful shell road which leads from the New Basin to the lake, and which in *ante-bellum* times was the proper drive for our sporting gentry, was opened through the almost impenetrable swamp during the years 1830-32, after the herculean task of hewing out the new canal had been completed. As the lower part of the city already enjoyed the old Carondelet, the idea of opening another outlet to the lake originated with an association of enterprising citizens, foremost among whom may be cited, Beverly Chew, an ex-collector of customs; ex-Senator Burthe, Samuel Jarvis Peters, the great city financier ; Hodge, of the *Bulletin*, and several

other equally spirited notables. Deeming that their
section would be wonderfully benefited by direct intercourse with the people of Bay St. Louis, Mobile and
Pensacola, they determined to organize themselves into
a banking corporation, styled the New Canal Banking
Association, which, having been incorporated by the
Legislature, soon went into operation.

On the topographical chart of Latourette the reader
will find the boundaries of the more than princely possessions of Antoine Michoud, erstwhile Sardinian consul. These stretched from Lake Pontchartrain to the
edge of Lake Borgne, and extended several miles on
both banks of Bayou Gentilly or Sauvage to within a
short distance from Fort Pike, on the Chef Menteur. A
Nimrod in his younger days, Michoud entertained a
particular predilection for this valuable tract, on account
of the great quantity and variety of game with which
it was always stocked. At the opening of every hunting season he would never fail, through the papers, to
issue warning notices to trespassers, as he claimed the
ownership of the countless flocks of wild geese and
ducks that were wont to settle, during the winter months,
in the immense lagoons and canebrakes which covered
his land.

Now, as no quantity of fences could possibly enclose
such a vast extent of open meadows, forests and marshes,
it may well be imagined that these fulminations on paper
were disregarded and ridiculed. Notwithstanding his
rage and inane threats, the amateur sportsmen of the city
and neighborhood continued their encroachments upon
his preserves, a practice which obtains even at the present
day, for this locality has always been noted for its excellent hunting grounds.

When Bienville, in the early part of 1700, first ex-
plored the nooks, recesses and meanderings of the Bayou
St. John, in the primitive pirogues of the friendly Cola-
pissas, nothing interesting met his view save a few low,
thatched, rough huts peering through the midst of a
dense, tangled forest, surrounded on every side by seemingly impenetrable morasses, and gloomy, dismal cypress marshes. This sluggish sheet of water was the
natural drain or outlet of a great swamp which formed
the background of the vast territory that extended from
the river bank to the lake. There were neither pathways
nor roads leading through the gloomy wilderness, as the
few Indians who lived in these regions were accustomed to
travel from place to place, whether engaged in the chase
or fishing, in light and swift canoes. From this general
description we must, however, except some more favored
localities; those, for instance, bordering Bayou Metairie,
and Bayou Sauvage, upon which bountiful nature had
scattered centenary trees, such as the ash and the live oak,
and a profusion of valuable shrubs and esculents. These
choice and fertile spots had been formed by slow degrees
from the alluvial deposits of the Mississippi, when, during
its yearly overflows, it spread over the wide expanse of
the adjacent lowlands. Hence it is we find that one
of the first back settlements of the city was established
upon these ridges, and that another had been located in
that part which stands midway between the river front
and the lake, on the Bayou St. John. The tourist who
will take the street car will soon reach this interesting
locality, now enlivened by beautiful villas and a spacious
park. Across the draw or spring bridge that spans the
bayou near that point he will see a historic spot, once
known as the "Magnolia Garden," in front of which
Bienville first set foot ashore. In those days it was the

site of a camping ground consisting of a few Indian
huts, whence a foot-path or trail led by a cut-off to the
settlements of the Tchoupitoulas, another small Indian
tribe, who lived in cabins huddled together along the
river bank below the present town of Carrollton.

At the period when these rural establishments were
being formed, in the last century, the Jesuit Fathers, with
the energy and rare intelligence characteristic of their
order, selected large tracts upon the high lands facing the
Bayous Sauvage and Gentilly for agricultural purposes.
Some of the buildings constructed on their wide domains
withstood the tooth of time for more than a hundred years,
as a few of them were still to be seen not very many
years ago.   These stood in the vicinity of the point
where the L. & N. railroad crosses the Gentilly as it
continues to follow the meanderings of the bayou of
that name to its final junction with the pretty stream
known as the *Chef Menteur.*

This water course, which alternatively flows from Lake
Ponchartrain into Lake Borgne, and *vice versâ*, according
to the stand of the waters in these two lakes, and according also to the prevailing winds or to the ebb and flow
of the tide, is for this reason called a *rigolet*, which signifies in the nautical parlance of that period a stream
flowing *both ways*.   Old people used to say that the Indians gave it the name of "Big Liar," because it talked
deceivingly.   Be this as it may, this stream is the most
beautiful one in the vicinity of New Orleans.   The water
is as pellucid as crystal, and its borders are decorated
with a gorgeous forest vegetation which has ever attracted the admiration of the sportsman and naturalist.

As I have already stated, a few Indian huts existed
along the Bayou St. John.   There may have been a few
more on Bayou Sauvage, for, in the immediate vicinity

of Daniel Clark's residence, at the intersection of the Bayou and Gentilly roads, an Indian graveyard was once to be seen. It was a small tract of very elevated ground. But the number of the aborigines around the city must have been very insignificant, indeed, for the reason that nowhere have they left any monuments of their existence. In fact, they seem to have suddenly disappeared from their primitive abodes, before the advance of the white man ; nobody knows how or where.

While this was the case with the small tribes of the Collapissas and Tchoupitoulas, there were annual visits of Choctaws and Natchez from over the lake and above the river, who were in the habit of repairing hither on New Year's Day to exchange compliments with the Governor and city authorities, and especially to receive the customary presents, which in ancient times had been stipulated by treaty. When by the lapse of time and the effect of prescription these resources were not forthcoming, the Indians would resort to *padegaud* shooting. The sport consisted in carrying about a wooden rooster decked with ribbons for target practice, around which they would dance and shout, begging from house to house a few picayunes for the " powder and shot " necessary to the warriors and squaws. That meant " whisky and rations." They were wont to keep up these carousals for several days in the outskirts or suburbs of the town. The same performances accompanied their Indian weddings and other ceremonies, from which they reaped rich harvests, as their exhibitions naturally attracted throngs of sojourners and sightseers.

The space of dry land upon which the city of New Orleans was originally built was extremely limited, and this may be better illustrated from the fact that the authorities were compelled to dig a draining canal through the middle of Bourbon street, on the very spot where now stands the French Opera House. It is not generally known that the location of a site for a city upon the banks of the Mississippi was for a considerable time a subject of serious contention between Bienville and his engineer. They were both agreed upon the necessity of selecting a point easy of access to, and of communication with, their early settlements and posts at Biloxi and in the Mississippi Sound and Gulf. This was an advantage which New Orleans offered. By means of the Bayou St. John the opening to Lake Pontchartrain was always convenient, and a constant intercourse with the colonies planted across the lake was available. But New Orleans was low, marshy, unhealthy and subject to periodical inundations. Here was the drawback. To remedy this evil, Manchac was suggested. The proposed site was high, comparatively salubrious, and offered, through the bayou of that name, since called the Iberville river, an outlet to the Gulf by the way of Lakes Maurepas and Pontchartrain. Bienville meditated long upon the availability of this location, and finally rejected the suggestion. The route was long, circuitous and dangerous. Besides it would have removed him at too great a distance from the mouth of the river, which it was his obvious policy to maintain, defend and secure at all hazards.

His will prevailed over all opposition, and the *carré de la ville* was laid out. It was a cesspool. The streets, few in number, had to be filled with the sand taken from the battures in front, and a sort of breastwork or dike was thrown up along the margin of the river to stem the force of the current. Reverting to the historical

fact that our drainage system began from Bourbon
street toward the rear, is it not possible, as some
have asserted, that the original founders intended to
have intersected the city with navigable canals, fed
by the great river flowing at our doors? This supposition is not totally groundless, as we know of cities in
tropical climates that are actually cut up by such appliances, and suffer no inconvenience either to health or
mercantile pursuits.

So slimy was the character of the soil in and around
New Orleans that Bienville, in his peregrinations around
the surrounding country, if he did not ascend one of
the branches of the Bayou St. John to the vicinity of
Rampart street, to which its several arteries generally
converged (immediately behind Congo Square), Bienville, I say, must have taken the Indian trail from the
Magnolia Garden station, through the dense forest extending along the ridge, and emerged into the Bayou
Road, on both sides of which were planted the first fruit
gardens and vegetable patches. This was the only ridge
of high ground by which the Indians usually reached
the river bank.

I believe that the project of introducing, by a system
of sluices and canals, the Mississippi river waters into
our city, was seriously contemplated, and this fact is
best proved by the prospectus of the company, which
was incorporated under the name of the Navigation
Company, one of whose achievements was to have conducted through Broad street the waters of the river into
the basin of Canal Carondelet. But this scheme was
never carried out, owing both to financial depression
and the opposition of speculators or interested parties.

There could be no doubt about its feasibility.
Witness the old Marigny canal, of which I have made

mention, which opened a direct communication with the
sea. The vestiges and ruins of this gigantic undertaking were visible as far back as 1816 at the lower end of
the city, and occupied precisely the present location of
the Pontchartrain railroad track. At the spot where
now stands the company's ticket office, on Elysian
Fields and Victory, were to be seen the massive walls,
built of solid masonry, which had been used as supports
to the sluice gates or locks that admitted the waters
of the river. This canal, turning at an angle or elbow,
at a short distance from where the first mile-stone is
standing now, conveyed its waters across the Gentilly road toward the Bayou St. John. At present, as I
have already said, the railroad track runs along a section of the former Marigny canal, which started from the
river's edge. There is hardly a remnant left of it now,
except a small draining ditch, near Claiborne street.
The branch, which proceeds toward the Bayou St. John
through the woods and marshes, has been improved by
the Draining Company, and now forms, I think, a part
of that system.

In the first decades of this century, the briny water
resort during the summer months was located near the
mouth of the Bayou St. John. There, and not over the
lake nor on the gulf coast, would the *élite* of New
Orleans society spend their leisure hours. They took
baths in the then clear and limpid waters of the bayou,
which was constantly refreshed and replenished by the
influx of the lake's swelling tide. There also were
many sailing and rowing boats for amateurs, who took
pleasure in excursions to the Fort. The grounds for
deep-sea swimming were around the lighthouse. It was
only later, some time in the 40s, that a smooth and
beautiful shell road was laid out, thus enabling thou-

sands to reach in buggies the small fishermen's village
at the entrance of the bayou, once noted by old *gourmets*
for its restaurants and hostelries.

A small tract of high ground, covered with latanier or
wild palm—a certain indication, by the way, that the
soil is not subject to annual immersions—was to be
found between the Canal Carondelet and the Bayou
Road Ridge. That portion of it which now lies almost
contiguous to Galvez street was denominated " *la terre
aux lépreux*"—Leper's Land—because, under the
administration of Galvez, this fell and malignant disease had raged with violence. To stamp it out, or
rather to arrest its further progress, the patients had
been removed to this distant and solitary waste, and
were secluded from all communication with the outer
world. They were regularly supplied with provisions
and water, but no one was permitted, under the penalty
of perpetual seclusion, to approach any of these outcasts.

Under the administration of Baron Carondelet, in
1794, the scheme of uniting New Orleans by means of
a navigable canal with the Bayou St. John was first
conceived and partially carried out. The drainage
canal, which had been extended from Bourbon street,
had gradually been enlarged and prolonged through
the cypress forest, connecting with one of the main
arteries of the bayou. In the course of time, the re-
quirements of trade demanded that it should be
widened and deepened so as to admit sailing vessels of
greater tonnage, capable of undertaking voyages to
the West Indies.

Thus it was that, after the subsidence of the flood
from the crevasse at Macarty's Point, in 1816, a number
of African slaves were put to work in pumping out the

water from one compartment into the other. The whole
length of the canal had to be divided and subdivided,
before it could be separated into sections by piles and
strong dams. Never was a severer task or more astonish-
ing work ever imposed. Although the herculean labor
of perforating the New Canal, which had been performed
by Irishmen, was attended by great sickness and
an incredible sacrifice of life, nothing of the kind occurred in the construction of the works done by slave
hands. There was no loss of life or health among
them. On the contrary, the black people, all of whom
were imported Africans, grew quite stout and lusty.
They spoke nothing but their native language (Congo),
and seemed to know, as if by instinct, the utility
of the enterprise. Never was work performed with
more cheerfulness and alacrity, for there were used no
drivers, or whips, but plenty of rations, and occasionally
a pull at the *tafia* jug. A *filet*, that is to say, a dram of
strong liquor, was what the slaves cared for above
all things. In all other respects they were very sober.
Their favorite beverage was a species of small beer, made
of Indian corn. In the extreme heat of the summer
solstice, with only their cotton trousers on, bared breasts
and shoulders, protected from the sun by large straw
hats or *tignons* merely, they would delve into the midst
of our murky swamps, hewing out with pickaxes enormous stumps, and spading and throwing up immense
clods of dirt without any apparent effort.

They had no machinery, no steam contrivance to
assist them in these arduous labors. Even the driving
of the piles had to be done by hand. The carpenters
and educated mechanics were whites and mulattoes,
and thus was this huge undertaking carried out toward
the main branch of the Bayou St. John. It may be

said to have been the great initial step toward the drainage of the immense territory, known later as the Faubourg Trémé.

From the moment that large sea-going schooners were enabled to reach the city by this new conduit, business in the thriving little town located on the banks of the bayou at once declined, and notwithstanding that grounds had been laid out for building lots and that streets had been regularly traced out, yet for a long time afterward this settlement or suburb of the city dropped into a lethargic sleep. A great many dairies in successful operation are now to be seen. Its industry there consists in gardening, shingle and picket making, and, I believe, in pottery works. As I have already said, this was the most ancient establishment, outside of the city proper, since as some of its oldest buildings date as far back as the period of the French occupation, and some of the titles to property, if we mistake not, descend from grants of the earliest colonial settlers. Hereabouts, no doubt, was the spot where the first explorers from Biloxi alighted from their frail crafts, partook of their meals and stretched their limbs under umbrageous oaks and magnolias before undertaking their perilous march across the woods and swamps to the banks of the Mississippi. Then it was that their eyes feasted on the aspect of the mighty river, "*le fleuve St. Louis*," as they called it, or *Le Méchacébé*, enriched by forests and canebrakes alive with game, for, if the statement of one of Bienville's companions is to be credited, wild turkeys settled on the tops of the trees and were so tame as to be caught with their hands.

Before the period of American occupation, as we all know, there were no paved streets or even passable roads. Very often, during the rainy winter months, or after a succession of long, wet weather, communication by land was no easy matter. The people were almost shut out from the outer world. But in the course of time a transformation began to manifest itself, and, under the administrations of Pitot, Watkins and Girod, decided improvements were steadily inaugurated. Stage coaches—an unheard-of innovation—had been introduced from the North, and in the few livery stables scattered about the town, in addition to saddle horses, some odd conveyance, as an old country *caléche*, might occasionally be secured. Whenever, however, these conveniences failed to materialize, the traveler would avail himself of an ordinary market ox cart, when bound to some country seat. Yet walking was the simpler way for short distances, and the one generally in vogue. There was but one highway leading above the river, and this was the "Tchoupitoulas road." Under the colonial *régime*, the city being completely surrounded by a deep and wide moat, the only route to the settlements above the city was through this road, the opening of which was guarded by a fort, established on Canal street, near the levee. No one from without could enter the city except through fortified gates, situated at the apexes of the four angles of the parallelogram, upon which the *carré de la ville* was built. Along this road, commencing about Delord street, the upper extremity of the Faubourg Ste. Marie, and extending toward the magnificent Livaudais plantation, was a succession of beautifully located villas and agricultural establishments.

All along Tchoupitoulas street there ran a low levee planted with willow trees, and during the season of high water, when the batture which was then forming was thoroughly immersed, the long Western keelboats and barges, as well as the unseemly flatboats, or *chalands*, would make fast to these trees, and thence discharge their cargoes. Sometimes their contents were retailed upon the pier. After the receding of the spring and summer floods, those flatboats, of enormous construction, and unfit for a return voyage, would be left high and dry upon the batture front, and then be broken up for fuel and building purposes. The strong side pieces, or gunwales, were used in the suburbs as footpaths or side banquettes in lieu of our present brick-paved sidewalks. Upon these wooden trails, as it were, pedestrians had to make their way through immense vacant spaces, for there were but few buildings toward the rural precincts leading to the Livaudais plantation, which constituted that portion of New Orleans which now forms the Fourth District.

As already stated, on the way to that wealthy estate the river front was lined with a continuous series of delightful rural residences, surrounded with orange hedges, orchards and well-tended gardens. Although no staple crops were raised on these lands, the owners, with the assistance of a numerous retinue of African slaves, derived a considerable income from their dairies, their orchards, gardens, timber and poultry. Sheep-raising was also a source of traffic. All these branches of industry and husbandry were exceedingly lucrative, by reason of the close proximity of our market, where a steadily increasing population afforded a ready sale for these necessary commodities.

The great Macarty crevasse, in the spring of 1816, submerged the rear portions of the numerous plantations existing between Carrollton and the city proper. The Livaudais estate was one of the heaviest sufferers

from this calamity.   I borrow from the rough but valuable note-book of an old-time merchant of this city,
now dead, his recollections of that event.   He says:

"When we reached the fine sugar estate of the late
François Livaudais we were put in possession of the
devastation which this inundation had wrought upon
the greater part of ground under culture of this farm.
All the lower or backward parts of the sugar lands had
been completely covered, and the planting of a crop of
several hundred hogsheads of sugar would not yield
the tenth part of an ordinary crop.

" So it resulted ; for it so happened that the commercial house in whose employ I then was became in
the fall of that year the purchaser of the entire crop of
sugar, of very fine quality no doubt, but only giving
twenty-eight hogsheads.   Now this, for the moment,
was no doubt a great misfortune for the owner, the
worthy Mr. Francois Livaudais, with whom, in after
time, we had a much nearer acquaintance, and it was
one of the causes why the splendid residence of his,
commenced about that time and never finished, afforded
even unto these latter days the spectacle of an abandoned castle, so much so that it went afterward by the
name of the 'Haunted House' (near Washington
avenue) ; but yet this very circumstance of the whole of
the back part of the plantation area being covered by
the Macarty crevasse waters finally turned out a most
beneficial accident, in raising the same ground several
feet by the remaining deposit or alluvial sediment of
the Mississippi water.   It was then that the value of
this plantation became greatly enhanced on account of
its being high and dry land to its uttermost limits
toward the woods, and when, some years after, a company of speculators acquired by purchase a great part of

this estate, the now beautiful Garden District, or the Fourth, took its rise from this very circumstance of the overflow.''

While speaking of the settlements on the Bayou St. John, I had occasion to refer to the residence of the once merchant prince and politician, Daniel Clark, father of the celebrated Mrs. Myra Gaines. It was situated at the fork of two roads ; one leading directly to the bayou, and the other to the Gentilly Road on the way to the Chef Menteur. Near the site formerly occupied by this mansion now stands the Bretonne market, sometimes called the Indian market, from the fact that it was once the bivouac of the vagrant Indians that abounded in that vicinity. As far back as 1816, the grand old house was in a very good state of preservation ; but, being afterward turned over to negligent tenants, it fell into complete ruin and gradually disappeared from view, having become the prey of covetous neighbors, who removed every vestige of brick or lumber from the dilapidated concern.

As it may be of interest to the reader to know how it happened that this historical relic of a past era was permitted to fall into such a state of decay, a few words concerning the wealthy proprietor may not prove out of place.

It is a well known fact that Daniel Clark was at one time the leading spirit of our city. I refer to the period immediately antedating the cession of 1803. Having by his commercial connection with the large house of Coxe & Co., in Philadelphia, established an extensive credit under the Spanish government, of which he was a sort of under secretary, and become a special favorite with the authorities, his relations with Havana, Vera Cruz and other Hispano-American seaports enabled him

to introduce into the territory not only the commodities
of those countries, but a large number also of African
labor hands, known as *bozales*. These proved a valuable
acquisition to the planters of Louisiana.   But as soon as
the country was purchased by the United States, this
branch of traffic was suppressed by the government.
The check put upon this enormous source of wealth to
the old colonists was an unexpected blow to Daniel
Clark, inasmuch as there was every reason to presume
that the same privilege which had been conceded to
South Carolina, Georgia and other States would have
been extended, until 1808, to Louisiana.   Had this *dou-
ceur* been allowed—had not Congress, in order to recon-
cile the extreme Northern States to the acquisition of
the new domain, lent a willing ear to their demand for
the prohibition of negro importations into it, Clark
would have had a chance of continuing his occupation
as a slave trader for a further period of five years.   The
halt produced by this determined resolve of Congress
became the cause of serious injury and annoyance to the
planting interest, and hence a bitter opposition sprung
up against the policy of the Washington cabinet among
many Louisianians.

Daniel Clark had been elected a delegate to Congress,
and from 1803 until 1812 he became the head and front
of the opposition in Louisiana, and as such had more
than one serious altercation with the State authorities.

Having been originally a warm partisan of Jefferson
in his diplomatic efforts to secure by purchase the immense tract of land embraced under the general name of
Louisiana, and having been also, in his capacity of
American Consul at New Orleans, an active co-laborer
in backing up the efforts of the administration in that
direction, he no doubt felt himself slighted and

neglected when he perceived that his influence was underrated, and that his advice and suggestions were not heeded. Hence arose those acrid feelings which sprung up between him and the Governor, and finally culminated into a hostile meeting on the field of honor.

When the war broke out in 1812 the business of the house of Coxe, Clark & Co. had been transferred to a new firm. It was composed of Richard Relf, late cashier of the Louisiana State Bank; Beverly Chew, ex-Collector of Customs, as active partners, and Daniel Clark as the partner *in commendam*. This association having made large advances to planters, now became a heavy dead weight owing to the blockade of the mouth of the Mississippi by English cruisers, and was compelled to suspend its payments, as was the case with the majority of the commercial houses of New Orleans, as well as all of the existing banks. Under these circumstances Daniel Clark, who had the greater part of the time been absent and attending to his duties in Congress, found his private affairs involved by the pecuniary difficulties of his commercial house. Although his means were ample and his fortune, which consisted in slaves, plantations, improved real estate and vacant lands, was quite considerable, yet such was the stringency of our markets that he was unable to procure at times even the necessary means to meet indispensable obligations. This humiliating situation chafed his spirit. Notwithstanding a very robust and active temperament, age had made inroads upon his former vigor and stalwart frame. Hence, when, after the erection of Louisiana into a State, his functions as a Delegate had ceased, he resolved to return home and put his private and commercial affairs in a proper train of liquidation. Sickness and death overtook him in the

midst of his affliction.   When this event took place, at
his residence on the Bayou St. John road, many of his
old friends, such as Dussuau de la Croix, who had
succeeded in the contract for enlarging Canal Carondelet; Messrs. Chew and Relf, close neighbors; old
Mr. Baron Boisfontaine, Colonel Bellechasse and others
attended his bedside.   A will was found in which
Messrs. Chew and Relf were named executors, and the
mother of the deceased was instituted sole heiress.   After
the lapse of several years another testament was discovered, in which the above named Dussuau de la Croix,
Baron Boisfontaine and Colonel Bellechasse were
declared executors, and his daughter, Myra, then living
with her grandmother in Philadelphia, was recognized
as his sole heiress and possessor of his estate.   I shall
not enter into a history of the trouble which these two
wills occasioned, nor wallow into the scandals which
entertained the wondering public during the whole period of the prolonged litigation that ensued.   It is only
necessary to say here that during its pendency all of
his property was neglected.   The reader can well imagine how it was that such a fine building, with its
beautifully laid gardens, orchards, flower *parterres*,
kiosks, statues and fountains was permitted to crumble
to pieces.   In the course of time it was rumored that
the house was haunted, and that ghosts had been seen
stalking in the dead of night along its corridors, and
no respectable tenant could be found willing to occupy
the premises.   Such is the story of a building of which
no traces now remain!

Perhaps some of my readers may have noticed an an-
tiquated building some fifty years ago, standing inside of
the yard midway from the corner of Bayou Road and

Claiborne avenue.　This was the residence of the great Scotch philanthropist and millionaire, Alexander Milne, after whom was named the once thriving little village on Lake Pontchartrain.　It was a singular looking building, frequently mistaken for the abode of some colonial Spanish governor.　It was flanked on either side by what seemed to be battlements made of solid granite and of unhewn stones cemented with rock mortar.　The enclosures, as well as the heavy massive doorways were composed of the same durable materials.　The gardens were ornamented by a great number of fine fruit trees, shrubbery and arbors, which it had required years to bring to absolute perfection.　Converted in later years into an asylum or hospital by a French charitable society, all traces of the peculiar architectural traits of this relic of generations long gone by have been removed by innovating hands, and naught now remains of its original structure and appearance, save its massive walls.　The work of renovation has been complete.　Alexander Milne was a most remarkable man.　He arrived here in Louisiana some time during the period of Galvez' administration, about 1776.　Having outlived the oldest inhabitant, although not his usefulness, he left behind him few data upon which to construct an accurate biography.　What his profession in the old country may have been was a riddle, but here in New Orleans, in addition to the hardware business in which he was engaged, he had devoted himself to the manufacture of country bricks, and with the assistance of his negro hands had amassed a colossal fortune.　Whether in this enterprise he was assisted by the Spanish authorities, or not, is a matter of conjecture ; but he must certainly have been upon an intimate footing with them to have obtained the valuable and vast tracts which he left

at the time of his death. These lay around the Gentilly farms, without including those that fronted the
lake, from the present terminus of the railway up to
the mouth of Bayou St. John, and even beyond, as old
maps of the city indicate.

This singular old man lived by himself in that old
castellated home, without a single white person in his
employ, in the midst of his slaves. He was eighty
years of age at the time of his death. Contemporaries describe him as small in stature, with head hanging down, eyes always bent on the ground, oblivious of
street surroundings and dressed in the seedy vestments
of a beggar, for whom he was often mistaken by strangers. He left at his death, besides a large number of
slaves, nearly a hundred thousand dollars in ready
cash, and property in every faubourg in the city. The
village of Milneburg, on the lake shore, was constructed
on a part of his domain. He bequeathed in his will
the bulk of his fortune to his native town in Scotland.
His slaves were manumitted, and to prevent their proving a burden upon themselves or the parish, he made
ample provision for their future maintenance. He set
apart, also, a portion of his fortune toward the erection
and support of a school and asylum for boys and girls,
but his benevolent intentions were never carried into
effect, as the revenues were squandered by faithless and
rapacious stewards and intermediaries.

L'ENVOI.

And now my work is done. It remains for the public to say whether I shall ever be induced to again make my bow before it. The theme I have selected is a prolific one, and the materials for its proper treatment, though not easy of access, are still available. To use the words of our own Washington Irving, I must candidly acknowledge that should my writings, with all their imperfections, be received with favor, it will prove a source of the purest gratification, for though I do not aspire to those high honors which are the rewards of loftier intellects, yet it is the dearest wish of my heart to have a cozy, though humble, corner in the good opinions and kind feelings of my countrymen. *Vale.*

INDEX.

348 INDEX.

HENRY C. CASTELLANOS

Mr. Henry C. Castellanos, one of the city's best known criminal lawyers, died at 8 o'clock yesterday morning at the Touro Infirmary. He had been in poor health for some time but took an active part in the last municipal campaign. He sat as a member of the state nominating convention, which met at Baton Rouge earlier in the year. His enfeebled constitution sustained but badly the strain placed upon it.

About a month ago he was compelled to take to his bed. As his illness progressed, it was found necessary to remove him to the infirmary where an operation was performed. Hopes were entertained that this would prove beneficial and for a time it seemed that they would not be disappointed.

However, his advanced age and prolonged illness had but poorly prepared Mr. Castellanos to resist the advances of disease and several days ago it was plainly evident that his end might be delayed, but not long. His death will be generally deplored. Probably no man in New Orleans possessed a wider acquaintance in professional or social circles.

Mr. Castellanos was descended from a distingushed Spanish family, his father, John Joseph Castellanos, having been an officer under Napoleon in the peninsular campaign. This gentleman immigrated to America in 1816. His wife was Maria Manual Sanchez, daughter of a noted cavalry general. Their son, the subject of this sketch, was born in this city sixty-eight years ago. He received his education at Georgetown College in the District of Columbia. After completing the course there, he went to St. Mary's College, Baltimore, where in 1847 he was graduated with the degree of master of arts.

Returning to New Orleans he began the study of law in the Office of Christian Rosellus, and then attended the lectures at the University of Louisiana [which later was incorporated into Tulane]. In his class at that time were George Eustis, D.C. Labatt, Peniston and others who afterwards rose to distinction in the state. He was admitted to the bar in 1848 and his eloquence and learning soon brought him into prominence. He participated in almost all the important cases of his time, and was considered to have been an authority on the criminal law. He took an active interest in politics, and at the age of 24, was elected a delegate to the constitutional convention of 1852. He subsequently gave up his practice to take a responsible position in one of the public schools. He served four years as a teacher and was then chosen a school director.

Finally, Mr. Castellanos entered the field of journalism, accepting a place on the editorial staff of the Louisiana Courier. At that time the paper was printed partly in English, partly in French, and Mr. Castellanos supervised both departments. His health giving way under the strain, he went to Franklin, La., where he established the Franklin Register. He resided in Franklin for several years, and then, returning to New Orleans, resumed the practice of his profession.

In 1858 he formed a partnership with E. North Cullom. The firm handled more than one celebrated case, among which must be included the defense of the returning board of 1875. The political significance of this case rendered it of national interest. The case in question came up after Rutherford B. Hayes was declared entitled to the presidency of the United States. It will be remembered that when the Hayes/Tilden election was left to the national returning board it was the vote of Louisiana that decided that Hayes should be seated. For a while nothing was said in this city regarding the action of the returning board, but when the Democrats once more got into power in Louisiana it was determined to prosecute the members of the returning board for fraud and bribery. The pent-up indignation of the populace of this state, which had been brewing for several years, burst forth, and there was a clamor from all quarters that the members of the returning board be prosecuted. Attorney General Ogden had the men put on trial and the case proved of national interest. The trial lasted several days and at each session the doors of the courtroom had to be locked, so dense were the crowds that flocked around seeking admission. When Madison Wells and the fellow members of the board were arraigned they pleaded not guilty, or rather, their attorneys, Mr. Castellanos and Judge Cullom, did so for them.

The outcome of the trial is well known, it was generally believed that a verdict of guilty, would be rendered, but such did not occur. An acquittal followed. The prosecution was most bitter and some very strong evidence was introduced, but points made by the attorney general were torn to shreds by the vigorous pleading of Mr. Castellanos and his confrere and a victory at the bar was accorded them by all the legal lights in the country which followed the circumstances in the case. Mr. Castellanos received a personal letter from President Hayes complimenting him on his efforts and even the prosecution acknowledged that the board owed their freedom to his talent.

After the partnership with Mr. Cullom was dissolved, Mr. Castellanos took his son, John H. Castellanos, into his business. The son bade fair to attain the same prominence as his father, but, at the age of 24, he died. His father, who fairly idolized him, withdrew from the bar shortly after this sad occurance and devoted himself to studies of an historical nature, his researches being embodied in the articles published over his signature in various magazines and periodicals. About a year ago, a collection of these papers was published in a book entitled "New Orleans as it Was". The volume is admittedly of the greatest value to the student of Louisiana history. Mr. Castellanos projected several other works all of an historical nature, the chief of which was to have dealt with the unwritten history of the state. That Mr. Castellanos did not carry out this project before his death, will be a source of regret to the future historian of the city .

Of late years Mr. Castellanos had to some extent resumed the practice of his profession, having been retained as counsel in a number of important cases, among them the Ford-Murphy trial, the Desforges, and the Gourdain cases, etc. He had also taken an interest in politics but the judgeship of the criminal court, which he at one time held, satisfied his ambitions. Entering the state campaign of 1892, he took an active part on behalf of the lottery, making a great many speeches, all over the state both in French and English. He believed that the money which the lottery agreed to pay the state would have been of benefit to the people. After the lottery bill was lost in the legislature, he was appointed to superintend over the opening of the lottery in Honduras. He went to that country and was the orator of the opening day. He returned to New Orleans soon after. He represented his ward in the last parish convention, which met in this city and as already said, he was a delegate to the recent state convention.

Mr. Castellanos was twice married. First to Miss Treme by whom he had a son, John Castellanos, a rising attorney, and then to Miss Gladey, who survives his death. This second marriage was blessed with several children, of whom a daughter, Miss Laure, and a son, Mr. Henry Castellanos, now in his 21st year, are now living. Mr. Castellanos had one grandchild, the present Mrs. John Coleman. He also has a brother and a sister who survive him, Dr. J.H. Castellanos and Mrs. Carmellite Grabiel.

The remains of Mr. Castellanos will be laid in state at St. Louis Cathedral today from 9-4 o'clock, after which the funeral will take place.

— From the New Orleans Picayune
August 8, 1896